Nigeria and the Politics of Unreason
A Study of the Obasanjo Regime

Published by
Adonis & Abbey Publishers Ltd
P.O. Box 43418
London
SE11 4XZ
http://www.adonis-abbey.com

First Edition, November 2003

Copyright © Victor E. Dike

British Library Cataloguing-in-Publication Data
A catalogue record for this book is available from the British Library

ISBN 0-9545037-4-0

Cover Design   Ifeanyi Adibe

Printed and bound in Great Britain by Lightning Source UK Ltd.

Nigeria and the Politics of Unreason
A Study of the Obasanjo Regime
By Victor E. Dike

Adonis & Abbey
Publishers Ltd

Other Books by Adonis & Abbey include:

Broken Dreams (Fiction/Town Crier Series 1)
By Jideofor Adibe

**Wooden Gongs and Drumbeats: African Folktales,
Proverbs and Idioms** (Fiction/Town Crier Series 2)
By Dahi Chris Onuchukwu

**The Making of the Africa-Nation
Pan-Africanism and the African Renaissance**
(politics/political economy/history)
Edited by Mammo Muchie

**The Challenge of Authenticity: African Culture and
Faith Commitment** (religion/philosophy/theology)
By Jacob Hevi

Flight From Fate (Fiction/Town Crier Series 3)
By Evans Kinyua

Contents

DEDICATION

To those whose lives were snuffed out in Nigeria through political assassination in the run-up to the 2003 elections.

Preface

Nigeria, for the most part of its history, has been vacillating between military dictatorship and civilian rule. Neither seemed to have benefited the common people. While political development has been arrested under the military, the civilian regimes were often characterised by bickering, the politicisation of ethnicity, brazen corruption and secessionist threats which make it often difficult to see the democracy dividends.

Nigeria has undergone countless crises - from the crisis of military rule to the June 12 1993 election annulment upheaval, *Shariah* law and *Miss World* riots, the 2003 election crisis, the *FG-ASUU* face-off and the 2003 fuel price increase crisis. This is not to mention rampant labour strike actions in the society. Educational institutions, social infrastructures and socio-political and economic developments have all been negatively affected. The cumulative effects of theses crises have been the upsurge in corruption, the worsening poverty profile of the citizens and the "the politics of unreason"* practiced by the politicians to acquire or retain political power. This politics of extremism seemed to have reached a new height during the 2003 electioneering campaigns.

This book analyses the unreasonable politics that has helped to weaken the economy and facilitated corruption, poverty, decay of educational institutions and social infrastructure. It calls for a change of attitude on the part of the politicians in order to move the nation forward. Its over-arching objective is to paint a picture of the ills of the society rather than to generate any grand theory of politics and government.

The book is expected to be highly valuable to students and teachers in the department of social sciences in tertiary institutions. It should also serve as a good reference source for policy-makers, political leaders and the general public. The book will, above all, be a very valuable resource to all who are interested in Africa in general and the Nigerian political economy in particular.

The book is divided into four parts. Part I deals with background issues on political activities in Nigeria and the nature of the 2003 electioneering politics;

Part II discusses leadership, corruption and poverty, which are among the major problems facing the nation. Part III focuses on the economy and the state of education in Nigeria, while Part IV deals with insecurity, political instability, political *godfathers* and Nigerian politics in general, and concludes with discussions of ways and means to control fraud in future elections in the country.

Part I consists of Chapters 1 and 2. Chapter 1 presents an overview of the book while Chapter 2 discusses the anomalies in the 2003 elections.

Part II comprises Chapters 3, 4, and 5. Chapter 3 focuses on leadership problems, Chapter 4 concentrates on corruption and Chapter 5 deals with poverty.

Part 111 comprises Chapters 6, 7, and 8. Chapter 6 deals with the economy, technology and productivity; Chapter 7 discusses the economy and inflation, while Chapter 8 discusses the state of education in Nigeria and the need to equip Nigerian schools with modern educational and information technologies.

Part IV is made up of Chapters 9, 10 and 11. Chapter 9 discusses insecurity and political instability while Chapter 10 is about political *godfathers* in Nigerian politics. Chapter 11 deals with the 2003 elections and recommends ways of reducing frauds in future elections in Nigeria.

The major impetus for this book comes from my desire to see the emergence of good governance and true democracy in Nigeria, which is anchored on true federalism. I showed from my analyses, especially the 2003 electioneering campaigns, that good governance and democracy will continue to elude the country for as long as the politics of unreason reigns.

My gratitude goes to all the authors whose works are cited in this book. I owe special thanks to Professor Enwere Dike of the Dept of Economics, Nnamdi Azikiwe University, Awka, for his encouragement and guidance throughout this work. I am also indebted to my friend, Dr Johnny Mez, and to all those whose constructive comments and suggestions contributed to the clarity of information in this book. In addition, I am grateful to Dr Jideofor Adibe and the editors at Adonis & Abbey Publishers in London, for their encouragement. Finally, this book would not have seen the light of the day without the personal sacrifices and support from my wife, Chizor and our five lovely children - Uchenna, Chiamaka, Chidiche, Chinyere and Ugochukwu.

Victor E. Dike
Sacramento, USA.
25 August 2003

* The title of this book is derived from *The Politics of Unreason* (Lipset and Raab, 1970).

Chapter 1

Introduction: Nigeria and the Politics of Unreason

In the following pages we shall present the synopses of the main problems facing Nigeria and highlight how they spiralled out of control during the 2003 electioneering campaigns. In a pro-development and pro-people democratic society, 'leadership' and 'democracy' possess positive meanings, but they seem to have assumed negative connotations in Nigeria. For the corrupt politicians at Abuja and the state capitals these would seem to be an excuse to rob, kill and get rich quick, while the governed remain in perpetual penury, hunger, ignorance and sickness. Nigeria has everything to build a vibrant society but its leaders are principally the causes of the poverty of the people and its backwardness.

Some of the major issues facing the polity include electoral frauds, politics devoid of ideology; the dismal state of education, weak economy, corruption, poverty, ethnicity and religious conflicts, frequent strike actions and political instability. These culminated in 2003 in numerous political assassinations, unprincipled decampments, insecurity and politics manipulated by *moneybags* and *godfathers*.

The 2003 Politics: Political Assassinations

Though the politics of extremism, bitterness and bloodshed have been with Nigeria since independence in 1960, it seemed to have reached a new crescendo during the 2003 electioneering campaigns. Some of the ugly hallmarks of this "politics of unreason" were the enthronement of a culture of insecurity of life and property and a wave of political assassinations as the table below shows:

Table A: **Political Assassinations****

Name	State (Party)	Name	State/Party
Chief Ajibola (Bola) Ige	Oyo (AD) Attor Gen/Min of Justice	Dr. Julius Kpaduwa (Gov. Asp)**	Imo (ANPP)
Odunayo Olagbaju (St Rep)	Ile-Ife -Osun State (AD)	Dele Arojo (Gov Asp)	Lagos (PDP)
Barnabas Igwe %%%	Anambra	Isyaku Mohammed (Chair)	Kano (UNPP)
Ahmad Ahman Pategi	Kwara State Chairman (PDP)	Akpan H. Ekpo (Univ of Uyo)	Cross River
Alhaji Yusuf Doma*	Plateau	John Oyom Okap (Dep Gov)**	Cross River (PDP)
Aliyu Maigari*	Plateau	Prophet Eddie Okeke	Anambra
Uche Ogbonnaya (OGB)	Imo (ANPP)	Ezeodumegwu G. Okonkwu	Anambra (LGA Chair)
Victor Nwankwo	Enugu	Ifeany Ibegbu (Anambra Ass.)***	Anambra
Mr. Emenike	Imo (ANPP)	4 PDP Stalwarts Killed****	Ebonyi State
Anthony Onyearugbulem	Imo (ANPP)	J.C. Amadi (Owelle Atta)	Imo (ANPP)
Prof. Chimere Ikoku	Enugu	Alhaji Isiaku Mohammed	Kano (UNPP)
Bukola Saraki	Kwara (PDP)**	7 killed in PDP/ANPP Clash++	Jato-Aka LGA, Benue
Sunday Ugwu	Enugu	14 persons died in a church?	Enugu
Many killed in party primaries	Ogbia & Kolukuma (PDP) Bayelsa	Theodore Emeka Agwatu	Imo (PDP)
Emmanuel Okocha	Asaba, Delta Satae (PAC)**** (a)	Alhaji Inuwa Musa Kubo**	Borno State (Speaker)
Mrs. Emily Omope**	Ado Ekiti, Ekiti (AD)	Harry Marshall (Rivers State)	Killed in Abuja (ANPP)
Monday Ndor (St Rep) Rivers	Port Harcourt	Ezendu Megwo Okonkwo	Nnew-South (ANPP)
Schnapps Omuvwiebese	Ughelli-North	Abel Chukwu (St Rep)**	Enugu (PDP)
Yan Doma (Senator)**	(PDP)	Joshua Boro **	Ughelli-South (PDP)
Alhaji Isa Ojibara**	Kwara State INEC (Ilorin)	Alhaji Adamu Waziri**	Yobe State
Mrs. Jumoke Anifowoshe**	Ondo St. Attry General	Momoh Lawal	Okene -Kogi State
Janet Oladape	PDP leader (Odigbo LGA)	3 killed in an ANPP/PDP clash++	Yoba State, Jan 18' 03
Chief Chekwas Okorie**	Abuja (APGA)	Uche Nwole**	Owerri –Imo State
Alhaji Umaru Shinkafi**	Kaduna	"Buhari's convoy attacked…."**	Adamawa
The convoy of Gani attacked**		200 houses burnt in PDP, ANPP clash**	Kebbi State
Moshood Gidado (two others)	Ilorin (Kwara) ANPP	Alhaji Issa Zaria (House of Assely Cand)	Kwara St (ANPP)

Sources: Compiled by the author from: *The Guardian*: "Police arrest seven suspects Over Ige's murder" Dec 27, 2001. *AP*: "Government critic killed in Nigeria" Sept. 3, 2002; *AP:* "Gunmen kill Nigerian ruling party official" Aug. 17, 2002; *The Guardian:* "Governor's aide, Beheaded in Plateau, six feared dead in Ondo" Nov 6, 2002; *ThisDay:* "Gunmen Kill ANPP Senatorial Candidate" Feb 11, 2003; *The Guardian* "Political assassination" Nov 21, 2002. Daily Independent: "Fresh facts emerge over Uche's murder," Feb 18, 2003. ThisDay: "In Abuja, Saraki Escapes Assassination," Feb 19, 2003. *NAMPA/Reuters:* "Gunmen kill outspoken Nigerian politician," Sept 23, 2002. ThisDay: "7 killed in PDP/ANPP Clash," Feb 22, 2003; *ThisDay:* "April Polls: Are the Police Ready?" Feb 22, 2003; *ThisDay*: "PAC Flagbearer Survives Acid Bath," Feb 27, 2003; *Vanguard*: "Ekiti AD women leader dies of acid attack," March 5, 2003. *Daily Trust:* "Borno

Speaker escapes death," March 5, 2003. Reuters: "Nigeria opposition chief killed in run-up to polls," March 5, 2003; *Daily Trust*: "Political Killings in the present dispensation," March 6, 2003; ThisDay: "The Lucky, The Not So Lucky," March 6, 2003. *Vanguard*: "ANPP chieftain, Harry Marshal shot dead — IG orders probe," March 6, 2003. *Daily Independent*: "Okorie, APGA chairman alerts on threat to life," March 7, 2003. Daily Independent: "Gunmen invade Shankafi's residence," March 11, 2003; BBC: "Nigerian Candidate attacked." March 14, 2003; Daily Trust: "Buhari's convoy attacked in Adamawa." March 14, 2003; Daily Trust: "200 houses burnt in PDP, ANPP clash." March 17, 2003; Daily Independent: "Lawal's cousin, two others killed by gunmen in Ilorin" March 21, 2003. Daily Independent: "ANPP chieftain killed in Kwara;" April 18, 2003.
? The stampede that caused the death was blamed on the agents of the state
****(a) Substance suspected to be an Acid was poured on the Gubernatorial Candidate of PAC in Delta State
* Beheaded
** Assassination attempts; Mrs. Emily Omope later died of acid attack;
***Tortured by Bakassi Boys
****As a result of the fuss between Senate President, Anyim and the Governor of Ebonyi State, Egwu, in Abakaliki, on August 24, 2001
%%% Local Bar chairman and his wife, Abigal Igwe, killed.
++Violent political clash and killing is common across the country

Another disturbing element of this politics of extremism is the blossoming of corruption despite the worsening poverty profile of the populace. It is obvious therefore that for the country to move forward – politically and materially, it should begin to develop a political culture that favours real competitive politics based on principles and ideological convictions as opposed to the current politics of unreason.

The 2003 Politics: Moneybags

The nation was shocked by the news of the extent of donations made to the Peoples Democratic Party (*PDP*) at fund raising parties organised for the re-election campaigns of Obasanjo/Atiku and other politicians. Huge amounts of money that sounded more like telephone numbers were donated by individuals – mostly by those connected in one way or the other to state power. These fundraising parties were in fact more like bazaars and provided corrupt government officials and favour-seekers the opportunity to channel their loots to the parties. This in turn ensures a perpetuation of corruption since these huge donations are seen by the donors as IOUs. In this regard, there is an urgent need to revise and update the law on donations to political parties by individuals to limit the influence of money in Nigerian politics. Already the debilitating effects of money politics has been vividly demonstrated in the recent failed 'coup attempt in Anambra State' organised by Chief Chris Uba - the so-called political *godfather* of Dr. Chris Ngige (governor of the State). The *godfather* in collaboration with others wanted to remove the political *godson* he allegedly single-handedly enthroned, through the equivalent of a civilian coup. (see Chapter 4 on corruption and Chapter 10 on political *godfathers*).

In more mature democracies, politicians use money to sell their political ideology. But in Nigeria the money is usually spent on bribing the voters, the police, electoral officials and in hiring and sustaining thugs. The nation needs a law to put a cap on the amount of money an individual or an organisation could donate to a candidate. Such a law should also require a proper documentation and declaration of donations received (*ThisDay Editorial* of July 27, 2003).

In 1925 for instance, the U.S Congress passed the Corrupt Practices Act, which placed limits on the amount of money that could be spent by candidates for Congress. In 1940 the Hatch Act was passed, which placed a limit on individual contributions to national party organisations. The Federal Election Campaign Practices Act of 1972 replaced the 1925 Act; this law placed limits on advertisement expenses, and so forth. In addition, the Campaign Finance Act of 1974 provides for public funding of presidential campaigns for candidates whose party drew at least 25 percent of votes in previous presidential election (Saffell 1975). Nigeria should borrow a leaf from the United States on this, and make necessary modifications to suit its purpose. Its politics should be issues-based. The 2003 general elections were for instance reportedly devoid of 'honesty and integrity' as the voting was coloured by massive 'election fraud in certain states' (*ThisDay*, April 22 and April 24, 2003; AP, April 22, 2003).

There were many other surprises and anomalies in the country during the 2003 electioneering campaigns. The Supreme Court for instance stunned everyone when it empowered civil servants to join partisan politics without minding that civil servants are traditionally shielded from the undercurrents of partisan politics. That would mean the death of career civil service if the verdict were implemented because workers could be hired and fired, harassed and demoted (or promoted) based on party affiliations. This could therefore turn the civil service into political battlegrounds and killing fields.

Valuable time was also wasted in unnecessary feuds and baseless impeachment proceedings against political office holders in the run-up to the 2003 elections. The National Assembly issued many impeachment threats to Chief Obasanjo. Some State Deputy Governors, including those of Cross Rivers, Abia, Lagos states, received their fair share of impeachment threats from their respective state legislature. President Obasanjo on his own waged relentless battles with university lecturers, the National Assembly, the labour union (NLC) and other organised labour and talked more about corruption than he acted on it. His apparent intransigence made it difficult to resolve many of these problems and led to very little being accomplished during his first term in office.

The religious dimension of 'the politics of unreason' bared its fang in the form of full-blown *Shariah* politics that the Zamfara Governor, Alhaji Sani Yerima, introduced into the polity. Other northern Governors followed his example, leading to many riots and loss of lives. The Muslims rioted during the botched *Miss World* beauty contest as they alleged that an article by Isioma Daniel in the *ThisDay* of Nov 16 2002 was 'blasphemous'.

Ethnic politics has been a major problem in the country (Nnoli 1978). As in earlier years, the various ethnic groups try to organise themselves to secure for their ethnic groups a bigger portion of the national cake. The Ibos for instance have Ohanaeze; the Yorubas, Afenifere, and the Hausa/Fulani, Arewa Peoples' Congress. Most of these ethnic groupings also have their own militias *(See the section on ethnic militias)*. In a situation like this, attachment to the nation becomes weakened, making it more difficult to mobilise and channel resources for national development since no one seems to belong to the nation. This is however not to say that ethnic identity does not have any role in development since politics should ideally start at the grassroots. The late Tip O'Neil (former Speaker of the United States House of Representatives, a Democrat) noted in his memoir that "All politics is local." This means that a candidate aspiring for public office should not take his or her constituency for granted because politicians may not win an election without solid support from their home base. Tip O'Neil lost an election because he took his "own neighbourhood for granted" (O'Neil with Novak, 1987).

In 2003 virtually everyone (the good, the bad, and the very ugly) wanted to become either the president of Nigeria, a State Governor, a Senator, Member of House of Representative or Member of the State Legislature. Because of this desperation, there were reports that some who did not even contest elections were declared winners by INEC after it was 'settled' (an euphemism for being bribed). In Anambra state for instance, Mr. Ikechukwu Abana and Dr. Ugochukwu Uba (the elder brother of *godfather* Chris Uba) who were not even nominated by their party (PDP) to contest the elections (they were not published by the INEC as candidates for elections) were declared winners (*Vanguard*, July 23, 2003 and Onyekamuo, August 8, 2003).

The Problem with Nigeria

Chinua Achebe (1983) is probably right that the problem with Nigeria is squarely that of leadership. As he puts it:

"The trouble with Nigeria is simply and squarely a failure of leadership. There is nothing basically wrong with the Nigerian character. There is nothing wrong with the Nigerian land or climate or water or air or anything else. The Nigerian problem is the unwillingness or inability of its leaders to rise to the responsibility, to the challenge of personal example, which are the hallmarks of true leadership."

If leadership were the main cause of Nigeria's backwardness, why haven't Nigerians elected virtuous leaders to move the nation forward? Is the society not tired of blame game politics? Is greed and selfishness not part of the trouble with Nigeria as well? Because of leadership ineptitude, political actors have been moving back and forth on policies, leading to policy instability and unsustainable programmes. Nigerians should conduct a National Conference to determine the causes of their problems because it is only Nigerians who can make Nigeria what Nigeria will become.

Oil, a source of huge income, seems to be one of the problems of Nigeria – rather than the blessing that it should be. Before the discovery of oil in the mid-1950s, the country was largely agrarian and things were relatively working all right. But the advent of oil diverted people's attention away from food crops. The neglect of agriculture in turn led to the country being dependent on a single commodity, oil, as the main source of revenue and chief foreign exchange earner. With the over dependence on oil, a chill in the world's oil market often turns into a serious 'financial pneumonia' in Nigeria. There is therefore an urgent need for the country to diversify its economy to reduce this unhealthy dependence on oil in order to ensure balanced and sustainable economic development (see for instance Dike, June 26 2003). Obviously lack of economic prosperity has been one of the barriers to true democratisation in the country.

Productivity is low and economic progress has been unsatisfactory for most of the population. It is a fact that increases in productivity would benefit both the consumers and producers. For this, the country should be serious with its privatisation of the inefficient and corruption-ridden government owned corporations. But the programme should be transparent and given a human face. If the programme were handled well, it would increase competition, improve productivity, create employment, and reduce poverty and the skyrocketing prices of commodities, which cause high inflation. During the period in review (1999-2003), the value of the Naira (the local currency) has massively depreciated, worsening the level of hardship for many. True democracy can hardly thrive in a society where poverty and hardship are rife and where basic infrastructures are either non-existent or in dilapidated conditions.

The middle class and the political process

It has been argued that a growing and affluent middle class would mean the gradual establishment of an economic and social structure independent of the party-state. This, it is argued, would give rise to demands for more meaningful participation in the political process. Support for this line of reasoning was found in the interpretation of developments in Taiwan and South Korea and in the arguments of Eastern European reformers (Saich 1994). Thus Andrain (1975) noted that wealthy nations would have the resources to produce "the economic surplus needed to satisfy" the demands of their citizens; but he warned that frustration and violence might occur in a society if the needs of the people are not satisfied. Mirsky (1994) supports the argument that economic development in a capitalistic "civil society" fosters "the emergence of a middle class and granting individuals controls over the material circumstances of their lives." Economic freedom is seen here as essential for political freedom (see also Lipset, 1960 and Raymond, 1978, Friedman 1979).

These views are relevant to the present sociopolitical and economic situations in Nigeria. With skyrocketing inflation and rising unemployment (a strange phenomenon economists brand stagflation) and debilitating infrastructure, the federal government seems to be doing very little, if anything at all, to help the masses. Instead, it seems to be worsening the situation by, for instance, increasing the price of fuel. Recently the Obasanjo administration tried to increase fuel prices from N26 to

N40 per litre, but the resultant national strike action forced it to reduce the price to N34 per litre. The strike action paralysed the nation's socio-economic activities for about two weeks. As I noted elsewhere, during that time, a litre of fuel sold for more than N100 in some areas as some greedy individuals took advantage of the situation to create artificial scarcity in order to make quick bucks. However the misery caused by this increase in fuel price seemed not to have perturbed Chief Olusegun Obasanjo and his ruling party, the PDP.

The government does not, and should not hold the answer to every socioeconomic problem because the culture of a society also plays an important part in their development efforts (Huntington & Harrison 2000). This is because the "gross and essential characteristics" of the culture of a people that affect their progress, cannot successfully be modified by government interventions (Will, Jan. 18, 1999). With limited access to resources, the cultural mandate to achieve material success in a country like Nigeria often exerts pressure on the people to succeed by fair means if possible, or foul means if necessary.

The 2003 Politics: Decampments and lack of Ideology

Political parties in most modern societies operate on set of coherent ideology and principles. For instance, the United States has Democrats and Republicans, with each espousing programmes based on their principles. And in Britain, there are the Labour and Conservatives and France has the Socialists and Republicans/Gaulists. Ideology is "a distinct group of beliefs about the social and political world and is a vehicle for the defence or advance of the interests of a social group" (Harris 1986). In addition, ideology is "a set of closely related beliefs or ideas, or even attitudes, characteristic of a group or a community" (Plamentaz 1970 and Glickman 1987). Similarly, a political ideology is "a set of ideas and beliefs" that people hold about their political regime and institutions and about their own position and role in it. Political ideology is sometimes used synonymously with "political culture" or "political tradition". In a sense political ideology moves people into action to bring about changes in their way of life and to modify the existing political, social, and economic relations (Macridis 1983).

Where are Nigerian politicians and political parties on this ideology spectrum? Could a leader govern a nation without a sound philosophical base? Is philosophical principle necessary in governance? What role can ideology play in establishing the norms by which power is exercised and policy made in Nigerian politics? The solutions to problems in societies often start, and should start, with an ideological base from which political issues can be worked out. Ideology, like money or numbers, can function as a political resource in a democratic political competition. In advanced and truly democratic societies, the proper channel to political power has normally been for a politician to espouse a better ideology. In Nigeria however, the politicians engage their political opponents, not by espousing better ideology, but often through physical elimination. Lack of ideology is a 'missing link' in Nigerian politics because it makes party politics not to be issues-based. Nigerian politics often revolves around regional, religious and ethnic groupings and therefore exploit the emotions of the gullible masses. And this, in electioneering years often turns the society into a wild and lawless place.

Most Nigerian politicians are opportunists at best because they often join the winning party, even if the philosophy of the party is contrary to their own personal principles (if they have any at all). They thus waffle on issues, displaying in the process what Lipset and Raab 1970 refer to as "common democratic commitment" as opposed to an "ideological democratic commitment." By, "common democratic commitment", the authors meant a pervasive popular attachment to democratic pluralism, which is essentially affective in nature. They defined "ideological democratic commitment" as an uncommon attachment to democratic pluralism, which is both cognitive and affective in nature. Thus 'common democratic commitment' exists more as a loyalty to institutions, groups and systems that support democratic procedure than is an internalised conceptual commitment. The authors argue that when the loyalty in this form of commitment to democracy is shaken or destroyed, the democratic commitment is also destroyed. In contrast, those who are committed 'ideologically' to democracy are not easily swayed. In other words, they do not fickle because they are solidly and deeply committed to democracy and all it represents. It may be tempting to wonder how many of Nigeria's politicians are ideologically committed to the cause of democracy, or to any set of principles – given the haste with which they change their party affiliations at the slightest opportunity. *(See Table B next page)*

With numerous registered political parties (30) in the country in the run-up to the 2003 elections, and with the politics of opportunism and the attendant decampment rife, violence and thuggery became part of the equation, turning the country into a theatre of the absurd (see Dike, Jan.30, 2003).

For Nigeria to remain united and prosperous, the country should restructure the system and entrust the leadership in the hands of individuals of probity. And there should be no room for individuals with narrow and selfish political objectives.

We shall discuss all the highlighted issues in more detail in the chapters that follow

Table B: Decampments***

Name	Old	New	Name	Old	New
Alhaji Kwatalo (Dep. Gov.)	ANPP	PDP	Emma Bassey (Rep)	PDP	ANPP
Ademu Argungu (Dep Gov.)	ANPP	PDP	Graham Ipingasi (Rep)	PDP	ANPP
Enyinaya Aberiba (Dep. Gov.)	PDP	ANPP	Gbenga Ogunniya	AD	PDP
John Okpa (Dep. Gov.)	PDP	ANPP	Kingsley A. Ogunlewe (Rep)	AD	PDP
Bucknor Akerele (Dep. Gov)	AD	NDP	Mrs. Dorcas Odunjirin (Rep)	AD	PDP
Bucknor Akerele	NDP	UNPP!	Leke Kehinde (Rep)	AD	PDP
Gbenga Aluko (Sen)	PDP	ANPP	Roland Owie	PDP	ANPP
Khairat A. Gwadabe	PDP	ANPP	Marshall Harry **	PDP	ANPP
Danie Saror (Sen)	PDP	UNPP	John Okpa (Dep. Gov)	PDP	ANPP
Peter Ajuwa (Aspirant)	ANPP	LDP	Sergeant Awuse**	PDP	ANPP
Chuba Okadigbo (Sen)	PDP	ANPP	Wahab Dounmu (Sen)	AD	PDP
Ike Nwachukwu (Sen)	PDP	NDP	Emmanuel Iwuanyanwu*	ANPP	PDP
Jim Nwobodo (Sen)	PDP	UNPP	Iyola Omisore (Dep. Gov)	AD	PDP
Chukwuemeka Ezeife	AD	UNPP	Jonah Jang	PDP	ANPP
Mohammed Goni	PDP	UNPP	Yemi Brinmo-Yusuf	AD	PDP
Chris Okotie	NDP	JP	Fidelis Okoro	AD	PDP
Obinna Uzor (Gov. Aspirant)	PDP	NDP	Gbolahan Okuneye (Rep)	AD	PDP
Haruna Abubakar (Gov. Asp)	PDP	NDP	Arthur Nzeribe	ANPP	PDP
Nuhu Audu (Gov. Asp)	PDP	UNPP	Laken Balogun (Sen)	AD	PDP
Mala Kachala (Gov Asp)	ANPP	AD	Alex Kadiri (Sen)	ANPP	PDP
Mike Mku (Gov. Asp)	PDP	UNPP	Funsho Williams	AD	PDP
Gbenga Olawepo (Gov. Asp)	PDP	NDP	Rochas Okorocha	PDP	ANPP
M.T. Mbu (Jnr., Sen)	PDP	ANPP	Damishi Sango	PDP	AD
Omololu Meroyi (Sen)	AD	PDP	Olusola Saraki*	ANPP	PDP
Alli Balogun (Rep)	AD	UNPP	Alhaji Abdul-aziz Tonku (Rep)	ANPP	UNPP
Appolos Amadi (Rep)	PDP	NDP	Muhammad Nura Khalie	PDP	ANPP
Alhaji Mohammed Koirana-Jada	UNPP	PDP	Mrs. Oluremi Adiukwu-Bakare	PDP	AD
Uche Ogbonnaya (OGB)	PDP	ANPP	Audu Dansa	PDP	ANPP
Ukeje O.J. Nwokeforo	UNPP	AD	Dapo Sarumi	PDP	PAC
Emmanuel Okocha	APGA	PAC	Salisu Matori	PDP	ANPP
Adamu Bulkachuwa	PDP	ANPP	Ibrahim Lame	PDP	ANPP
Kura Mohammed	PDP	ANPP	Annie Okonkwo	PDP	ANPP
Chief Idowu Odeyemi****	PDP	AD	Chief Akin Akomolafe****	PDP	AD
Chief Ade Akilaya****	PDP	AD	Chief (Mrs.) A. Olaye****	PDP	AD
Olufemi Ojo****	PDP	AD	Tunde Owolabi****	PDP	AD
Kayode Oguntoye****	PDP	AD	Ademiluyi Adelanke****	PDP	AD
Emeka Nwajiuba	ANPP	NDP	Don Etiebet	PDP	ANPP
Florence Ita-Giwa	ANPP	N/A	Bob Nwanunnu	ANPP	N/A
James Mako (States Rep) Ebonyi	AD	PDP	Magus Ngie Abe (St. Rep) Rivers	ANPP	PDP
Fidelis Ogodo (St. Rep) Ebonyi	AD	PDP	Prince Ugorji Ama Oti (St Rep)	ANPP	PDP
Arinze Egwu (St Rep) Ebonyi	ANPP	PDP	Ben Oke Obasi (St Rep) Ebonyi	ANPP	PDP
Patrick Edediugwu (St Rep)	ANPP	PDP	Joseph Egwuta (St Rep) Ebonyi	ANPP	PDP
Ray Akanwa (St Rep) Ebonyi	PDP	ANPP	Linus Okorie (St Rep) Ebonyi	PDP	ANPP
Bode Olajumoke (St Rep) Ondo	ANPP	PDP	Jafar Bio Ibrahim (St Rep) Kwara	ANPP	PDP
Hassan Y. Bagudu (St Rep) Kwara	PDP	ANPP	Raheem Agboola (St Rep) Kwara	AD	ANPP
Ambali Amuda (St Rep) Kwara	ANPP	PDP	Uche Nwole (St Rep)	PDP	ANPP
Khinde Ayoola	AD	PDP	Peter Adeyemo	AD	PDP
Alli Balogun	AD	PDP	Ayoka Lawani	AD	PDP
Peter Oyetunji (St Rep)	AD	PDP	Olubunmi Odumbaku (St. Rep)	AD	PDP
Ramota Okemakinde (St Rep)	AD	PDP	Prince Elvis Jude Agukwe	PDP	AD
Nnanna Onyenekwu (St. Rep)	ANPP	PDP	Effiong Edunam	NDP	PDP
Catherine Acholonu	PDP	UNPP	Catherine Acholonu	UNPP	NDP
Chinwoke Mbadinuju (Anambra Gov)	PDP	AD	Bukar Mai Lafiya (Gombe St)	ANPP	PDP
Alhaji Baffa Ahmed Garkuwa	ANPP	PDP	Col. Magji Deb (rtd)	ANPP	PDP
Abdulmuminu Abubakar	ANPP	PDP	Alhaji Sa'idu Shehu Awak	ANPP	PDP
Sa'adu Muhammad	ANPP	PDP	Muhammad Dukku (Rep)	ANPP	PDP
Muhammad Abubakar Umar (St, Rep)	ANPP	PDP	Mr. Lebetek (Gombe State)	ANPP	PDP

Name	Old	New	Name	Old	New
Alhaji Sada Yakubu (Katsina St)	ANPP	NDP	Ademola Adegoroye (Ondo St)	AD	NDP
George Okpagu (Anambra St)	UNPP	ANPP	Ichie Mike Ejezie (Anambra St.)	UNPP	ANPP
Alhaji Ibrahim Ali Amin (Kano St.)	ANPP	PRP	Emmanuel Aguariavwodo (Rep)	ANPP	PDP
Isa Kachako (Kano St.)	ANPP	PDP	Toyin Anifowoshe	NDP	JP
Toyin Anifowoshe	JP	NDP	Alhaji Ibrahim Apata (AJG group)	ANPP	PDP

Sources: Compiled by the author from: *Daily Independent*, "The decampment Option" Feb 5, 2003; *The Guardian*,
"Four PDP Senators Decamp To ANPP, AD Whip Joins PDP," Jan 11, 2003; *ThisDay*: "Okadigbo Decamps to ANPP," Nov 30, 2002;
ThisDay: "Carpet-crossing: The Fourth Republic Experience," May 26, 2002; *New Nigeria*: "3 AD Defect To PDP, " May, 17, 2002;
The Guardian: "Saraki was expelled, ANPP insists," July 5, 2002; Weekly Trust: "Nura Khalil deserts PDP, joins ANPP" Nov 15, 2002;
Daily Trust: "Aggrieved legislator defects to UNPP, bids for Senate," Feb 18, 2003; The Guardian: "UNPP adopts Bucknor Akerele as governor-
Ship candidate, Balogun quits AD," Feb 18, 2003; The Guardian: "Adiukwu-Bakare, ex-Lagos PDP governorship aspirant, supporters join AD,"
Feb 21, 2003; *ThisDay*: "Why I Quit PDP – Sarumi" Feb 27, 2003; *ThisDay*: "PAC Flagbearer Survives Acid Bath," Feb 27, 2003;
ThisDay: "2 PDP Senators Defect to ANPP," Feb 28, 2003; ThisDay: "Ex-PDP Chieftain Lauds Buhari-Okadigbo Ticket," Feb 28, 2003
ThisDay: "PDP Loses 1,000 Members to AD in Ekiti," March 1, 2003; ThisDay: "2003: Sidelined State Law Makers (1)," March 1, 2003; Daily Trust:
"Another ANPP chieftain shot in Imo." March 7, 2003; The Guardian: "Four Oyo legislators dump AD for PDP." March 11, 2003;
ThiDay: "Udenwa's Aide Decamps to AD." The Guardian: "Akwa Ibom NDP executive decamp to PDP." March 11, 2003; The Guardian: "Acholonu dumps UNPP,
Joins NDP;" March 10, 2003; Daily Independent: "Mbadinuju to dump PDP for AD;" March 11, 2003. Daily Trust: "Four ex-aides of Gov Hashidu decamp to PDP."
March 10, 2003; ThisDay: "Why I Quit ANPP – Guber Candidate." March 14, 2003; ThiDay: "Why I Quit AD, By Adegoroye," March 16, 2003; ThiDay: "UNPP Decampees Swell Moghalu's Rank." March 15, 2003; ThisDay: "Amin, ANPP Chieftain Joins PRP." March 17, 2003; The Triumph: "Kachako dumps ANPP for PDP...calls former party 'a broken calabash'" March 25, 2003; Daily Independent: "Anifowoshe replaces Amure as Lagos NDP candidate" March 25, 2003; Daily Independent: "Kwara: ANPP supporters decamp to PDP;" April 16, 2003.
March 9, 2003
*One of the founding members of APP (now, ANPP)
**One of the founding fathers of PDP
***This is just a sample of those who decamped
****The PDP in Ekiti State suffered a major set back with about 1,000 of its members decamping to AD (see ThisDay, March 1, 2003)
! "NDP expels Bucknor-Akerele" Vanguard: Feb 15, 2003
N/A= Not available

References

Achebe, Chinua The Trouble with Nigeria. [Enugu, Nigeria: Fourth Dimension, 1983]

Andrain, Charles F; *Political Life and Social Change: An Introduction to Political Science.* (2nd edition.), [Belmont, California: Duxbury Press, 1975]

AP: "Obasanjo Wins Re-Election in Nigeria;" April 22, 2003

Dike, Victor E. *Democracy and Political Life in Nigeria.* [Zaria, Nigeria: ABU Press, 2001]

--------------------; "In need of a democratic Leader;" *Daily Trust,* July 8, 2003

--------------------; "Fuel price increases and distributive consequences;" *Daily Trust,* June 26, 2003

--------------------; "To Sustain the Unity of Nigeria;" *Daily Independent,* Jan 30, 2003

--------------------; "Automatic Re-election and Corruption," Online: *Nigerdeltacongress.com,* February 2003

Glickman, Harvey; "Reflections on State-Centrism as Ideology in Africa." *The African State in Transition,* Zaki Ergas (ed.) [New York: St. Martins Press, 1987]

Harrison, Lawrence E. and Samuel P. Huntington. *Culture Matters,* (eds.), New York: Basic Books, 2000).

Mirsky, Yehuda; "Democratic Politics, Democratic Culture: Democratisation and Civil Society." *Current History,* January 1994

Macridis, Roy C; *Contemporary Political Ideologies.* (2nd Ed.) [Boston & Toronto: Little, Brown and Company, 1983]

Machiavelli, Niccolo; *The Prince.* [Dover Publications: (unabridged), 1992].

Nnoli, O; Ethnic Politics in Nigeria; [Enugu, Nigeria: Fourth Dimension, 1978]

Lipset, Seymour; *Political Man.* [New York: Doubleday, 1960]

Lipset, Seymour Martin and Eral Raab; *The Politics of Unreason* [2nd ed.; 1970]

Onyekamuo, Charles; "Abana, Anambra Senator, Loses Seat;" *ThisDay,* August 8, 2003

Plamenatz, John; *Ideology* [London: Pall Mall Press, 1970]

Raymond, Walter J; *Dictionary of Politics;* [Brunswick Pub Company, 1978]

Will, George F. "The Primacy of Culture." *Newsweek,* January 18, 1999

ThisDay: "The Enemies Within," Feb 23, 2003

----------: "Buhari: Don't Recognize Obasanjo After May 29;" April 24, 2003

----------: "Obasanjo Re-elected, Extends Hands of Fellowship;" April 22, 2003

----------: "Mass Action: I'm Prepared to Go To Jail, Says Okadigbo." May 15, 2003

----------; "A Law on Campaign Finance;" (Editorial) July 27, 2003

The Guardian: "A lid on campaign donations" Feb 25, 2003

Vanguard: See Anayo Okoli on "'INEC didn't register Abana'" July 23, 2003

Chapter 2

2003 Elections: Political Parties and Electoral Commissions

Brief Survey of Party Activities

Though party politics in Nigeria dates back to pre-independence era[1], Nigerians actually began to participate fully in partisan politics during the 1959 general elections that ushered in the First Republic. Twenty-six political parties were authorised to contest the elections leading to the First Republic (1960-1966) including the Democratic Party of Nigeria and Cameroon (DPNC), Northern Elements Progressive Union (NEPU), United Middle Belt Congress (UMBC), Borno Youth Movement (BYM), and United National Independent Party (UNIP). There were three main political parties, each dominated by one of the three main ethnic groups in the country - the Northern People's Congress (NPC), the Action Group (AG), and the National Council of Nigeria and the Cameroons (later called the National Council of Nigerian Citizens (NCNC).

The 1964 general elections witnessed the alliance of parties, which produced two political alliances - the Nigerian National Alliance (NNA) and the United Progressive Grand Alliance (UPGA). [2] The NNA was made up of the Northern Peoples Congress (NPC), the Nigerian National Democratic Party (NNDP), the Midwest Democratic Front (MDF), the Dynamic Party, the Republic Party, the Niger Delta Congress, and the Lagos State United Front. The UPGA was an amalgam of the National Council of Nigerian Citizens (NCNC), Action Group (AG), Northern Elements Progressive Union (NEPU), United Middle Belt Congress (UMBC) and Northern Progressive Front (NPF). But the alliance eventually disintegrated (Andrain 1975). The elections were riddled with cases of intimidation and killing of political opponents and the destruction of properties.

In November 1962, Chief Obafemi Awolowo was jailed for treasonable felony, while the crisis generated by the contentious

26

1963 census added to the tension in the polity. These crises eventually led to the first military coup in 1966 and the suspension of political parties. There was a bitter civil war and eventually general elections in 1979 to usher in the Second Republic.

The 1979 general elections, which came after 13 yeas of military rule, saw the creation of new political parties in the polity. There were five political parties - the National Party of Nigeria (NPN), the Unity Party of Nigeria (UPN), the Peoples Redemption Party (PRP), the Great Nigeria Peoples Party (GNPP), and the Nigerian Peoples Party (NPP). However, these parties, like the previous ones, were more or less controlled by particular ethnic groups [3]

During the 1983 general elections the Nigerian Advance Party (NAP) joined the main parties in the race. But its impact was not much because the party could not control any State. There were, as usual, allegations of frauds and massive rigging of elections during the period. Three months into the second Shehu Shagari administration, the military intervened again, and once more suspended political activities.

The 1989 and 1993 elections came after years of military misrule. New parties were also created. However, the political parties -the Social Democratic Party (SDP) and the National Republican Convention (NRC) were not established by the people, but by General Ibrahim Babangida. Chief Moshood Abiola of the SDP, who was believed to have won the 1993 presidential elections, received 4.3 million of the 6.6 million votes counted, against 2.3 million for Bashir Tofa of the NRC. However, the final official result was halted by the military government of General Ibrahim Babangida, leading to the historic election annulment of June 12, 1993 (Suberu, 1994). The annulment generated a wave of political protests, forcing President Babangida to step aside and set up an Interim National Government (ING), headed by Ernest Shonekan. On 27 August 1993, the ING was toppled by General Sani Abacha.

During the transitional programme of General Sani Abacha five political parties were created. The parties were - Congress for National Consensus (CNC), Democratic Party of Nigeria (DPN), Grassroots Democratic Movement (GDM), National Centre Party of Nigeria (NCPN) and the United Nigeria Congress Party (UNCP). However contrary to democratic tenets, all the five political parties adopted General *Sani Abacha* as their sole presidential candidate during the elections (Suleiman, July 22-28, 1998). The late Chief Bola Ige who branded the five political parties 'five leprosy fingers' adopted the principle of aloofness -'*Siddon look*' -during the transitional programme of General Ibrahim Babangida and General Sani Abacha because he predicted (and rightly, one might add) that the transitions would not lead Nigeria anywhere.

The death of General Sani Abacha in June 1998, brought to an end these political parties. General Abdulsalami Abubakar was chosen to succeed Abacha and he is best remembered for supervising the 1999 transitional programme. The 1999 general elections (the Fourth Republic) witnessed the creation of many new parties but only nine were given provisional registration to contest the 1999 elections. However only three parties – the Peoples Democratic Party (PDP), the All People's Party (APP), which is now ANPP, and the Alliance for Democracy (AD) had the political wherewithal to contest the general elections (Dike, 2001).

The journey through the memory lane of party activities in the country is to note how far Nigeria has come with party politics. The *brouhaha* that occurred during the 2003 electioneering campaigns was not good for the image of Nigerian politicians. The PDP increased the number of States under its control to 27 in the 2003 elections from 21 (1999) and ANPP went down to 8 from 9 and the AD down to 1 from 6.

The pattern of politics with bitterness continued into the 2003 elections with more horrifying episodes. As noted in *The Guardian* of Jan 17, 2003, before the 2003 party primaries, intra-party squabbles, protests, ethnicity and corruption littered the political landscape. And according to the *Reuters* (Sept 23, 2002) and *ThisDay* (Feb 19, 2003) political assassinations (*see* Table, A) and corruption were on the increase during the 2003 politics. The more terrifying aspect of it all was that the Nigerian police were ill-equipped to track down those involved in the assassinations. The *BBC had* for instance on 17 January 2003 reported that the police had uncovered a plot by some unscrupulous party members to print a huge number of fake voters cards in Lagos. Despite this however, and the signs that the 2003 elections were not going to be free and fair, the police still failed to prevent the large scale frauds that reportedly marred the elections. The table below shows the 30 political parties registered by INEC to contest the elections.

Table C: **30 Political Parties**

1	Action Renaissance Party (ARP)	16	New Democrats (ND)
2	United Democratic Party (UDP)	17	Nigeria Advance Party (NAP)
3	National Conscience Party (NCP)	18	Nigeria Peoples' Congress (NPCO)
4	All Peoples Liberation Party (APLP)	19	Party for Social Democracy (PSD)
5	Better Nigeria Progressive Party (BNPP)	20	Peoples Mandate Party (PMP)
6	Community Party of Nigeria (CPN)	21	Peoples Redemption Party (PRP)
7	Democratic Alternative (DA)	22	Peoples Salvation Party (PSP)
8	Justice Party (JP)	23	Progressive Action Congress (PAC)
9	Liberal Democratic Party of Nigeria (LDPN)	24	The Green Party of Nigeria (GPN)
10	Masses Movement of Nigeria (MMN)	25	Alliance for Democracy (AD) [*]
11	Movement for Democracy and Justice (MDJ)	26	People's Democratic Party (PDP) [*]
12	National Action Council (NAC)	27	All Nigeria Peoples Party (ANPP) [*]
13	National Mass Movement of Nigeria (NMMN)	28	United Nigeria Peoples Party (UNPP)
14	National Reformation Party (NRP)	29	National Democratic Party (NDP)
15	New Nigeria Peoples Party (NNPP)	30	United Progressive Grand Alliance (UPGA)

Sources: Compiled by the *Author* from, *The Guardian*: "INEC Okays two parties, new groups get certificates," Dec 18, 2002. *The Guardian*: "Applause, Criticism Greet New Parties'
Registration," June 23, 2002. *Daily Independent Newspaper*: "INEC registers 22 new parties," Dec 3, 2002.
ThisDay: "Supreme Court Orders Registration of New Parties," Sept 11, 2002.
ThisDay: "Now, to Real Politics,"
June 23, 2002
[*]= AD, APP (now ANPP) and PDP are the 3 old political parties

Though 30 political parties were registered, only 17 submitted presidential candidates to the INEC on time for the elections (parties had until Feb 11, 2003 to do that).

Table D: **The 17 Parties with Presidential Candidates and the 13 without Presidential Candidates**

Political Parties	Presidential Candidates	Running Mate	Political Parties without Presidential Candidates
People's Democratic Party (PDP)	Gen Olusegun Obasanjo	Atiku Abubakar	Alliance For Democracy (AD)
All Nigeria Peoples Party (ANPP)	Gen Muhammadu Buhari	Dr. Chuba Okadigbo	Nigerian Peoples Congress (NPC)
National Conscience Party (NCP)	Chief Gani Fawehimi	Jerome Tala Topye	Community Party of Nigeria (CPN)
All Progressive Grand Alliance (APGA)	Gen Odumegwu Ojukwu	Alhaji Sani Bayero	All Peoples Liberation Party (APLP)
National Democratic Party (NDP)	Gen Ike Nwachukwu	Alhaji Aliyu Habu-Fari	Peoples Salvation Party (PSP)
United Nigeria Peoples Party (UNPP)	Jim Nwobodo	Alhaji Mohammed Goni	United Democratic Party (UDP)
Progressive Action Congress (PAC)	Ms. Sara Jubril	Chief Mohammed Shittu	New Democrats (ND)
Peoples Mandate Party (PMP)	Chief Arthur Nwankwo	Otubo Raymond	Better Nigeria Progressive Party (BNPP)
African Alliance Party (AAP)	Alhaji Yahaya Ndu	Hajiya Asma'u A. Mohammed	Masses Movement of Nigeria (MMN)
National Action Council (NAC)	Dr. Olapade Agoro	N/A	National Reformation Party (NRP)
Peoples Redemption Party (PRP)	Alhaji Balaraba Musa	Ngozi Okafor	Party for Social Democracy (PSD)
Democratic Alternative (DA)	Dr. Abayomi Ferreira	Edoibge Ihi Emmanuel	National Mass Movement of Nigerian (NMMN)
Justice Party (JP)	Pastor Chris Okotie	Hajiya Mairo B. Habib	New Nigerian Peoples Party (NNPP)
Movement for Democracy and Justice (MDJ)	Alhaji M.D. Yusuf	Emantor Patrick Wales	
Liberal Democratic Party of Nigeria (LDPN)	Chief Pere Ajunwa	N/A	
Green Party of Nigeria (GPN)	Chief Olisa Agbakoba	N/A	

Sources: Compiled by the author.
N/A=Not Available

Despite the disagreement between Chief Olusegun Obasanjo and the PDP members in the National Assembly, Chief Olusegun Obasanjo still won the party's nomination (some would say rigged out Dr. Alex Ekwueme, his main rival) and other candidates in the 2003 PDP primary at Abuja on Jan 5, 2003. He received 2642 votes while Dr. Alex Ekwueme got a paltry 611 votes. Other contestants were Abukakar Rimi, who received 159 votes and Barnabas Gemade who got 17 votes (*BBC,* Jan 6, 2003 and *ThisDay,* Jan 6, 2003). One should recall that Chief Obasanjo had defeated Dr. Alex Ekwueme in the 1999 primary elections in Jos. Dr. Alex Ekwueme tried unsuccessfully through the courts to stop Chief Obasanjo from becoming the PDP flag bearer.

Electoral Commissions (1959-2003)

An electoral commission has always been set up to supervise elections in Nigeria since 1959. Some of these include FEDECO, NECON, NEC; and the Independent National Electoral Commission (INEC), which was established to supervise the General Abubakar transitional programme. INEC was chaired by Justice Epharim Akpata. Generally the responsibilities of electoral commissions include voter registration, public enlightenment, preventing electoral fraud and generally ensuring the integrity of the electoral process. The viability of a nation's democracy is sometimes judged by how 'free' and 'fair' the process of choosing their leaders is, and the effectiveness and neutrality of the electoral body charged with conducting the elections. Obviously, if the politicians bribed their ways to "victory", common sense dictates that they are bound to be corrupt and dishonest since they would try to recoup whatever they spent during the elections and also appease their supporters before serving the public.

The table below shows the five Electoral Commissions, which Nigeria has had since independence. *(next page)*

While it may be unrealistic to expect any election to be totally free of malpractice, the overall result should reflect the will of the electorate, even if some doubts may be raised over the outcome in an "odd constituency" (Wiseman 1990). This is not the case with the 2003 elections, where most people questioned its fairness while many seemed alienated by the central role-played by retired military Generals.

Table E: **Electoral Commissions and Chairmen** (1959-2003)

Commission	Year
Electoral Commission (a)	1959
The Electoral Commission of Nigeria – ECN	1964-1965
The Federal Electoral Commission – FEDECO	1979-1983
National Electoral Commission – NEC	1987-1993
National Electoral Commission of Nigeria –NECON	1994-1998
The Independent National Electoral Commission –INEC	1998-Present
Chairman	**Year**
R.E. Wraith – a Briton (a)	Electoral Commission (1959)
Eyo Esua *	ECN (1964)
Michael Ani **	FEDECO (1979)
Victor Ovie-Wiskey ***	FEDECO (1983)
Eme Awa****	NEC (1987)
Prof Humphrey Nwosu +	NEC -replaced Awa
Okon Uya ++	NEC (1993) – replaced Nwosu
Sumner Dagogo Jack +++	NECON (came in and out with Abacha)
Justice Epharim Akpaka ++++	INEC (1998)
Dr. Abel Guobadia *+	INEC (May 2000-Present)

Sources: Compiled by the author; (a) The election that ushered in the First Republic.
See Nwokocha, March 1999; *The Comet*: May 18, 2000; *Vanguard:* May 30, 2000;
(a) Mr. R.E. Wraith (senior lecturer in Pub Admin, Univ. College, Ibadan) supervised the 1959 general elections
Eyo Esua, a civil servant, headed the ECN in 1964.
** *Michael Ani* became the chairman of FEDECO in 1979.
***Justice *Victor Ovie-Wiskey* took over the chairmanship of FEDECO after Ani, and conducted the controversial 1983 general elections.
****In 1987 President Babangida appointed Eme Awa, a professor of political science at the University of Nigeria, Nsukka, as the chairman of NEC.
+Professor *Humphrey Nwosu* replace Prof. *Eme Awa*, another political science professor from UNN.
++ *Okon Uya* also another university professor replaced Nwosu when Babangida annulled the 1993 election. Uya's NEC was getting ready to conduct fresh elections when General Abacha struck.
+++*Sumner Dagogo Jack*: General Abacha set up his own electoral commission – NECON, headed by *Sumner Dagogo Jack*. The era of NECON ended with the death of Abacha on June 8, 1998.
++++Justice *Epharim Akpata*: After that, General Abubakar inaugurated the INEC in August 1998, with Justice Epharim Akpata as the chairman. This commission

was mandated to complete the transitional democratic programme bungled by Babangida and Abacha.

*+Dr. Abel Guobadia became the new chairman of INEC, in May 2000, after the death of Justice Akpata

2003 Politics and the Retired Generals

Retired army officers dominated the 2003 politics. Four retired Generals participated actively as presidential candidates. They are Generals Olusegun Obasanjo (PDP), Muhammadu Buhari (ANPP), Chukwuemeka Odumegwu Ojukwu (APGA) and Ike Nwachukwu (NDP). Many other officers participated actively in other capacities - Tunde Ogbeha and David Mark were elected Senators while Diepreye Alamieyeseigha and Mohammed Lawal were elected Governors of Bayelsa and Kwara states respectively. Other retired Generals who participated actively in the politics of the Fourth Republic include Augustus Aikhomu, Olabode George, Abdukareem Adisa, Lawrence Onoja Joshua Madaki, Jerry Useni, Isa Mohammed, David Jemibewon, Theophilus Danjuma, Aliyu Mohammed Gusua, Col.Yohanna Madaki, Elias Nyiam, John Shagaya and Jonah David Jang (see *Daily Independent*, Jan 14, 2003, *ThisDay*, Jan 12, 2003 & Jan 26, 2003 and *The Guardian* of Jan 16, 2003). This is not to mention General Ibrahim Babangida who reportedly has been remotely controlling political activities in the country.

Many Nigerians were quite displeased with the involvement of the retired military officers in politics, especially given the role most of them played in derailing previous transition programmes. As Jato Ibrahim puts it, "these generals who are conveniently elbowing politicians out of the political space were architects of whatever woes Nigeria is suffering today, and they ought not be allowed to assume the kind of role they are playing in the polity." Others see their dominance of the political landscape as a sign that the politicians have failed (see for instance *ThisDay* of Jan 1, 2003). Dennis Austin (1993) has rightly noted that many African autocrats "who are less keen to become democrats than they appear to be so always conjure up various programmes for democracy" which they seek to manipulate.

And the result is often a kind of 'African masquerade with intent to deceive'

Two good examples of this 'intent to deceive' in Nigeria are the annulment of the June 12 19993 elections by General Babangida and the General Abacha's 1998 election charades. Both Generals planned and manipulated their transitional programmes. The military's transitional programmes were often aimed at legitimating the regime in power while deflecting attention from their incompetence and lack of serious programmes for the country. Col. Abubakar Umar, in his resignation letter during the Babangida regime for instance stated that, "the military, as represented by our present leadership has become a stumbling block to the development of the nation's democracy" (Suberu 1994). The incursion of the military into Nigerian politics has led to an increasing pathological political ambition among its officers, with the officers either remotely controlling the political process or physically and actively involved in the process. For instance, many military Generals are chairman of boards of rich corporations; and some influential military officers have been state governors or administrators. As a result, many of them live in flamboyant excesses and are boastful owners of multi-billion Naira businesses, including banks and other financial institutions. Many of the military officers were known to have spent too much time fretting over the spoils of office, with little or no time allocated in doing their duties as professional soldiers (*The Economist,* Aug 21, 1993; Lawal, Aug 10, 1998). The money they amassed during their years in government helped them to come back in full swing in the 2003 elections, taking complete charge of the political process, with the professional politicians playing second fiddles.

Notes and References

1. The first Nigerian political party was the *Nigerian Democratic Party*. Herbert Macaulay led the party, founded in 1922, and it won the three seats for the Lagos Legislative Council, while the Calabar Improvement League won the only seat for Calabar. But those who could vote, or be voted for, during that period were only British citizens living in the cities and British Protected Persons with a minimum gross income of 100 Pounds a year. Consequently, many Nigerians were not allowed to vote (see *ThisDay*: "1922 to 2002: Evolution of Political Parties in Nigeria." Dec 12, 2002; See also Online: www.nigeriafirst.org: "The Nigerian Electoral Process in perspective." Accessed on March 5, 2003.

2. See Online: www.nigeriafirst.org: "The Nigerian Electoral Process in perspective." Accessed on March 5, 2003; also see The Guardian: "Zik, NCNC and political evolution," June 13, 2002. Also see Perspectives on Nigeria's Fledging Fourth Republic (ed.), M. Adejugbe. Malthouse Press, Lagos, Nigeria, 2002; *ThisDay*: "2003: The Usual Suspects." March 3, 2002

3. See *ThisDay*: "1922 to 2002: Evolution of Political Parties in Nigeria." Dec 12, 2002; *ThisDay*: "2003: The Usual Suspects." March 3, 2002

Andrain, Charles F. *Political Life and Social Change: An Introduction to Political Science.* (2nd Ed) [Belmont: California, Duxbury Press, 1975].

Anele, Douglas. "The democratisation process in Nigeria: A critical notice." *Vanguard:* Jan. 24, 1999.

AP: "Government critic killed in Nigeria," Sept. 3, 2002

AP: "Gunmen kill Nigerian ruling party official," Aug. 17, 2002

Austin, Dennis. "Reflections on African Politics: Prospero." Ariel and Caliban, *International Affairs;* Vol. 69, No. 2., 1993

Brett, E. A. "Neutralizing the Use of Force in Uganda: the Role of the Military in Politics," *The Journal of Modern African Studies,* 33, 1, 1995

BBC News: "Nigerian party backs Obasanjo," January 6, 2003

BBC News (on the fake voter's cards): January 17, 2003

BBC News: "Nigerian Candidate Attacked." March 14, 2003

Daily Independent: "The decampment Option," Feb 5, 2003

------------------------: "INEC registers 22 new parties," Dec 3, 2002

------------------------: "The year of the generals." Jan 14, 2003

Daily Trust: "Buhari's convoy attacked in Adamawa." March 14, 2003

Dike, Victor E; Democracy and Political Life in Nigeria. [Zaria, Nigeria: ABU Press, 2001]

------------------; Leadership, Democracy, and the Nigerian Economy: Lessons from the Past and Directions for the
Future [Sacramento, California: The Lightning Press, 1999]
Esajere, Akpo, Saxone Akhaine and John Abba-Ogbodo; "My Ordeal, By Ngige;" *The Guardian,* July 13, 2003
French, Howard W; "Nigeria, a Proud Nation in a Free Fall, Seethes under a General's Grip." *New York Times,* April 4, 1998
Igboanugo, Sunny; "Crushing another madness in South East politics;" *Daily Independent* Online, July 15, 2003
Lawal, Sola; "Beating the Military in Their Own Game." *Post Express,* Aug. 10, 1998.
Maier, Karl: See article on Nigeria: *Africa Report;* July/Aug. 1992, pp.47-48.
New Nigeria: "3 AD Defect To PDP, " May, 17, 2002
NAMPA/Reuters: "Gunmen kill outspoken Nigerian politician," Sept 23, 2002
Otteh, Joseph; "Demanding Accountability for Abuse." *Post Express,* Oct 10, 1998.
Saffell, David; *The American National Government* (4th ed.). [Mass: Winthrop Pub. Company Cambridge, 1975]
Skidmore, Thomas E. & Peter H. Smith; Modern Latin America; [New York, Oxford: Oxford Uni. Press, 1984]
Suberu, Rotimi T. "The Democratic Recession in Nigeria." *Current History,* May 1994
The Economist-*Online*: www.economist.com/countries/Nigeria/ (accessed 2/27/03)
The Guardian: "Four PDP Senators Decamp To ANPP, AD Whip Joins PDP," Jan 11, 2003
------------------: "INEC Okays two parties, new groups get certificates," Dec 18, 2002
------------------: "Applause, Criticism Greet New Parties' Registration," June 23, 2002
------------------: "Political assassination" Nov 21, 2002
------------------: "Governor's aide, Beheaded in Plateau, six feared dead in Ondo," Nov 6, 2002
------------------: "The party primaries: matters arising," January 17, 2003
------------------: "Police arrest seven suspects Over Ige's murder," Dec 27, 2001
------------------: "Saraki was expelled, ANPP insists," July 5, 2002

------------------: "Adiukwu-Bakare, ex-Lagos PDP governorship aspirant, supporters join AD,"
                    Feb 21, 2003
------------------: "2003: The battle of the Generals and their plot to conquer Nigeria." Jan 16, 2003
ThisDay: "Why I Quit ANPP – Guber Candidate." March 14, 2003
-----------: "The Generals' New Symphony." Jan 26, 2003
-----------: "Return of the Generals." January 12, 2003
-----------: "PDP Loses 1,000 Members to AD in Ekiti," March 1, 2003
-----------: "PAC Flagbearer Survives Acid Bath," Feb 27, 2003
-----------: **"Why I Quit PDP – Sarumi," Feb 27, 2003**
-----------: "In Abuja, Saraki Escapes Assassination," Feb 19, 2003
-----------: "Supreme Court Orders Registration of New Parties," Sept 11, 2002
-----------: "Now, to Real Politics," June 23, 2002.
-----------: "Obasanjo Wins by Landslide," January 6, 2003
-----------: "Gunmen Kill ANPP Senatorial Candidate," Feb 11, 2003
-----------: "Okadigbo Decamps to ANPP," Nov 30, 2002
-----------: "Carpet-Crossing: The Fourth Republic Experience," May 26, 2002
Weekly Trust: "Nura Khalil deserts PDP, joins ANPP," Nov 15, 2002
Wiseman, John; *Democracy in Black Africa: Survival and Revival* [New York: Paragon House Pub Company, 1990]

Chapter 3

Virtue and Leadership Challenges in Nigeria

In the preceding chapter we sketched the issues surrounding the 2003 election campaigns and argued that if these issues were not redressed, the system would not evolve into a true democracy. It is believed by many in the society that the dismal performance of the political leadership in Nigeria is one of the central problems facing the nation. This section discusses leadership types, factors that sustain 'instrumental' leaders, and solutions to the leadership issues facing the nation.

Who is a Leader?

The definition of a 'leader' is as diverse as the myriad of books and articles written on the subject. No matter the angle from which one views leadership it is essential to understand that a leader is one who exerts unusual influence and considerable power. McFarland (1969) defines a leader, as "one who makes things happen that would not happen otherwise." If the leader causes changes that he intended, he has exercised power, but if the leader causes changes that he did not intend or want, he has exercised influence, but not power." Hook's (1943) view of a leader is similar to that of McFarland. In *The Hero in History*, Hook depicts a heroic leader as one who makes things happen that ordinarily would not have happened. "The hero in history," he notes "is the individual to whom we can justifiably attribute preponderant influence in determining an issue or event, whose consequences would have been profoundly different if he had not acted as he did." In addition, the hero is "an event-making individual who re-determines the course of history." Here a "leader" refers to persons who occupy important positions in the formal polity, such as Presidents, Prime Ministers, Ministers, Governors, Legislators, Party Officials, Local Government Chairmen, Council Members, and of course, the local Chiefs.

Students of leadership would share the views of Hook and McFarland that the prerequisites of leadership are influence and power. A person, who is endowed with these qualities in the context of a group, community or nation, has the personality of a leader (Kofele-Kale 1976). And Henry Kissinger (US Secretary of State in Nixon Administration) pointed out in one of his famous speeches that a leader has the power to invoke the 'alchemy of great vision.' This means that a leader is expected to possess the power or influence of transforming something common into something precious. This is among the ingredients lacking in Nigeria's leaders.

Leaders have duties too. The task of leaders, according to Gardner (1978), is to help societies understand the problems that all must face, and to aid in the setting of goals and priorities. Leaders must work with others in finding paths to those goals chosen, maintaining public morale and motivation and nurturing a workable level of public unity. Leaders must activate existing institutions in pursuit of the society's goals, or when necessary, help redesign institutions to achieve that result. Leaders must also help people know how they can be at their best "...with malice toward none, with charity for all..." In a free society, leaders perform these functions within a framework of constraints, including an uncorrupted electoral process, the rule of law, institutional checks and balances and a free press. The institutional checks on power must be effective or the laws of the land would be circumvented. Thus every society needs good leaders to move forward.

Types of Leaders

There are many leadership types, and each has peculiar attributes. We shall discuss the two dominant types of political leadership common in contemporary African societies, their attributes, and their methods of affecting changes in the society. These two types are *instrumental leadership* and *societal leadership*.

Instrumental Leadership: The main concern of the *instrumental* leader is how he can use his office to achieve personal goals (i.e.

satisfy personal ambitions and the needs of his/her family, friends and cohorts). Community objectives are secondary to an instrumental leader. He or she may not be lacking in social/community commitments, but in practice more considerations are given to self over the interests of the society, which he governs (Eulau 1963). And the instrumental leader, as Kofele-Koale (1976) points out, would hold on to power as long as private objectives are being achieved. The instrumental leader does not really care whether the community derives any benefit from his rule or not.

Societal Leadership: The *societal* leader is a public servant first, and only secondarily a private person. While the instrumental leader uses official position to promote private and selfish goals, the societal leader subordinates private narrow goals to broader community objectives. For the societal leader, power and influence are important only if they can be used to solve societal problems. The societal leader is likely to resign if he is convinced he cannot influence changes to the benefit of the public (Kofele-Koale 1976).

The above two categorisations are of course ideal types because in reality, leadership in Africa is often a combination of the two, with one type being dominant. In Nigeria, most of the country's leaders would fit more into the category of *instrumental leaders*. Their opportunism seemed to be epitomised by the brutal reign of General Sani Abacha, who stole and hoarded as much money as he could possibly put his hands on, without minding the effect of his actions on the society. As Adesida (Nov. 9, 1998) noted, over $600 million and £75,306,884 were recovered from his family as part of the money he acquired illegally. At the time of writing this (August 2003), the federal government was still working with the international community to repatriate the loots he banked in foreign financial institutions.

Instrumental Leadership: Favourable Conditions

There are many conditions that make instrumental leadership possible in a society. These include:

1)*The guaranteed loyalty of the masses to the leaders:* In Africa, including Nigeria, the masses through socialisation have come to internalise the norms of respect for authority. They find it difficult to criticise or challenge authority (though this is gradually changing).

2)*The title of officeholders -Chief, General, Minister, Commissioners, and so forth:* This allows its holder to insist on being treated like one. And if the behaviour and performances of the present leader is the same (or similar) to that of the past leader, some people may not worry about any change (Mazrui 1966). That would apparently make it a 'usual' behaviour.

3)*Cluster of factors:* a) the symbols of office; b) Ceremonies surrounding the office; c) Material resources. In Africa, even the "ubiquitous walking stick," or a "staff" confers respect to the holder (Schapera 1967; Kofele-Kale 1976).

4)*The deeds of African leaders:* African leaders are usually showered with lengthy eulogies composed while in office by praise singers and hangers-on. These eulogies are often recited to honour the leaders at public gatherings (Schapera, 1967). A friend once noted that Nigerian musicians have a tendency to sing the praises of leaders and men of wealth, without minding how corrupt they might be.

5)*Seeing the leader as the "first citizen" and or the "Great comrade" the omnipresent and omnipotent leader:* Myth-making often confers on African leaders supernatural powers or talents and visions far above what they really possess. Good examples of this include Dr Nnamdi Azikiwe (Zik of Africa), Chief Awolowo (Awo, the legend) in Nigeria, and Nkrumah in Ghana (Nkrumah, the philosopher and Pan-Africanist).

6) *Weak or absence of institutional checks and balances* (Gardner 1978, and Bienes 1993): African societies lack effective institutions that will hold leaders to accountability and check their excesses.

7)*The availability of resources to tap and steal:* Obviously the availability of resources, and the belief they could steal them and get away with it, has helped in perpetuating the instrumental type of leadership in the continent. The story of the mammoth looting of the Nigerian treasury under General Sani Abacha has demonstrated why the checks on power must be made effective and seen to be effective.

Instrumental *leaders* also corrupt their followers, making corruption to become more or less an acceptable national practice. With this, is it any wonder that the economy of a rich country like Nigeria remains perpetually in comatose? As Shakespeare mused in *Julius Caesar* '...the fault is not in our stars but in ourselves.'

Nigeria and the Politics of Virtue

Politics - the management of political affairs, decides what activities are performed in a nation, as it employs all arts (beyond the skill of persuasive oratory), to legislate what 'we should and should not do.' The end of politics is for 'the good of man' and for building 'a well-organised society.' As *The Philosophy of Aristotle* notes, 'virtue and justice [are the] subject matter of politics.' Liebig in *Business Ethics: Profile in Civic Virtue* (1990) notes that virtue is a disposition or trait acquired, at least in part, by teaching, practice, or perhaps, by grace (that is virtue from God). Virtue involves the core belief system of a person such Prudence, Justice, Fortitude and Temperance. It requires the acceptance of equity in human relations and the commitment to act accordingly. In *After Virtue*, MacIntyre (1981) notes that virtue is an acquired human quality, the possession and exercise of which enables us to achieve those goods which are internal to practices, and the lack of which effectively prevents us from achieving any of such goods. Virtue means recognising and doing the right thing.

Virtue is of two kinds: *Intellectual* and *Moral* virtues. The *Nicomachean Ethics* (1996) notes that intellectual virtue, which is acquired through teaching, requires experience and time, while moral or ethical virtue is the product of habit (ethos) and practice. Although intellectual virtue is important in a society, the author emphasises moral virtue, as it relates to politics and leadership. As Aristotle notes, we learn an art or craft by doing the things that are required to learn them. Therefore, men become builders by building houses, become *just* by doing just acts, *temperate* by doing temperate acts, and *brave* by doing brave acts (Gould 1982). Children, Aristotle observed, learn virtue by following rules of good behaviour, hearing stories of virtuous people, and imitating virtuous models: parents, friends, and worthy public figures. Thus a child born by bad parents or a citizen of a corrupt society has little chance of becoming a virtuous adult. In other words, good constituencies produce good leaders.

To be a good leader one has to have good character. As *Newsweek* (June 13, 1994) noted, the *Greek* word, *kharakter* signifies the 'constellation of strengths and weaknesses' and good and bad that forms and reveals the person we are. A person of good character, then, is someone who, through repeated good acts, achieves an appropriate balance of these virtues in his life. Like a successful tennis player or soccer/football professional, the virtuous person plays consistently a good game. This applies to people in business as well as those in government. But a person cannot have good character without being guided or directed by a philosophy that will enable the individual to do what is right. Again, as Aristotle rightly noted, 'We are what we repeatedly do.' Good character comes from living in societies - family, neighbourhoods, religious and civic institutions - where virtue is encouraged and rewarded. However, as Jean Bethke Elshtain notes, '...you can't have strong virtues without strong institutions, and you can't have strong institutions without moral authority' (*Newsweek*, June 13, 1994). Without moral authority one would not be virtuous. Virtuous persons, then, are those of high ethical standards who pursue (or have pursued) activities purely for the good of society – and also for themselves. A virtuous citizen is one who understands that personal welfare depends on general welfare and therefore acts accordingly. And virtuous leaders are persons of honesty, integrity and trust. Virtuous business leaders are those who are sensitive of the fact that the needs and realistic expectations of others in the society in which they carry out their businesses must be satisfied as a condition for their own needs and realistic expectations being met.

Given the nature of things in Nigeria, the preceding philosophical discussions are important lessons for the society. Most politicians, statesmen and business leaders have not been practising the politics of virtue. With prevalent crude politics and its associated political assassinations; with intolerance and politics devoid of ideology; with ethnic politics and politics of political patronage, fraud and resource mismanagement, the leaders of Nigeria have not been working for the welfare of the society. Their self-serving excesses, their lust for power and insatiable appetite for money, which have destroyed the fabric of the society, provide inappropriate models for emulation. For instance General Abacha could not have been a virtuous leader, given the abandon with which he pillaged the nation's treasury and imprisoned or killed innocent citizens during his infamous regime (see for instance *BBC,* July 12, 2002). In the same vein, the annulment of the June 12, 1993 presidential election by General Ibrahim Babangida could not have been right. Also the mysterious death of Dele Giwa under his regime remains unsolved (see for instance *Vanguard,* August 15, 2001; Ugborgu, Sept 23, 2001; Nkwocha, June 24, 2002; and Giwa, June 21, 2002). Although the country does not regard Alhaji Shehu Shagari as a corrupt individual, his administration allowed corruption to blossom, and the economy to be pillaged. The tyrannical General Mohammed Buhari who sent many politicians to prison after the Dec 31, 1983 coup (Babatope, Dec 9, 2001) and promised to stamp out corruption and lawlessness in Nigeria, was himself believed by some to be lawless and corrupt. He has, for instance, been accused of leaving the Petroleum Trust Fund (PTF), which he chaired, in shambles, and with many uncompleted projects.

Corrupt leadership has crippled the engines of NITEL, NEPA, NIPOST and Nigerian Airways, which should help to propel the economy. As noted by the *Daily Trust (July* 23, 2002), and ThisDay (June 24, 2002 and Jan 26, 2003), the Chief Olusegun Obasanjo's civilian administration is perceived as having failed in its avowed war on corruption and poverty. The protracting echoes of corruption from the National Assembly in Abuja since the inception of the Fourth Republic speaks volume. The National Assembly seemed to have been turned into a place where how fast one moves around with *'Ghana-Must-Go'* bags matter more than one's intelligence, conscience or principle.

If 'politics is supposed to build a nation' and 'bring people together for development,' why does it seem to be tearing Nigeria apart? In many democracies lawmakers are remembered for the policies they championed. In Nigeria, the lawmakers are often the main lawbreakers (Dike, Nov 28, 2002). Many countries set high standards for their politicians such that even a casual, politically or socially unacceptable comment by a politician could get that politician in political hot water. For instance, in the USA, public pressure forced Senator Trent Lott to resign as the Senate Majority Leader because of an unguarded comment. In Nigeria however, anything goes! We do not advocate that Nigerians should scrutinise their leaders with the same compulsive thoroughness with which Americans search their leaders for hidden flaws. Though the American society sometimes over flogs issues, Nigeria could learn a lot from the activities and philosophy of America's Founding Fathers: they crafted a Constitution, which is today the envy of the world and believed that the stability and success of their democratic republic rested on the maintenance of virtue among its citizens.

What are the philosophies of Nigeria's Founding Fathers? As I wrote in the *Daily Trust* (July 14, 2003), how well a nation performs economically, politically and socially depends, in some ways, on the creativity, boldness and vision of its founding fathers. The forebears of Nigeria were entangled in tribal and ethnic issues and, therefore, could not lay a solid socio-political and economic foundation for the nation. Many countries were able to wade through their initial crises in nation-building and set up enduring economic and political systems. For most of the Nigerian leaders, beyond the myth, is the reality that they were mostly ethnic champions whose inability to craft an enduring

45

Constitution or set up a true democratic framework has led to the baneful *ethnicisation* of Nigerian politics.

The political class panders to tribal/regional and religious sentiments, leaving serious national issues unresolved. Party leaders and their followers keep running around, jumping from one apparently losing party to another perceived to be likely to win, even if the new party's ideology is not compatible with their own ideological inclination (if they have any, that is).

With visionless leadership, the youths are currently vacillating between hope and anxiety regarding opportunities and challenges posed by modernisation because they lack the means to deal with modernity. As a result, they resort 'to get-rich-quick' ploys, with '419' scams being the favourite. The greedy and selfish political leaders should stop exploiting the masses. They should instead try to control and direct social development by providing basic human needs that will enable the people to cope with the challenges of modernity. As noted in Schleicher (1989) 'many aspects and trend of modernisation must be controlled in order to harmonise them with basic human needs and values.'

There have been unending crises in the oil producing areas of Niger Delta, which has led to a number of high-handed responses by the government, such as the Jesse incident and the *Odi* massacre of Nov 20, 1999 by the military. There have also been threats by some women in the area to go stark naked to protest their squalid living conditions (see *AP* of July 15, 2002 and Onishi Dec 22, 2002), all which go to demonstrate that the government has not been able to find a lasting solution to the problems of the oil-producing areas of the Niger-Delta.

There have also been threats of secession by some leaders from the South-South geo-political zone allegedly because of Chief Olusegun Obasanjo's delay or refusal to sign the *Onshore/Offshore* dichotomy Bill, which they perceived as a mistreatment in the hands of the federal government (see for instance the *Vanguard*, Dec 14, 2002).

The oil companies that degrade and damage the environments in the Niger-Delta area are not virtuous because they are not putting enough money back into the communities from which they drill billions of dollars worth of oil so as to improve their living conditions. They do not seem to understand the fact that virtuous 'business leaders are those leaders who are mindful that the needs and realistic expectations of others in the society, in which they carry out their businesses, must be satisfied if their own needs and realistic expectations are to be met.' Some of the communities in the oil-producing area of *Niger-Delta* do not have good roads, schools, drinking water, health clinics, and even gas stations (Blunt, Oct 21, 1998; Dike, 2001, p. 189; Onishi, Dec 22, 2002). Thus the neglect of human needs and values on the part of the oil companies in the area has contributed immensely to the continued crises in the Niger-Delta area.

The crises enumerated above exacerbate the nation's socio-political and economic problems and help to discourage both local and foreign investors from investing in the economy. Many Nigerians remain poor despite the nation's oil wealth. For fairness, peace and justice, the oil companies operating in the area (and the federal government) must work toward the development of these communities. As the work of *Aristotle* and contemporary philosophers show, the woes of Nigeria emanate from the fact that much of the nation's political and business leaders are not virtuous.

Obasanjo regime and the *Ostrich* leadership Style

Ordinarily, one would not expect that an *Ostrich* would have anything to teach human beings. The *Ostrich* is a swift-footed large bird, that when pursued, hides its head in the sand and believes that it will be unseen. Chief Obasanjo seems to have adopted this approach when confronted with the numerous problems and challenges facing the polity. In order words, since he became the civilian leader of Nigeria on May 29, 1999, Chief Olusegun Obasanjo has, like an *Ostrich*, avoided solving any problem by refusing to face it. This *Ostrich* leadership style has turned the nation into a society where sociopolitical and economic problems remain unresolved.

47

Leadership is not about hiding away from problems or making promises that are never fulfilled; it is about meeting the needs of the people. Nigerians are tired of listening to polished speeches that are mellifluous but cannot solve the problems of the country. The present problems facing the country should be boldly confronted before any sustainable plan could be made for the future. Chief Olusegun Obasanjo displayed an *Ostrich* style of leadership when the *Sharia* crisis erupted; when the politicians were slaughtering one another during the 2003 electioneering campaigns and during the six-month *ASUU* strike and the fuel price crisis. When the PDP adopted Iyiola Otunba Omisore (who was implicated in the murder of Chief Bola Ige) to run for a senate seat, Chief *Obasanjo*, like an *Ostrich* buried his head in the sand and kept mum. Even the recent 'attempted coup' in Anambra state by a political *godfather* could not force the *Ostrich* to get his head out of the sand.

Nigerians are not asking Chief Olusegun Obasanjo and his administration to take them to the moon, or to provide for them anything out of the ordinary. The people are simply asking for basic things like clean streets, maintaining the roads, controlling traffic, making fuel and food available, providing employment, paying the workers regularly and keeping the schools open and funded adequately. Nigerians also want basic healthcare services, electricity, portal water, among other simple things that directly touch on the lives of the citizens. These are basic thing that the citizens of many societies take for granted.

The success of any administration depends on how its policies improve the living standards of the ordinary citizens, and not how richer they make the few rich ones in the corridors of power. The federal government has rolled out a ten-year economic plan that is asking Nigerians to bury their head in the sand like an *Ostrich* and wait for the economy to improve. The Nigerian economy could grow only when the necessary infrastructure and institutional frameworks that would help to improve the nation's industrial base and public utilities are operational and efficient. I do not want to sound pessimistic, but with all the on-going political somersaults in the society, the ten-year economic plan could become another broken dream!

The hungry needs food and employment now, not in ten years' time. Things are already unbearable for them, with rising inflation, worsening poverty level, deterioration in the levels of crime and insecurity, non-functional schools and epileptic NEPA. Yet, the Obasanjo regime, which appears impervious to constructive criticisms, seems not to care. The citizens want promises to be translated into action because action speaks louder than words. When there are problems in a society, a forward-looking leader would immediately probe the issues and proffer solutions. Real leaders are always looking for solutions to the problems facing the citizens and making sure that the provision of the basic necessities of life is his or her top priority. The success of a leader depends on how he or she helps others to achieve what is important to them.

Good quality education, which is among the basic needs of any society, has been noted as the food for the soul that provides the wherewithal and the means for the people to appraise past civilisations and interrogate the present leaders. And the educational level of the citizens is a measure of how far a society has travelled and how close or far away it is from its destination. The Obasanjo regime however seems fond of casting the educators in a negative light for fighting for the welfare of the nation's educational institutions. As has been noted, an 'ostrich-like behaviour only gets one [a leader] a mouthful of sand' while the problems facing the people remain unresolved.

Ethics and Governance

Ethics is action, the way we practice our values, a guidance system used in making decisions. Ethical decisions are often tougher to make than other decisions. The issue of ethics in the public sector encompasses a broad range, including a stress on obedience to authority, on the necessity of logic in moral reasoning, and on the necessity of putting moral judgments into practice (Bowman 1991). The ethical standards are grossly inadequate in all the agencies of government in Nigeria. Many officeholders in the society (appointed or elected) do not have clear conceptions of the ethical demands of their positions, and little attention, if any, is being given to this. Consequently, people abuse and misuse official positions. Custom officers delay the clearance of goods at the ports in order to attract *'dash'* or tips from frustrated traders and travellers. Some police officers demand bribes before they could perform their official duties, and they often set up illegal roadblocks and unauthorised tollgates to extort money from the gullible public. They also harass and sometimes kill innocent citizens who refuse to offer them bribe.

Lack of laws, and/or the failure to effectively utilise existing laws as instruments for regulating the affairs of the society and the failure of law enforcement officers to remain within the confines of law as they carry out their duties, are some of the main issues facing the nation today. This condition is approaching an alarming proportion. The society has many renowned individual performers in numerous fields of endeavour. It has great scientists, artists, great economists and writers. It has world-class surgeons, football players and athletes. But it lacks leaders with depth, dimensions, character, and confidence to serve the society as a whole. To advance the cause of true democracy, the nation has to challenge the status quo. In fact, Nigeria needs *societal* leaders to move forward.

Nigeria needs effective, self-critical, visionary and dynamic national leaders who can put in place structures and reforms that will strengthen the rule of law, support true democracy, promote greater accountability and transparency. The core elements of good character should be the cornerstone of the behaviour of such leaders. These characters include trustworthiness, honesty loyalty, respect, responsibility, self-discipline and hard work. They also include fairness and caring (compassion) and citizenship (including obeying the laws of the land, staying informed and participating actively in the political process - voting, and so forth). This is because "if we want our children to possess the traits of character we admire, we need to teach them what those traits are..." Children imitate what they see and hear (Bennett 1994). And as Stephen L. Carter rightly noted (Newsweek, June 13, 1994), a society that ignores the moral side of life is going down the tubes.

Nigeria needs leaders who are concerned about what they can do for the nation, and not what they can gain from it. As the former U.S. President John F. Kennedy admonished in a speech, 'ask not what your country can do for you, but what you can do for your country.' Nigerian leaders (civilian and military alike) must be among the most myopic leaders in the world. They loot the state and buy most expensive cars the industrial world can build, but they cannot think it wise to build good roads to drive the cars on. They build mansions with looted money, but are not bothered about the epileptic nature of power supply by NEPA. They want good schools, but do not want to adequately fund the country's schools and research institutes. They admire the good healthcare and hospitals abroad (they usually go there for treatment) but do not care that the ones in the country are grossly under-funded.

References

Aristotle; As cited in James A. Gould. Classic Philosophical Questions (4th ed.); [Columbus: Charles E. Merrill Pub. Company, 1982]
Associated Press (AP: Escravos, Nigeria); "Oil company appeases Nigerian women;" July 15, 2002
Babatope, Ebenezar; "Buhari, Politicians and History;" The *Guardian Online*, December 9, 2001
BBC – Africa: "Nigerians divided over Abacha ruling;" July 12, 2002
Bennett, William; *The Book of Virtues: A Treasury of Great Moral Stories.* [Touchstone Books, 1994].
Bienen, Henry; "Leaders, Violence, and the Absence of Change in Africa." *Political Science Quarterly, 1993*
Bowman, James S. "Introduction: Ethical Theory and practice in Public Management." In *Ethical Frontiers in Public Management: Seeking New Strategies for Resolving Ethical Dilemmas.* (ed.). James S. Bowman [San Francisco: Jossey Base, 1991]
Blunt, Liz; "Oil Wealth: An unequal bounty." *BBC: Africa*, October 21, 1998

Bretton, Henry L; *The Rise and Fall of Kwame Nkrumah.* [London: Pall Mall Press, 1967].

Carter, Stephen L. Cited in *Newsweek,* June 13, 1994, p.36

Daily Trust: See "Economic Crimes: Obasanjo admits failure of anti-corruption drive;" July 23, 2002

Dike, Victor E; *Democracy and Political Life in Nigeria.* [Zaria, Nigeria: Ahmadu Bello Univ. Press, 2001]

--------------------: "Lawmakers and Lawbreakers." *Daily Independent,* Nov 28, 2002

--------------------: "Reward System in Nigeria: Workers Morale and Productivity." Online: *www.Nigeriaworld.com,* May

               17, 1999

--------------------: "Reward System and Labour Productivity;" *Daily Independent,* May 15, 2003

--------------------: "Toward Labour Productivity;" *Daily Independent,* May 22, 2003

-------------------; "State Administration and True Federalism;" *Daily Trust,* July 14, 2003

-------------------; "Obasanjo and the *Ostrich* leadership Style;" Online: *www.Gamji.com,* August 2003

Elshtain, Jean Bethke; As cited in *Newsweek,* June 13. 1994, p.36.

Eulau, Heinz; The Behavioural Persuasion in Politics [New York: Random House, 1963]

Gardner, John W. *Morale,* [New York: W. W. Norton and Company, 1978].

Giwa, Yemi; "Oputa Panel IBB can't dictate;" *Nigerian-Tribune,* June 21, 2002

Gould, James A; *Classic Philosophical Questions* (Ed); Charles E. Merrill Publishing Co., Fourth Edition, 1982

Hook, Sidney. *The Hero in History: A study in Limitation and Possibilities.* [New York: The Humanities Press, 1943].

Kofele-Kale, Ndiva; "The Problem of Instrumental Leadership in Contemporary African Political Systems." *Journal of Asian and African Studies,* xiii, 1976.

Lakemfa. Owei; "The military's endless transition." *Vanguard:* July 21, 1998

Liebig, James E; *Business Ethic: Profiles in Civic Virtue;* [Golden, Colorado: Fulcrum Publication, 1990]

MacIntyre, Alasdair C; *After Virtue.* [University Of Notre Dame Press, June 1981]

MacFarlan, Andrew S. *Power and Leadership in Plural Systems* [Stanford: University Press, 1969]

Nkwocha, Jossy; "An all-out War;" *Newswatch*, June 24, 2002

Onishi, Norimitsu; "As Oil Riches Flow, Poor Village Cries Out" *The New York Times*, Dec 2002

Schapera, I. Government and Politics in Tribal Societies [New York: Schocken Books, 1967]

Schleicher, Klaus; "The Future Generation in Industrialized and Developing Countries;" In John Oxenham (ed.), *Education and Values in Developing Nations*. [New York: Paragon House, 1989

ThisDay: "The Poverty Time Bomb;" January 26, 2003

-----------: "Anti-Corruption Panel: The Battle So Far;" June 24, 2002

Ugborgu, Victor; "Above the Law;" *Newswatch*, Sept 23, 2001

Vanguard: "On-Shore/Off-Shore Bill: Obasanjo's parley with N/Delta leaders deadlocked;" Dec 14, 2002

------------: "I'm not afraid to appear before Oputa- IBB –Atmosphere must be conducive, says lawyer;" Aug. 15, 2001

Chapter 4

Corruption in Nigeria: Understanding and managing the Challenges

In the preceding chapter we discussed the types of leadership and their impact on the polity. In this chapter we shall deal with corruption, which I will argue, is related to the leadership problem in the country. The menace of corruption affects the entire social fabric of Nigeria; even the mad people on the streets seem to recognise the havoc caused by this social cancer because the funds allocated for their welfare usually disappear into the thin air – or more correctly into private pockets.

It should be pointed out that corruption is not peculiar to any continent, region or ethnic group. It cuts across faiths, religious denominations and political systems and affects both young and old alike. Corruption is found in both *democratic* and *dictatorial* regimes; *feudal, capitalist* and *socialist* economies. *Christian, Muslim, Hindu,* and *Buddhist* cultures are equally bedevilled by corruption. And corrupt practices did not begin today; the history is as old as the world. Ancient civilisations had traces of widespread 'illegality and corruption.' Thus "corruption has been ubiquitous in complex societies from ancient *Egypt, Israel, Rome,* and *Greece* down to the present" (Lipset and Lenz 2000). Though corruption could be found in every country and society, the degree and magnitude of this differs from country to country.

In Nigeria and other African and Asian countries, the level of corruption seems unacceptable and also seems to defy the usual medicine. Both the leaders and the followers are corrupt. This makes it especially difficult to "cure". The pervasive nature of corruption in virtually every stratum of the society reminds one of the old saying: "When water chokes you, what do you take to wash it down?" (*The Philosophy of Aristotle*). This book will adopt a broad definition of corruption and will suggest, what I consider a novel approach to tackling the problem in Nigeria.

Definition

There are various definitions of corruption – partly because of the extensive attention accorded to it in the literature and by virtually every society in the world. It has for instance been broadly defined as a perversion or a change from good to bad. Corruption or "corrupt" behaviour also "involves the violation of established rules for personal gain and profit" (Sen 1999). Corruption is "efforts to secure wealth or power through illegal means (private gain at public expense); or as Lipset and Lenz, 2000 note, a misuse of public power for private benefit. (Osoba 1996) defined it as an "anti-social behaviour conferring improper benefits contrary to legal and moral norms and which undermine the authorities" ability to improve the living conditions of the people.

Corruption is a behaviour, which deviates from the formal duties of a public role, because of private gain, or expectations of private gain (personal, close family, private clique and so forth). It is a behaviour, which violates rules against the exercise of certain types of duties because of private gains (Nye 1967). This includes bribery (the use of a reward to pervert the judgment of a person in a position of trust); nepotism (bestowal of patronage by reason of *ascriptive* relationship rather than merit); and misappropriation (illegal appropriation of public resources (Banfield 1961). Corruption has been given many funny names in Nigeria including 'settlement,' 'kola,' 'kick back,' 'kick front,' 'goro,' and *'alheri'* (which is an *Hausa* word for 'goodness and righteousness' (Abdulkarim, March 19, 2003).

We have in Nigeria witnessed the phenomenon of reckless conversion of public money, sometimes running into billions of US dollars by some unscrupulous serving and retired army generals and politicians. Under Obasanjo's first term, democracy was more or less turned into "lootocracy" (Edevbaro 1998) as the 'lawmakers' became the 'lawbreakers' influencing legislation with *Ghana-Must-Go bags* (Dike, Nov 28, 2003). It is unreasonable for any political leader to allow corruption to spin out of control, as it appeared to be under Obasanjo's first term in office. Corruption manifests in different forms in Nigeria.

Understanding the forms and nature of corruption

Some studies have sought to understand corruption better by dividing it into many forms and sub-divisions. The various categories include: **1)** political corruption (*'grand'*); **2)** bureaucratic corruption (*'petty'*) and **3)** electoral corruption. Political corruption takes place at the highest levels of political authority, such as with the new phenomenon of 'political *godfathers' (see below)*. It occurs 'when the politicians and political decision-makers, who are entitled to formulate, establish and implement the laws in the name of the people, are themselves corrupt.' It also takes place when policy formulation and legislation is tailored to benefit politicians and legislators. Often times, political corruption is seen as similar to 'corruption of greed.' This is because it affects the manner in which decisions are made, as it manipulates political institutions, rules of procedure and distorts the institutions of government for selfish gain (NORAD, 2000 and The Encyclopaedia Americana, 1999; Williams 1987 and Kibwana et al, 1996; and Lipset and Lenz 2000).

Bureaucratic corruption occurs 'in the public administration" or 'the implementation end of politics.' This kind of corruption has been branded 'low level' and 'street level.' It is the kind of corruption the citizens encounter daily at places like the hospitals, schools, local licensing offices, the police and taxi offices. Bureaucratic 'petty' corruption – also known as the 'corruption of need,' occurs when one for instance obtains a business from the public sector through inappropriate procedure (NORAD, 2000). Electoral corruption includes the purchase of votes with money, promises of office or special favours, coercion, intimidation, and interference with freedom of election. Nigeria provides a good example of this form of corruption.

Votes are routinely bought and people killed or maimed in the name of election; 'losers' are often declared the winners, and the votes are usually counted and collated in areas where votes were not cast. Corruption in office involves such practices as the sale of legislative votes, administrative, or judicial decision, or governmental appointments, which are not based on merit. It also involves any relationship that sacrifices the public interest and welfare, with or without the implied payment of money. (The Encyclopaedia Americana: 1999; Williams 1987; Kibwana, et. al, 1996; Lipset and Lenz 2000). Other forms of corruption include;

◊   *Bribery*: The payment (in money or kind) that is taken or given in a corrupt relationship. These include *kickbacks, gratuities, pay-off, sweeteners, greasing palms*, etc. (Bayart et. al 1997).

◊   *Fraud:* It involves some kind of trickery, swindle and deceit, counterfeiting, racketeering, smuggling and forgery (Ibid. p.11).

◊   *Embezzlement*: This is theft of public resources by public officials. It is when a state official steals from the public institution in which he/she is employed. In Nigeria the embezzlement of public funds is one of the most common ways of capital accumulation, perhaps, due to lack of strict regulatory systems.

◊   *Extortion*: This is money and other resources extracted by the use of coercion, violence or threats to use force. It is often seen as extraction *'from below'* [The police and custom officers are often the main culprits in Nigeria] (Bayart et. al 1997).

◊   *Favouritism:* This is a mechanism of power abuse implying a highly biased distribution of state resources. However, this is seen as a natural human proclivity to favour friends, family and anybody close and trusted.

◊   *Nepotism*: This is a special form of favouritism in which an office holder prefers his/her *kinfolk* and family members. *Nepotism,* [which is also common in Nigeria], occurs when one is exempted from the application of certain laws or regulations or given undue preference in the allocation of scarce resources (*NORAD*, 2000; *Amundsen*, 1997; *Girling* 1997; *Fairbanks*, Jr. 1999).

For effective control of corruption in Nigeria, the country must develop a culture of relative openness, in contrast to the current bureaucratic climate of secrecy. There is also a need for a vigorous promotion of a merit system in employment and the distribution of scarce national resources (instead of the current system that favours ethnicity, state of origin and nepotism). More importantly, the leadership must muster the political will to tackle the problem head-on (see the report of the Second Global Forum on Fighting and Safeguarding Integrity, May 28-31, 1999). Regardless of where it occurs, its causes or the form it takes, the simple fact remains that corruption is likely to have a more profound and debilitating effects in less developed countries, than in wealthy and developed societies. This is due to a number of reasons, many of which can be traced to the nature and causes of their own underdevelopment (see for instance Nye 1967).

Causes of Corruption

It is 'luminously evident' that corruption is not peculiar to Nigeria, but it is a viable enterprise in the country largely because of the absence of an effective system to track and control it. Recently, the International Olympic Committee (IOC), had to relieve some of its officials of their posts because they had taken bribes. And all the commissioners of the European Union (EU) once resigned because they, too, had been found to be corrupt beyond acceptable limits. In the United States and Europe, the law often descends furiously on all found to be corrupt – no matter their standing in the society. The energy trading giant, Enron Corporation, and the telecommunications group, WorldCom, collapsed and filed for Chapter 11 bankruptcy protection because it was found that they 'manipulated their balanced sheets, profit and loss account and tax liabilities.' Enron's accountant -Arthur Andersen also collapsed largely because of its role in the scandal. It was accused of obstructing justice in connection with the Enron probe (*Reuters,* June 27, 2002 and *The Observer* (UK), June 9, 2002). Sam Waksal, the founder of the drug discovery firm, *ImClone Systems* was also found guilty of insider trading and sentenced to seven years and three months in prison and also ordered to pay fines of $4.3 million and back taxes. Martha Steward, owner of a home-decorating empire, was equally implicated in the *ImClone* scandal and indicted on conspiracy charges.

The above examples show that corruption is not an exclusively third world phenomenon – contrary to what some analysts will have us believe. One writer in fact cynically noted that it would *probably* be "difficult to secure [by honest means] a visa to a developing country that would be the subject of a corruption study (Nye 1967). Though corruption is also prevalent in the developed countries of North America and Europe, our examples also show that the law is no respecter of persons or titles when it comes to fighting the menace in these countries. This, sadly, cannot be said of Nigeria.

One may be tempted to pose the question of why corruption is such a viable enterprise in the *Third World,* nay, Nigeria? Some evidence points to a link between 'corruption and social diversity, ethno-linguistic fractionalisation, and the proportions of a country's population adhering to different religious traditions' (Lipset and Lenz, 2000). And studies also show that corruption is widespread in most non-democratic countries, particularly those branded 'neo-*patrimonial*,' '*kleptocratic*' and '*prebendal*' (NORAD, 2000). Thus the political system and the culture of a society could make the citizens more prone to corrupt activities. We shall focus on the fundamental factors that engender corrupt practices in less developed nations, including Nigeria. Some of the factors include:

- o   Great inequality in the distribution of wealth

o   Political office as the primary means of wealth accumulation
o   Conflict between changing moral codes;
o   The weakness of social and governmental enforcement mechanisms; and the
o   Absence of a strong sense of national community (Bryce 1921).

In addition to the above, corruption in Nigeria is also caused by obsession with materialism, compulsion for a shortcut to affluence and the glorification and approbation of wealth, even if ill-gotten (Ndiulor, March 17, 1999). In Nigeria, one of the indices of good living is a display of *flamboyant affluence* and *conspicuous consumption*. Because of this, some people get into dubious activities, including 'committing ritual murder for money-making' in order to have, and be seen to have this good life.

Cases of *ritual* murder abound in Nigeria. The newspaper, *ThisDay, of* July 7, 2002 for instance reported of a middle-aged woman and a high school female student who were beheaded in Akure, the *Ondo* State capital. There was also the celebrated case of Vincent Duru (Otokoto) in Imo state in 1996. A well-known proprietor of *'Otokoto'* hotel, Vincent Duru was reported to have indulged in killing and selling the body parts of some of the travellers that checked into his hotel at Owerri.

The lack of sincerity on the part of the government in tackling corruption, including a manifest absence of ethical standards throughout the agencies of government and business organisations in Nigeria, is a serious drawback. As Bowman (1991) noted, *ethics* is action, the way we practice our values; it is a guidance system to be used in making decisions. The issue of ethics in public service [and in private life] encompasses a broad range, including a stress on obedience to authority, on the necessity of logic in moral reasoning, and on the necessity of putting moral judgement into practice. Unfortunately, many officeholders in Nigeria do not have clear conceptions of the ethical demands of their position. Even as corrupt practices are going off the roof, little attention, if any, seems to be given to this ideal. In fact, the Obasanjo administration had to remove Mr. Vincent Azie as the Acting Auditor-General simply because he produced a financial report exposing the corrupt practices of the federal government. The action contradicted the government's anti-corruption posture (*The Guardian,* Feb 21, 2003). Who then will fight corruption in Nigeria if the government is seen to descend heavily on those who expose corrupt practices?

Poor reward system and greed are also causes of corruption in Nigeria. Nigeria's reward system is, perhaps, among the poorest in the world. Nigeria seems to be a country where national priorities are turned upside down. Hard work does not seem to be rewarded or respected, while known rogues, in so far as they are wealthy, are glorified. As Arthur Schlesinger said of America in the 1960s, "Our [the] trouble [with Nigeria] is not that our capabilities are inadequate. It is that priorities - which means our values-are wrong" (quoted in Howard, 1982).

Peer community and extended family pressures are also causes of corruption (Onalaja and Onalaja, 1997). The influence of extended family system and pressure to meet family obligations are more in less developed societies. Harrison (1985) acknowledged that the extended family system "is an effective institution for survival," but also a big "obstacle for development."

According to Lotterman (April 25, 2002), bad rules and 'ineffective taxing system,' which makes it difficult to track down people's financial activities, breed corruption. Ineffective taxing system is a serious problem in Nigeria. The society should institute an appropriate and effective taxing system where everyone is made to explain his or her sources of income, through *end-of-the-year* income tax filing system. Recently, the Nigerian Deposit Insurance Corporation (NDIC) reported the disappearance of almost $10m from Nigerian banks through employee fraud in 2002 (*BBC,* May 22, 2003). Although this type of fraud does not occur only in Nigeria, the unique thing is that such crimes (forgeries) often go undetected because of poor control systems. The lukewarm attitude of officers charged with enforcing the laws (judges, police officers and other public officials) often encourage corrupt behaviour. They often let the culprits off hook when they are 'settled.'

Bad economic policy is also a problem. The recent ban on the importation of *Tokunbo* (used cars) over five years old is an example of a bad policy that could breed corruption. The importation policy was limited to cars under five years old (the Federal Government reviewed the policy to cars under eight years due to public pressure). If this anti-business ban is not reviewed or discarded completely, it will, as many critics have noted affect the economy, as those making a living in the business will be exposed to poverty, and subsequently, corruption. Businessmen would be forced to bribe the corrupt custom officials (to allow the cars in), causing the state to lose the needed tax revenue. In addition, the policy will divert business to other neighbouring countries (*Vanguard*, June 4, 2002). To tame corruption, the country should try to get rid of regulations that serve little or no purposes.

The lukewarm attitude of those who are supposed to enforce the laws of the land (judges, police officers and public officials) could lead to people engaging in corrupt behaviour, knowing they could get away with it. Some cultural and institutional factors also lead to corruption. For instance, nepotism and the strength of family values are linked to feelings of obligation. The work of Merton (1968) has demonstrated the relationship between culture and corruption. His "means-ends schema" implies that corruption is at times a motivated behaviour responding to social pressures to violate the norms, so as to meet the set goals and objectives of a social system.

The recent trial of Chief Iyiola Omisore and others implicated in the murder of Chief Bola Ige and election petition against Senator Wabara are like pimples on the face of Nigeria. With money allegedly exchanging hands, witnesses were allowed to change initial testimonies. Mr. Dan C. Imo, who was believed to have defeated Adolphus Wabara in the senatorial election suddenly withdrew his lawsuit challenging the declaration of

Wabara as the victor allegedly because he was 'satisfactorily settled'.

Members of the national assembly were also involved in '419' scam. The Economic and Financial Crimes Commission (EFCC) arrested a Member of the Federal House of Representatives, Mr. Maurice Ibekwe in May 2003 "for allegedly obtaining $300,000 and 75,000DM under false pretence" from a German national. This kind of behaviour would work against the efforts of many honest and genuine businessmen and women as well as impede 'foreign capital inflow' into the economy (Ushigiale, 2003).

Lipset and Lenze (2000) note that those using corrupt means (through the *back door*, so to say), to achieve their objectives have little or no access to opportunity structure. The hindrance to economic opportunity, according to the study, could be a result of their race, ethnicity, lack of skills, capital, material and other human resources. They note "that cultures that stress economic success as an important goal but nevertheless strongly restricts access to opportunities will have higher levels of corruption. This probably explains the high incidence of corrupt behaviours in Nigeria. Many Nigerians are highly achievement-oriented, but they have relatively *low access to economic opportunities.* For example many civil servants in Nigeria work for months without getting paid (see for instance *ThisDay*, July 7, 2002 and *Daily Trust*, July 9, 2002). Yet, the society expects them to be honest and productive. Many of those civil servants working without being paid are parents, who are expected to train their children in schools with empty wallet. How can they do that? Are they magicians? Under this condition, many of the unpaid workers would innovate (even if it means criminally) to make ends meet. There are many problems in Nigeria, but that which involves non-payment or late payment of workers salaries for months, is very difficult to understand. It is no longer news that workers' salaries and retirement benefits are not paid regularly. The country is a place where payment of workers makes news headlines and state governors usually list the payment of workers' salaries as part of their achievements. Employers and managers of labour in the society seem ignorant of the fact that salary, at the end of each month's work, should not be negotiable (Osadolor, 2003).

The brazen display of wealth by public officials, whose source they are often unable to explain is an indication of how pervasive corruption has become in Nigeria. The irony is that many of the officials engaged in this brazen display of wealth had little or modest income prior to their election (or selection) or appointment into public office (see ThisDay, June 24 2002). This is in contrast to the developed countries where elected officials make efforts to be seen as living modestly. In the USA for instance, the 2000 financial disclosure forms released in 2001, which is required annually of all the 535 members of Congress (House and Senate members), show that many of them live relatively modest. The financial forms show sources of outside income, assets, liabilities, speech honoraria, donations to charity and travels paid for by private interests. The forms revealed that the main assets of the Senate Majority Leader, Tom Daschle (the nation's highest-ranking Democrat, with direct influence over billions of federal dollars), is "a one-half share in a house in Aberdeen, South Dakota, given by his mother and worth between $50,000 and $100,000 in income" (*CNN*, June 14, 2001). If he were a Nigerian, he certainly could have owned many million-dollar homes in beautiful areas in London and the United States (and all over Nigeria too), and decorated himself with countless traditional titles.

The work of Banfield (1958) shows a relationship between corruption and strong family orientation. The study, which helped to explain high levels of corruption in southern *Italy* and *Sicily* notes that "corruption is linked to the strong family values involving intense feelings of obligation." That was the case with the *Mafia* in Italy where some people were seen to have the attitude of "anything goes that advances the interests of one's self and family."

Moral laxity is also a problem. People for instance engage in various dishonest schemes such as the Advance *Fee Fraud,* otherwise known as -'419', in order to make quick money. *(Formally, "419" refers to 'section 419 of the Nigerian Criminal Code,' which regards obtaining money under false pretences as a criminal offence)*. Someone has suggested that it is almost impossible to live in Nigeria without being corrupt because morality is relaxed and people struggle for survival without any assistance from the government (Moore, 1997; Dike 2001).

Lack of social justice (or distributive justice) and human rights will also inevitably lead to violence and corrupt behaviour. A case in point is the frequent vandalisation of gas pipeline in the Niger Delta area. While no one will condone vandalism, it is sometimes a weapon of the weak, especially in situations where they feel they are denied access and control over the resources in their communities for community development programmes, and on top of that impoverished in the mist of plenty.

Effects of Corruption

The effects of corruption on a nation's sociopolitical and economic development are myriad. The negative effects impede economic growth as it, among other things, reduces public spending on social services and infrastructures such as education (Mauro, 1997 and 1995). Lipset and Lenz (2000) note that the effect on growth, is in part, a reduced level of investment, as it adds to investment risks. The effect of corruption on education comes from the fact that the government spends relatively more on items that will make more room for *"graft"* (Shleifer and Vishny, 1993; Lipset and Lenz, 2002). Corrupt government officials often shift government expenditures to areas in which they can collect bribes easily. Large and hard-to-manage projects, such as airports or highways or the national stadium at Abuja, become therefore favoured.

Despite the adverse effects of corruption, some scholars have argued that it could be beneficial to political development or "political modernisation" (Pye, March 1965). Political modernisation or development means growth in the capacity of a society's governmental structures and processes to maintain their legitimacy over time by contributing to economic development, national integration and administrative capacity

65

and so on (Nye 1967). We would not get entangled with the different scales used for measuring political development. Nevertheless, Gluckman (1955) opined that scandals associated with corruption sometimes have the effect of strengthening a value system of a society as a whole. This is probably true in relation to Nigeria. The scandals associated with the *Abacha* era (looting of the treasury and human rights violations) have given the nation some food for thought. Nigeria seems determined, on the basis of the Abacha experience, to strengthen the nation's essential governmental structures to avoid the re-occurrence of the kind of looting and human rights abuse that characterised his regime.

Some writers have also noted that corruption may help to ease the transition from traditional life to a modern political life. Some have argued that the vast social gap between literate officials and illiterate peasants may be bridged if the peasant approaches the official bearing traditional gifts or their (corrupt) money equivalent. In this respect, McMullan (July 1961) points out that "a degree of low-level corruption" can 'soften relations of officials and people.' And *Shils* (1962) notes that corruption can 'humanise government and make it less awesome.' These observations are common occurrences in Nigeria where communities pay political visits to their Governors, Commissioners and top civil servants with (cows, wines, cola nuts and *'Ghana must go'* bags) to get them to attend to their local problems. The apparent benefits of corruption notwithstanding, we are here mainly concerned with its negative effects.

As we have noted earlier, many studies have been conducted that show the negative effects of corruption. The widespread corruption in Nigeria has given the wrong impression to many Nigerians that it does not pay to be honest, hardworking and law-abiding. With the blatant display of wealth by political office holders, Nigerians have come to think of politics as lucrative business because anything spent to secure a political office is regarded as an investment, which matures immediately one gets into office.

Corruption wastes skills as precious time is often wasted to set up unending committees to fight corruption, and to monitor public projects. It also leads to denial of aids by the donor community. Some foreign donors do not give aid to corrupt nations. For instance, the International Monetary Fund (IMF) has withdrawn development support from some nations that are notoriously corrupt. The World Bank has introduced tougher anti-corruption standards into its lending policies' to corrupt countries. Similarly, other organisations such as the Council of Europe and the Organization of American States are taking tough measures against international corruption (*OECD*, Dec 1997).

Corruption is politically destabilising, as it could lead to social revolution and military takeovers. Corruption has often been one of the points used to rationalise military coups by the new regime. The General Buhari's post-coup broadcast to Nigerians in 1983 was a case in point (Welch, Jr., 1987). However, with the history of the military in government in most parts of Africa, and with many retired and serving senior army officers known to be very corrupt, it is unlikely that the military will in future successfully use allegations of corruption to rationalise their seizure of power

Corruption causes a reduction in the quality of goods and services available to the public as some companies could cut corners to increase profit margins. Corruption also affects investment, economic growth, and government expenditure and choices. It equally reduces private investment (Mauro 1997). The Lord Bishop of Guilford has for instance noted that bribery and corruption, the culture of late payment, delays or refusal to pay for services already delivered are among the factors that scare away foreign investors from Nigeria. He notes that those who fail to pay companies for services rendered seem to forget that the "life blood of any company is its cash flow." The *Daily Trust* (July 9, 2002) rightly points out that the "the price of corruption is poverty." Because of the pervasiveness of "petty" and "grand" corruption, the international business community regards the whole of Africa as a "sinkhole that swallows their money with little or no return" (Callaghy 1994). With the recent changes in the political economy of Eastern Europe, the attention of the business world has been turned to this area where they may reap quicker returns from their investments. One African diplomat could not put it any better: "Eastern Europe is [now] the most sexy beautiful girl, and we [Africa] are an old tattered lady. People are tired of Africa. So many countries, so many wars" (see *Newsweek Education Programme*: Fall/1994). As we have seen, what is happening in Africa is a blueprint of the problem facing Nigeria. The nation's "unworkable economic policies, blatant corruption..." in fact, the "fossilised system" of government, has brought almost everything to a halt (Adams, 1995). Corruption discourages honest effort and valuable economic activities as it breeds inefficiency and nepotism. It also leads to possible 'information distortion' as it 'cooks the books;' and 'a high level of corruption can make public policies ineffective' (Sen 1999 and Jessica Hall on *WorldCom*, June 27, 2002). Above all, corruption can tarnish the image of a country. As we have seen, Nigeria suffers more than most nations from an appalling international image created in large part by its inability to deal with corruption and bribery.

A 1996 study of corruption by Transparency International and Goettingen University ranked Nigeria as the most corrupt nation, among 54 nations listed in the study, with Pakistan as the second most corrupt (Moore 1997). The 1998 Transparency International corruption perception index (CPI) of 85 countries ranked Nigeria 81 out of the 85 countries polled (Lipset and Lenz 2000, see also table next page, beating only Bangladesh which was perceived to be the most corrupt.)

Corruption upsets ethnic balance, and exacerbates problems of national integration in developing countries. For instance, if a corrupt but popular ethnic leader is replaced in his or her position, it 'may upset ethnic arithmetic' and the cohorts may revolt. The social brawl that followed the annulment of the 1993 presidential election, perceived to have been won by Moshood Abiola is a case in point. Southerners (mainly Yorubas from his ethnic *Southwest*) rioted, as they felt they were mistreated by the northern oligarchy. Similarly, some politicians from the northern part of the country seem to have forgotten the atrocities committed by Generals Buhari, Babangida, and Abubakar during their regimes (they even refused to testify before the *Oputa Panel*), because they are their 'home boys.'

Table F: **Corruption Perception Index (1998)**

Country	Rank	Country	Rank	Country	Rank
Denmark	1	Namibia	31	Argentina	61
Finland	2	South Africa	32	Nicaragua	62
Sweden	3	Hungary	33	Romania	63
New Zealand	4	Mauritius	34	Thailand	64
Iceland	5	Tunisia	35	Yugoslavia	65
Canada	6	Greece	36	Bulgaria	66
Singapore	7	Czech Repub	37	Egypt	67
The Netherlands	8	Jordan	38	India	68
Norway	9	Italy	39	Bolivia	69
Switzerland	10	Poland	40	Ukraine	70
Australia	11	Peru	41	Latvia	71
Luxembourg	12	Uruguay	42	Pakistan	72
United Kingdom	13	South Korea	43	Uganda	73
Ireland	14	Zimbabwe	44	Kenya	74
Germany	15	Malawi	45	Vietnam	75
Hong Kong	16	Brazil	46	Russia	76
Austria	17	Belarus	47	Ecuador	77
United States	18	Slovak Repub	48	Venezuela	78
Ireland	19	Jamaica	49	Colombia	79
Chile	20	Morocco	50	Indonesia	80
France	21	El Salvador	51	Nigeria	81
Portugal	22	China	52	Tanzania	82
Botswana	23	Zambia	53	Honduras	83
Spain	24	Turkey	54	Paraguay	84
Japan	25	Ghana	55	Cameroon	85
Estonia	26	Mexico	56		
Costa Rica	27	Philippine	57		
Belgium	28	Senegal	58		
Malaysia	29	Ivory Coast	59		
Taiwan	30	Guatemala	60		

Sources: *The Transparency International Corruption Index,* 1998; and Lipset, Seymour & Salman Lenz, *"Corruption, Culture, and*

Markets," (2000), In *Culture Matters,* Harrison and Huntington (eds.), 2000

Corruption is also destructive of governmental structures and capacity. *TheNEWS* (July 11, 1999), in an issue entitles, *The Face of a Liar,* broke the news of "forgery" and "perjury" committed by the former Speaker of the House of Representatives, Alhaji Ibrahim Salisu Buhari. He was said to have corruptly amassed wealth when he worked for *NEPA* and had bribed his way to the fourth highest position in the land. He later admitted that he lied about his academic qualifications and was forced to resign as Speaker of the House of Representatives. President Olusegun Obasanjo disappointed the world by granting him a state pardon, despite his apparent campaign to transform Nigeria into a corruption-free society (Obasanjo's Inaugural Speech: May 29, 1999). The 'Buharigate,' as the scandal was later called, nearly destroyed Nigeria's nascent democracy.

Corruption can also destroy the legitimacy of a government. The Shehu Shagari regime for instance was written off as inept because of the magnitude of corruption in the regime, and its lack of policy direction (Suberu 1994). Corruption may alienate reform-oriented civil servants and may cause them to reduce or withdraw their service or even to leave the country (see Table G next page)

Corruption is one of the reasons for the 'brain drain' phenomenon in Nigeria (talented professionals leaving the country in search of employment elsewhere). In Nigeria, you can hardly enter an office and get your file signed except if you 'drop' some money. Even the security personnel at the door of every office will ask for tips (bribe). In other words, corruption leads to 'slow moving files that get through the desk of officers once the interested parties have compromised themselves.' According to *The Guardian* (April 21, 2002), it also leads to "missing files that [would] resurface immediately the desk officer is settled," unnecessary bureaucracy and "delays until fees are paid." Thus, by corruptly dolling out money to politicians, General Abacha got many of the nation's political class to commit political suicide in 1998. Many of them lined up en masse to proclaim him as a 'dynamic leader' and the only person qualified to lead Nigeria. Similarly, many politicians from the ruling Peoples' Democratic Party (PDP) trooped to President *Obasanjo's Ota Farm* in *Ogun State* to 'beg him' to run for a second term.

Table G: **Corruption Index Report (2001)**

COUNTRY	RANK	COUNTRY	RANK	COUNTRY	RANK
Finland	1	Tunisia		Guatemala	65
Denmark	2	Slovenia	34	Philippine	
New Zealand	3	Uruguay	35	Senegal	
Iceland	4	Malaysia	36	Zimbabwe	
Singapore	5	Jordan	37	Romania	69
Sweden	6	Lithuania	38	Venezuela	
Canada	7	South Africa		Honduras	71
The Netherlands	8	Costa Rica	40	India	
Luxembourg	9	Mauritius		Kazakhstan	
Norway	10	Greece	42	Uzbekistan	
Australia	11	South Korea		Vietnam	75
Switzerland	12	Peru	44	Zambia	
United Kingdom	13	Poland		Cote d'Ivoire	77
Hong Kong	14	Brazil	46	Nicaragua	
Austria	15	Bulgaria	47	Ecuador	79
Israel	16	Croatia		Pakistan	
United States		Czech Republic		Russia	
Chile	18	Colombia	50	Tanzania	82
Ireland		Mexico	51	Ukraine	83
Germany	20	Panama		Azerbaijan	84
Japan	21	Slovak Republic		Bolivia	
Spain	22	Egypt	54	Cameroon	
France	23	El Salvador		Kenya	
Belgium	24	Turkey		Indonesia	88
Portugal	25	Argentina	57	Uganda	
Botswana	26	China		Nigeria	90
Taiwan	27	Ghana	59	Bangladesh	91

Estonia	28	Latvia	
Italy	29	Malawi	61
Namibia	30	Thailand	
Hungary	31	Dominican Rep	63
Trinidad & Tobago		Moldova	

Source: The Transparency International Corruption Index (2001)
General Abubakar's visible timidity to address the issue of corruption in Nigeria was alarming and discouraging as he retained the military officers accused of looting the national treasury with General Sani Abacha.

Corrupt military is however not peculiar to Nigeria. Juan D. Peron of Argentina and Batista of Cuba, among others, were also known to have deposited their ill-gotten wealth in Swiss banks and other foreign financial institutions instead of investing the loots in their local economy (Sklar 1965; Lewis, May/June, 1994; Adams 1995). And with brute force Augusto Pinochet of Chile bastardised the nation's economy and killed many of the people who opposed his regime.

During his inaugural speech on May 29, 1999, Olusegun Obasanjo vowed to tackle the menace of corruption in Nigeria. He said: "Corruption will be tackled head-on. No society can achieve its full potential if it allows corruption to become the full-blown cancer it has in Nigeria." And he vowed that "there will be no sacred cows" in his campaign to stamp out corruption in the country (*Inaugural Speech*: May 29, 1999). It is however now self-evident that sacred cows are exempt from his so-called corruption campaigns. A crucial question is whether it will be at all possible for Nigeria to effectively tame corruption.

Towards an effective management of corruption

Some human ailments could require many doses of medicines to be treated. Similarly, the menace of corruption, which has eaten deep into the fabric of Nigeria, would require all the necessary *medicines* to effectively control it. In other words, no single and simple remedy will do it; and the problem cannot be solved overnight, because, as we have noted, corruption has been ingrained into the fabric of the society. Nigeria has, in theory, the solutions in the book to tackle corruption; but like other issues bedevilling the nation (such as poverty), implementations of the laws are the Achilles heel *of* the country.

One of the authors whose work we reviewed noted (and rightly, we might add), that one of the reasons why the measures against corruption have not been effective in Nigeria is that they have "operated at a level [of mere] symbolism" (Osoba 1996). Yes, corruption has defied all measures adopted to combat it in Nigeria, apparently, because those who wage the war against corruption are themselves corrupt. In the name of turning Nigeria into a corruption-free society, the nation has experimented with many policies. It has tried the judicial commissions of enquiry, the Code of Conduct Bureau, and the Public Complaints Commission but to no avail. Also it fiddled with War Against Indiscipline, the Mass Mobilisation for Social Justice and Economic Recovery (MAMSER), and the National Open Apprenticeship (NOA) programme but rather than these outfits helping to reduce corruption, corruption actually blossomed under them. Now the current civilian administration of President Olusegun Obasanjo has instituted an Independent Corrupt Practices Commission (ICPC), which seems to have power only over the corrupt poor without connections.

I have argued elsewhere that Nigeria cannot effectively control the menace of corruption by merely instituting probe panels. It was suggested that to tame the surge of corruption in Nigeria, the general population should be re-orientated to a better value system. This is because Nigerians have for long been living on the 'survival of the fittest' and grab-whatever-comes-your-way mentality (Dike, Oct 6, 1999 and Feb 5, 2002). The re-orientation of the youth in Nigeria to a good value system could help in the war against corruption. The *World Values Surveys* (1990-1993) found a relationship between values and corruption (*World Values Study Group*, 1994). Preaching the gospel of virtue and at the same time practising it was found to be effective in inducing behavioural change and reducing corruption. It was also found to correlate with increased productivity, which would mean enough goods and services being put into circulation, prosperity and economic growth. These would in turn allow the citizens the *'freedoms'* to live a meaningful life.

To win the war on corruption in Nigeria, President *Obasanjo's* vow that there must 'be *no sacred cows'* in the crusade against corruption should not be a mere political rhetoric. It should be put into practice by prosecuting all the known corrupt political *heavy weights* in the country as they contribute in making the nation's inchoate laws inoperable. Kanu Agabi, the former Attorney General and Minister of Justice noted at a meeting with state commissioners of police that:

> "Some of our leaders are doing everything they can to make the work of the police impossible. Big men are the greatest criminals and except you go after the big criminals and bring them to book, the rate of crime may not reduce. [But] If you bring three or four of these big men to book, the rate of criminal activities would reduce."

> He added, "Arrest ministers, arrest [the] big people and others would fear"(*Vanguard*, March 30, 2002).

But why has President Obasanjo made a deal with the Abacha family if his chief law enforcement officer has such a wonderful idea? He should have used the opportunity afforded by the Abacha saga to show the world that he was serious with his avowed war on corruption. The agreement made by the Obasanjo regime with the Abacha family would allow them to keep $100 million (of the money stolen by the late General), so that they could return about $1 billion of the loot to the federal government (BBC, May 20, 2002). As many critics have noted, this deal would encourage the many opportunists hanging on the fence waiting, to grab whatever government funds they can lay hands on, since the federal government would allow them to keep a part of the money, if and when, they are apprehended.

To win the war against corruption, all revenue generating and collection agencies in the nation must be transparent in their activities and give comprehensive account of the revenues collected. Some of the critical agencies, as noted by ThisDay ((July 30, 2003), are the Nigerian Custom service, Inland Revenue, the Central Bank, Nigerian Ports Authority, the Nigerian Maritime Authority, and the Nigerian National Petroleum Corporation, among others. And as has been noted, to win the war on corruption, adherence to ethical standards in decision-making must be the foundation of the nation's policies. Without ethics (defined by Webster's New Collegiate Dictionary, 1980, as a set of moral principles or values or principles of conducts governing an individual or a group) in the conduct of the affairs of the nation (public and business), the apparent war on corruption in Nigeria will not be won. In other words, without ethics, any money budgeted toward fighting corruption in Nigeria is a thing cast to a wild cat. Nigeria has to make laws and implement them to the letters. As Aristotle noted, the aim of ethical philosophy is 'to make us better men' (Bambrough, not dated and ThisDay, May 26, 2002). To win the war against corruption, Nigeria has to fortify the institutional 'checks and balances among the country's major social institutions and the separation of powers within the government' (Dahl 1998). The nation has to make sure that those entrusted to execute the war on corruption are men and women of *virtue* - those who recognise what is right, and will always strive to do it. For MacIntyre (1981) 'virtue' is an acquired human quality, the possession and exercise of which enables us to achieve those goods which are internal to practices, and the lack of which effectively prevents us from achieving any of such goods. Virtuous leaders [in government and business] are persons of honesty, integrity and trust (see also Liebig 1990, Frankena 1963 and Dike 2001).

Armed with ethics and virtue, the nation should then set out to reduce personal gains from corrupt behaviour with tough penalties against the culprits. Making tough rules with vigorous enforcement can deter corrupt behaviour. The nation should not grant too much discretionary power to officers who are in position to grant favour to others (businessmen in particular), such as officers who issue out licenses and passports. These officers often create artificial scarcity to attract bribes from the desperate public. There is the temptation to be corrupt when officials who have a lot of power are themselves poor (Sen 2000). One of the reasons for the upsurge in corrupt activities in Nigeria is that many Nigerians have not had the chance to live under the rule of law, as the country has, for the most part since independence from Britain in 1960, been under the claws of the military. As De Bono (1990) notes: "Law and order are a basic part of the fabric of society. Society needs to give a high priority to this aspect of life, because poor quality here downgrades everything else." The Nigerian police need to be upgraded in status, and be well trained, well equipped and well paid (and on time too!). The police should become an elite profession, which would be open only to those with good moral character. If the police and other security agents, including customs and the military will learn and understand their limits (for instance not to harass and kill innocent citizens) and follow the rules, things might improve in Nigeria.

This is not to suggest that upper level officers could not be corrupt. Top bureaucrats with excessive powers could abuse them. Cases abound of the abuse of power by top military Generals, governors, senators and members of the House of Representative. The effects of power on those who wield it are well stated in 1887 by Lord Acton, who noted that "Power tends to corrupt; absolute power corrupts absolutely." Before this time a British statesman, William Pitt observed in a speech that unlimited *power* "is apt to corrupt the minds of those who possess it" (Dahl 1998). The mass media have a crucial role to play in the campaign to educate the people of their rights as citizens, and in exposing the rogues. The nation should erect permanent structures in the society to constantly tackle corruption, instead of setting up *ad-hoc* corruption-panels here and there. The citizens have a role to play in the war against corruption: they should always try to resist the temptation to offer bribes to corrupt government officials, as 'it takes two to tango.'

To deal with corruption in ancient China many bureaucrats were paid a "corruption-preventing allowance" (*yang lien*) as an "incentive to remain clean and law-abiding"(Alatas 1980 and Klitgaard 1988). For Sen (2000) a payment system of this kind can help reduce corruption through what he called its "income effect," as the officer who gets this payment may be "less in need of making a quick buck." This type of payment will also have what he called "substitution effect." The officer receiving the payment "would know that corrupt behaviour may involve serious loss of a high-salary employment if things were" to go bad (that is, if he or she is caught with his or her hand in the cookie jar). In some cases, how people behave in a society depends on how they believe that others behave. If the prevailing behaviour in a country is bad, others could imitate the behaviour. The lousy argument would be that "others do the same." This was one of the cited "reasons" for corrupt behaviour when the Italian parliament investigated "the linkage between corruption and the *Mafia* in 1993." Thus corrupt behaviour, especially if rewarded or not sanctioned, encourages others to behave in the same manner. But respect for rules, honest and upright behaviour is certainly "bulwarks against corruption" in many societies (Sen 2000).

In Nigeria, corruption is endemic, with those occupying political offices as the main culprits. Very few of them, if at all, are ever prosecuted despite media reports of corruption against some, and their lifestyles that cannot be justified by their salary. Many of the political officeholders often engage in frivolous overseas trips (with hordes of cronies and praise-singers) while civil servants in their states go for months without getting paid their salary (the President is also guilty of this). Some are known to have acquired landed properties in the United States and Britain. An Independent Corrupt Practices Commission (ICPC), presided over by Justice Mustapha Akanbi, was instituted to fish out those whose hands were tainted while in office. Now the commission has its bait in the water, but so far it has not landed any 'big fish'. Or, has it caught any fish at all? Whether this commission will succeed in curing the country the cancer of corruption remains to be seen.

It may be necessary to emphasise the importance of good and enforceable policies in controlling corrupt practices. Policies should for instance be reviewed periodically to close any loopholes and to catch-up with events in the society. Toward this, Robert S. McNamara, former president of the World Bank and the Ford Motor Corporation, has enumerated the critical elements, which must be present in any policy to successfully combat the plague in sub-Saharan Africa. The policy, he argues, must:

◊   Require direct, clear and forceful support of the highest political authority: the president or prime minister.
◊   Introduce transparency and accountability in government functions, particularly in all financial transactions.
◊   Encourage a free press and electronic media to forcefully. report to the public about corrupt practices in the society.
◊   Organise civil society to address the problems of corruption brought to light by the process of transparency and the activity of the media.
◊   Introduce government watchdogs - anti-corruption bureaus, inspectors-general, auditors-general and ombudsmen [government officials appointed to receive and investigate complaints made by individuals against abuses or capricious acts by public officials, etc] - which will identify corruption practices and bring them to public attention.
◊   Minimise and simplify government regulations, particularly those involving the issuance of licences, permits and preferential positions, thereby restricting opportunities for rent seeking behaviours.
◊   Insert anti-bribery clauses in all major procurement contracts, and with the assistance of both international financial institutions and bilateral aid agencies insist that international corporations bidding for African procurement contracts must accept such clauses and the penalties associated with their violation.

◊   Introduce similar anti-bribery clauses into contracts relating to privatisation of government enterprises, and the development of natural resources.

◊   Ensure that enforcement is predictable and forceful; and

◊   Criminalize the acts of bribery; prohibit the deduction of bribes for tax purposes; and erect barriers against the transfer to western financial institutions the financial gains derived from corrupt practices (United States Information Agency: Nov 17, 1997).

Other steps authorities could take to control corruption include:

Declaration of Assets: The state should require that all high-level Nigerian officials (Presidents, Ministers, Legislative officers, Central Bank governors, Police and Customs Chiefs, Military Generals etc), sign a statement granting permission to banks (both local and foreign), real estate or investment houses to disclose any personal assets they may hold. Breaking this veil of secrecy, it has been argued, is crucial if assets declarations are to be verified and accountability enforced (Diamond 1992).

Withholding of Aid: International donors (the IMF and World Bank) can be helpful by cutting off assistance to any country noted for high-level corruption.

Scrutiny for sources of income: As noted earlier, scrutinising the sources of wealth of those who deposit huge sums of money in financial institutions would go a long way to curbing the looting of the national treasury by civil servants. The Commonwealth of Nations and the African Union (AU) should emulate other international organisations and work toward stamping out corruption and dictatorship from their midst.

In conclusion, many laws are already in the book to fight corruption in Nigeria (including those crafted by the international organisations). But what is important now, as Peter Eigen, chairman of the corruption watchdog, Transparency International, has noted, is "the political will to fight corruption at home…" Robert McNamara rightly remarked at the end of the Second Global Forum on Fighting Corruption and Safeguarding

Integrity at The Hague (May 31, 2001): "Every country has to determine it own priorities" on the war against corruption. But each, as Odessey (May 31, 2001) noted, should "focus on concrete actions that can yield measurable results," and "...publicly report whether results are being achieved."

Finally, Nigeria cannot be seen as secure and free until people's human rights are respected and protected by the government. As Mikhail Gorbachev points out, "...the world cannot be considered secure if human rights are being violated...And more importantly, the world cannot be considered secure if a many people lack the elementary condition for life worthy of man." Similarly, Nigeria cannot be considered secure if millions of people go hungry, do not have a roof over their heads and or remain jobless and sick indefinitely. More importantly, to seriously tame corruption, Nigeria has to use *words* as well as *actions* – a multifaceted approach. Finally, good governance, transparency, accountability and the rule of law are the keys to tackling corruption in the country, as corrupt leaders cannot wage an effective war against corruption.

References

Abdulkarim, Siraj B; "The devastating monster of corruption;" Daily Trust, March 19, 2003

Abubakar, Shehu;"Edo civil servants call off strike;" Daily Trust, July 9, 2002

Adam, Paul; "Nigeria: Next Pariah?" African Report, May-June, 1995, p.43; p.45

Alatas, Syed Hussein; The Sociology of Corruption, Singapore, Times Book, 1980

Amundsen, Inge; "In search of a counter-hegemony. State and civil society in the struggle for democracy in Africa." Unpublished Ph.D. Thesis, Institute of Political Science, University of Tromso, 1997

Amundsen, Inge; "See ch.1, ch.2, and ch.4: corruption – Definitions and Concepts." The report was commissioned by the Norwegian Agency for Development Cooperation (NORAD), by was prepared by Inge Amundsen, Chr. Michelsen Institute (CMI), January 2000.

Anyikwa, Levi; "World Bank faults govt's audit system;" The Guardian, June 3, 2003

Bambrough, Renford; (With introduction and commentary), The Philosophy of Aristotle. A Mentor Book, 451-ME2783 (nd), p.355

Banfield, Edward; The Moral Basis of a Backward Society (Chicago: Free Press, 1958)

Bayart, Jean-Francois; Ellis, Stephen and Hibou, Beatrice; *La criminalisation de l'Etat en Afrique Paris, 1997* **(Ed) Complexe The Criminalisation of the State in Africa,** Oxford, 1999, James Curry.

BBC News: "Nigerian bank fraud up 40%" May 22, 2003

Bivere, Godfrey; "Ban on importation of over 5 years old vehicles: Ministry of Finance urged to extend deadline." Vanguard June 4, 2002

Bowman, James S; "Introduction: Ethical Theory and practice in Public Management," in Ethical Frontier in Public Management: Seeking New Strategies for Resolving Ethical Dilemmas; James S. Bowman, editor, San Francisco: Jossey Base, 1991

Bryce, James; Modern Democracies, New York, 1921

Dahl, Robert; On Democracy (New Haven and London: Yale University Press, 1998), p.73; p.112

De Bono, Edward; Future Positive, Penguin Books, 1990, p.208

Callaghy, Thomas;"Africa: falling off the Map;" Current History, January 1994, pp.31-36

Cooksey, Brian; "Corruption and Poverty: What are the Linkages?" Paper prepared for the 9th International Anti-Corruption Confer-ence, Durban, Oct10-15, 1999

Daily Independent: "Auditor-General exposes multi-billion Naira fraud;" January 8, 2003

-------------------------: "Azie's blow against corruption;" February 26, 2003

CNN News:"Tom Daschle: A man of modest means," Washington (AP), June 14, 2001

Dike, Victor E; "Corruption, so dismal." Daily Independent, Nov 20, 2002

------------------. "Tackling Corruption in Nigeria." Daily Independent, July 27, 2002

------------------. Leadership, Democracy and the Nigerian Economy: Lessons from the Past and Directions for the Future.
[Sacramento, CA: The Lightning Press] 1999

------------------. "Corruption in Nigeria: A New Paradigm for Effective Control." Online Publication: Gamji.com, 2002

------------------. "The philosophy of Transforming Nigeria into a Corruption-free Society: Are the probes the Solution?" Online
Publication: Nigeriaworld.com/feature, October 6, 1999

-------------------. Democracy and Political Life in Nigeria [Zaria, Nigeria: A BU Press, 2001], pp. 97-113

-------------------. "The State of education in Nigeria and the health of the nation." NESG Economic Indicators, January – March,
Vol. 8, No 1, 2002

Edevbaro, Daniel Osakponmwen; "The Political Economy of Corruption and Underdevelopment in Nigeria;" [Helsinki: a Ph.D. Dissertation, University of Helsinki, Department of Political Science, 1998

Ekwowusi, Sonnie; "A Kingdom of Open Robberies;" ThisDay, July 23, 2003

Ewulu, Bright; "Why British investors shun Nigeria." Daily Trust, July 9, 2002

Ezema, Malachy; "Global Financial institutions options for poverty reduction." The Guardian, July 10, 2002

Fairbanks Jr. Charles H. "The Feudalisation of the State." Journal of Democracy; vol. 10, No.2, 1999, pp.47-53

Frankena, Williams K; Ethics, 2nd Edition, Prentice Hall, Inc., Englewood Cliff, NJ, 1963

Girling, John; Corruption: Capitalism and Democracy, London, 1997, Routledge

Gluckman, Max; Custom and Conflicts in Africa, Oxford, 1955

Hall, Jessica; "WorldCom Faces Fraud Charge," Reuters: (Philadelphia), June 27, 2002.

Harrison, Lawrence E. Underdevelopment Is a State of Mind: The Latin American Case. [Cambridge: Centre for International Affairs, Harvard Univ.; Lanham, Md., University Press of America, 1985], p.7

Hope, Ronald Kempe, Sir and Chikulu, Bornwell C. (eds.); Corruption and Development in Africa: Lessons From Country Experiences [London: Macmillan Press, 2000

Kibwana, Kivutha; Wanjala, Smokin & Okehowiti; The Anatomy of Corruption in Kenya: Legal, Political and Socio-Economic Perspectives; Nairobi, Claripress, Ltd., 1996

Kilson, Martin;"Behind Nigeria's Revolts," New Leader, Jan 1966, pp.9-12

Klitgaard, Robert; Controlling Corruption (Berkeley: University of California Press, 1988), p.7

Lewis, Peter; "The Politics of Economics," African Report, May/June, 1994, p.47

Liebig, James E; Business Ethics-Profiles in Civic Virtue; Fulcrum Publication, Golden, Colorado, 1990

Lipset, Seymour Martin, and Gabriel Salman Lenz;"Corruption, Culture, and Markets." In Culture Matters, Lawrence E. Harrison, and Samuel P. Huntington, eds., (New York: Basic Books, 2000), p.112.

Lotterman, Edward;"Bad rules breed corruption; " Pioneer Press: April 25, 2002

MacIntyre, Alasdair C; After Virtue, University of Notre Dame Press, June 1981

Maduekwe, Ojo; "Corruption and The Nigerian Project-Issues," ThisDay, May 26, 2002

Madu, Onurah and Alifa Daniel; "PDP governors say Anambra crisis is a 'family affair;' The Guardian, July 15, 2003

Mauro, Paolo; "Corruption and Growth," Quarterly Journal of Economics, 110, no. 3, 1995.

------------------; **"The effects of Corruption on Growth, Investment, and Government Expenditure: A Cross- Country Analysis."** In **Corruption and the Global Economy** (ed.,), Kimberly Ann Elliot [Washington, D.C.: Institute for International Economics, 1997].

------------------; "Why Worry About Corruption," editor, IMF Publications: Economic Issues, No. 6, 1997

Merton, Robert K; Social Theory and Social Structure (New York: Free Press, 1968), pp.246-248

Moore, Stephen; Power and Corruption, Visions Paperback, 1997

Mohammed, Suleiman; "We failed in war against corruption – Danjuma confesses;" Daily Trust, May 22, 2003

Nas, Wada; Weekly Trust, March 8, 2003

Mohammed, Aminu; "Political Corruption and its Nemesis;" Weekly Trust, July 26, 2003

Momodu, Shaka."Sacked Aviation Officials to Face Akanbi Commission;" ThisDay, June 23,'02.

Morrison, Donald; Mikhail Gorbachev: An Intimate Biography; A Time Book, 1988, p.250

McMullan, M; "A Theory of Corruption," The Sociological Review (Keele), 9, July 1961, p.1961

Ndiulor, Tony;"Price Nigeria is paying for Corruption," The Guardian, March 17, 1999

Newsweek Education Program - Fall/1994; see 'conflict in Africa'

Nwakanma, Obi; "Treason in Anambra State;" Vanguard, July 20, 2003

Nye, J. S. "Corruption and Political Development: A Case-Benefit Analysis," The American Political Science Rev, 1967, pp. 417-427

Obasanjo, Olusegun; 'Inaugural Address' May 29, 1999

Odessey, Bruce; (Washington File Staff Writer), "Delegates at Global Forum on Corruption Urged to Take Action Now." U.S. Dept. of State: International Information Program, May 31, 1999.

Oditta, Chika;"Imo Workers Begin Strike Action;" ThisDay, July 8, 2002

Odivwri, Eddy; "The Governors, Their Godfathers;" ThisDay, July 19, 2003

Ogbodo, Abraham; "Primaries Of Blood" The Guardian, July 14, 2002

Ogugbuaja, Charles; "Violent protests in Imo over alleged ritual killing," The Guardian, May 16, 2002

Okpowo, Blessyn; "AGABI: Reformist at war," Vanguard, 30th March, 2002

Oloja, Martins."How Civil Servants Engage In Corruption, By Experts;" The Guardian, April 21, 2002

Orwell, George; Animal Farm (with a New preface by Russell Baker and introduction by

Onalaja, Taiwo & Kehinde Onalaja; How Polygamy Wrecks Nigeria, Africa. CAPWONA Books, 1997

Osadolor, Kingsley; "Elements of law and order;" The Guardian, June 4, 2003

Pye, Lucian;"The Concept of Political Development," The Annals, 358, March 1965, pp.1-19

Sagay, Isaac; "Political warlords: Threat to Nigerian democracy;" Vanguard, July 20, 2003

Schlesinger, Arthur; "The New Mood in Politics;" in The Sixties; Gerald Howard (ed.), Washington Square Press, 1982

Sen, Amartya; Development as Freedom (New York: Anchor Books, 1999), p.275

Shekarau, Ahmed I; "Political killings in the present dispensation;" Daily Trust, March 6, 2003

Shils, Edward; Political Development in the New States, The Hague, 1962, p.385

Shleifer, Andrei, & Robert W. Vishny; "Corruption," Quarterly Journal of Economics, 103, No.3, 1993, pp. 599-617

Sklar, Richard L. "Contradictions in the Nigerian Political System." Journal of Modern African Studies, 3, 2, 1965, p. 385

Suberu, Rotimi T. "The Democratic Recession in Nigeria," Current History, May 1994, p, 216; p.213

The Observer (UK); "US Capitalism is in the dock," Sunday, June 9, 2002.

The Guardian; "EMU chieftain, others condemn auditor-general's removal," Feb 21, 2003

------------------; January 2, 1999

The NEWS – a weekly Magazine (Nigeria), "The Face of a Liar," July 11, 1999

The Organization for Economic Cooperation and Development (OECD); see 'The OECD Convention on Combating Bribery of Foreign Public Officials in International Business Transactions,' December 1997

The Transparency International Corruption Index (CPI), 2001; pp.234-236

The United States Information Agency; Nov 17, 1997

ThisDay: see Ahamefula Ogbu on "Fiscal Indispline, Corruption Bane of Economy;" July 30, 2003

------------: "Corruption at Code of Conduct Bureau;" May 22, 2003

------------: "How the Polls Were Rigged;" May 11, 2003

------------: "Gunmen Kill ANPP Senatorial Candidate," Feb 11, 2003

------------: "Corruption, Major Cause of Injustice Against Women – Minister;" July 7, 2002

Treisman, Daniel; The Causes of Corruption: A Cross-National Study (1998), pp.22-23.

Uko, Utibe; "Anti-Corruption Panel: The Battle So Far," ThisDay Sunday, June 24, 2002

Ushigiale, Joseph; "419-House Member, Ibekwe, Arrested." ThisDay, May 30, 2003

Vanguard: "Education: ASUU's armor cracks; 11 varsities out of strike;" May 22, 2003

-------------: "Constitutionality of campaign donations;" March 21, 2003

-------------: "Halliburton's $5 m tax evasion scandal attracts call for disclosure;" May 27, 2003

-------------: March 21, 2003

Wallerstein, Immanuel; "Autopsy of Nkruma's Ghana," New Leader, March 14, 1966, pp.3-5

Webster's New Collegiate Dictionary: G. & C. Merriam Company, Springfield, Mass, USA, 1980

Welch, Claude Jr. "The Military and the States in Africa: Problems of Political Transition." In Zaki Ergas, editor, The African States in Transition, St. Martin's Press, New York, 1987

Williams, Robert; Political Corruption in Africa; Aldershot: Gower Pub. Inc, 1987

World Values Study Group; "World Values Survey Code Book," ICPSR 6160 (Ann Arbor, Mich., August 1994).

Wraith, Ronald & Edgar Simpkins; Corruption in Developing Countries; [London, 1963], pp.11-12

Chapter 5

The Poverty profile of Nigeria

We have in the preceding chapter discussed the adverse effects of corruption, and how it has worsened the problem of poverty in the country. There are variations in living standards around the globe, as economic growth rates and productivity vary from nation to nation. Some countries are poor, some are fairly well off, and others are rich, just as some individuals are poor, some are fairly well off, and others are considered rich. However, everything is relative, and that is certainly the case with poverty. Although "millions of Americans can't make a decent living" (Schwarz, Oct 1998) what most people in the United States today regard as "stark poverty...would seem like luxury in parts of Asia and Africa..." (Mansfield 1977). Similarly, a poor person in Nigeria might not be perceived as such by other Africans in dire economic needs. Thus poverty is partly a matter of how one person's income stacks up against another person's.

If you were to determine how a person is doing economically, you would first look at the person's income. A person with a high income could afford life's necessities and luxuries. But "inadequate income is a strong predisposing condition for an impoverished life" (Sen 1999). And when judging whether the economy of a nation is doing well or poorly, it is common to compare the total income of everyone in the economy with that of another country or the global economy. The most common economic tool for this is the *Gross National Product* (GNP). This is the total income earned by a nation's permanent residents at a given period, (Mankiw 2001). The average income of a citizen of any country is the GNP per capita, calculated by dividing the *GNP* with the population. Nevertheless, *GNP* differs from *Gross Domestic Product* (GDP), which is the market value of all-final goods and services produced within a country in a given period of time, by including income that a nation's citizens earn abroad and excluding income that foreigners earn in the country. For instance, if a Ghanaian citizen works temporarily in Nigeria, his production is part of Nigeria's GDP, but it is not part of the GNP (It is part of Ghana's GNP.)

Definition of Poverty

In spite of Nigeria's oil wealth (the nation is the 6th largest oil producing nation in the world), the poor constitute about 70% of the Nigerian population. Recent report by the United Nations Development Programme (UNDP) ranked Nigeria as the *26th poorest* nation in the world (The Guardian, July 26, 2002; Dike, Oct 6, 2002). Worse still, despite the vast mineral, oil, water, land and human resources, many Nigerians live on less than $1.00 (one U.S. dollar) a day. Is this statistics not bad enough to wake the nations political leaders up from their deep slumber? It is unreasonable for any leader to allow the citizens he or she governs to live in such abject penury.

Poverty has *narrow* and *broad* definitions, partly, because it is a physical matter, and partly, because it is relative. It is physical, because one can note its effects on those afflicted by it. And it is relative, because a poor person in one country may not be perceived as such in another country. However, the poor are those that 'have limited and insufficient food, poor clothing [live in] crowded...and dirty shelter...' (Galbraith 1955). It also includes those who cannot afford medical care and recreation; cannot meet family and community obligations and other necessities of life. And people are "poverty-stricken when their income, even if adequate for survival, falls markedly behind" the average obtainable in their immediate community. Poverty is a serious issue in Nigeria, because many people are struggling daily for survival without assistance from the state. Worse still, the nation does not have any guideline to measure the construct, which are available in some countries. In the *US* for instance, the 1995 official federal policy poverty guidelines 'carry precise dollar amounts' of about $15,150 for a family of four. Poverty *guidelines,* which are issued by the Department of Health and Human Services, determine financial eligibility for federal programmes and household incomes for basic necessities. Any family whose income is below the set benchmark is considered as living below the poverty line The *poverty threshold*, which is the statistical version of the poverty guidelines, is used by the *Census Bureau* to calculate the number of poor people in the United States, individual States or Regions (Schwarz Oct.1998 and UNDP 2002).

Who are the poor in Nigeria? No precise definition is really needed in Nigeria for one to understand what poverty is, as poverty is indelible on those afflicted by it. The poor are those who cannot afford decent food, medical care, recreation, decent shelters and clothing. It also includes those who cannot meet family and community obligations, and other necessities of life. With this, it is not surprising that poverty is regarded as a form of oppression (UNDP *Conference Report*, 15-17 March 2001). Thus, a poor person could not afford the life style a rich individual would regard as the minimum for decent and acceptable living in a particular community.

The *Webster's New Twentieth Century Dictionary* defines poverty as the condition or quality of being poor, need, indigence, and lack of means of subsistence. It is also deficiency in necessary properties or desirable qualities, or in a specific quality, etc. The *Journal of Poverty* notes that poverty means more than being impoverished and the lack of financial means but is also "an overall condition of inadequacy, lacking and scarcity, and destitution and deficiency of economic, political, and social resources." This is a *broader* perspective of poverty, which reflects its true dimensions. Therefore, people are living in poverty "if their income and resources (material, cultural and social) are so inadequate as to preclude them from having a standard of living which is regarded as acceptable" by their society generally (Ireland: *NAPS*, 1997). Because of the nature of Nigeria's underdevelopment and the effects of corruption, the poor are found both in rural and urban settings in Nigeria, living in different categories of poverty.

Poverty Profile of Nigeria

Given the indices currently used by international organisations, Nigeria's current GNP per capita of about $260 is below that of less affluent countries such as Bangladesh with a per capita income of $370. And Nigeria's low per capita income compares with those of smaller African countries with less endowment in natural resources, such as Tanzania with a per capita income of $260 and Mozambique with a per capita income of about $220. African countries that enjoy impressive standards of living are South Africa with a per capita income of $3, 170, and Botswana with a per capita income of $3, 240 (*The Commonwealth Yearbook*, 2002; The Guardian, March 17, 2002). Nigeria's low per capita income becomes more frightening when compared with those of some western nations. For instance, the GNP per capita in the United States was about $27,086 in 1996 (USAID 2002); and recently that of Britain was put at $23, 590 (*The Commonwealth Yearbook*, 2002). This is not to mention the impressive economic performances of the four Asian Tigers of Singapore, South Korea, Taiwan and Hong Kong. Thus as ThisDay (July 30, 2003) rightly noted, "poor economic performance" in Nigeria, as in many other African countries, is worsening the poverty profile of the country.

A nation's standard of living is determined, among other things, by the economic condition of the nation and the productivity of her citizens - the quantity of goods and services that a worker can produce for each hour of work (Mankiw 2001). A country may prosper if her citizens are productive and do not possess many anti-growth behaviours such as *corruption* and *bad work ethic*. The mention of work ethic takes us to the issue of "culture" that is a significant determinant of a nation's ability to prosper. This "shapes individuals' thoughts about risk, reward and opportunity" (Lindsay 2000). There are different views of what prosperity is and how to create it. Prosperity could be both a "flow" of *income* and a "stock" of *capital*. It is a "flow" of *income,* that is the ability of a person to purchase a set of goods, or capture value created by someone else. It is a "stock" of *capital* that is the enabling environment that improves productivity (Fairbanks 2000; Sen 1996). Prosperity, therefore, is the ability of an individual, group, or nation to provide shelter, nutrition, and other material goods that enable people to live a good life (Ray 1998). Prosperity helps to create space in people's hearts and minds so that they may develop a healthy emotional and spiritual life and become "unfettered by the everyday concern of the material goods they require to survive" (Fairbanks 2000). Therefore, the life of any person burdened with the vices of poverty is miserable and short with their daily struggle for survival. This is, unfortunately, the case with many people in present-day Nigeria.

There is need for the Nigerian leadership to provide the enabling environment that would attract and retain local and foreign investors and spur economic growth. This, *ceteris paribus*, would lead to more jobs, increase in goods and services, improvement in the health of citizens and the poverty-profile of Nigeria. A World Bank study of Nigeria shows that there are differences between regions in the concentration of the poor and non-poor in the society. This, according to the study, poverty varies from the north to the south, with more concentration of the poor in the northern agro-climatic zone (*The World Bank*, August 1996). But generally people of low-income live in the rural agricultural areas from where they struggle to eke out a living from barren lands and by raising animals.

Categories of Poverty

The life of those afflicted by poverty is comparatively miserable and brief. *Galbraith* (1958) has classified modern poverty into two categories, namely: *Case Poverty*, and *Insular Poverty*.

◊ *Case Poverty* is the kind of poverty seen in every community - rural and urban. It manifests in poor family with "junk-filled yard and dirty children playing in the bare dirt" (Galbraith 1958). Other qualities peculiar to the individuals or family afflicted by *Case* poverty are, mental deficiency, bad health, inability to adapt to the discipline of modern economic life, excessive procreation, alcohol, insufficient education, or perhaps a combination of several of these handicaps. These conditions hinder these individuals from participating in general well-being.

◊   *Insular Poverty* manifests itself as an *Island*. In this imaginary island everyone or nearly everyone is poor (Galbraith 1958). He notes that it is not easy to explain *insular* poverty by individual inadequacy, because the environment in which the people found themselves may have made them poor or may have frustrated them.

Given these explanations, it is appropriate to note that poverty assumes *social, political,* and *economic* dimensions. The social dimensions of poverty include lack of educational opportunity and lack of access to healthcare, while the political dimensions of poverty exists where civil rights are denied and political power rests in the hands of a few people. Although the economic dimension of poverty is broader than lack of finance, it includes a 'lack of employment opportunities and uneven distribution of resources' (journalofpoverty.org). However, some people are poor due to factors beyond their control.

Causes of Poverty

The classical Greek philosophers, especially, Socrates, Plato, and Aristotle believed that anything human beings could experience or think about was worth investigating. Aristotle, in particular, noted that all human beings, by nature, 'desire to know' what affects them. Poverty and squalor are among the social ills that affect human beings, which they should investigate and study. Alfred Marshall (1842-1924), a renowned British economist, in *The Study of Poverty* (1927), observed at the turn of the 20th century that poverty "is the study of the causes of the degradation of a large part of mankind." He noted that many people "had insufficient food, clothing, and house room" and that they "were [and are still] over-worked and under taught, weary and careworn [and] without quiet and without leisure" (Marshall 1927).

One should remember that this study was conducted at the early 20th century. Yet despite the advancement in modern technology at the dawn of the 21st century, many people are still poor all over the globe. Although there are traces of poverty in every nation, the situation in Africa in general and Nigeria in particular, is dismal. Many people are without access to safe water and lack the ability to read or write. Consequently, Africa is often referred to as a "Paradox of poverty in the midst of plenty" (Ndulo 1999). Why is the region very poor? The causes of poverty are myriad and complex. And they vary according to their settings. In most cases, those the people have elected to protect them from poverty worsen the situation. This is the case with Nigeria, where the political leaders with access to the national treasury convert public funds to their private use.

Insular poverty is caused by the nature of the resource endowment or the fertility of the land inhabited by the people, as it has something to do with a place of birth. For instance, the "homing instinct" (the desire of a large number of people to spend their lives at or near the place of their birth), which operates mostly among the poorly educated, prevents them from leaving the 'island of poverty' in which they were born. If the groups remain in the area, they will be committed to a pattern of agricultural land use or mining, petty industrial, and unproductive, or otherwise "un-remunerative" activities. The poverty of the community also ensures that educational opportunities will be limited, and that health services will be poor. Consequently, subsequent generations will be ill-prepared, either for mastering the environment into which they are born, or for migration to areas of higher income outside (Galbraith 1955). *Case* poverty could be caused by illiteracy, lack of economic opportunities, and indulgence in illegal drugs, alcoholism, excessive procreation, polygamous household, and bad health, among others. These conditions hinder people's active participation in the affairs of their community.

Reports show that HIV/AIDS contribute to the worsening poverty situation at household level in many countries in Africa. The Nov 2001 Government of Nigeria sentinel survey reported that Nigeria had "5.8% HIV prevalence rate." And the United Nations ranked Nigeria as the fourth-worst affected country in 1999, based on the number of *HIV* infections. With life expectancy of 55 years, illiteracy rate of 50%, and under-five mortality of 143 per 1, 000 live births, *HIV/AIDS now* affects over 2.7 million people in Nigeria (USAID 2002). With poor economic performance, corruption, the paltry expenditure of $0.03 per capita funding for HIV/AIDS (as at 1996), and the citizen's inability to pay for treatment once infected, the number of HIV/AIDS in Nigeria is expected to increase in future (*UNAIDS* 1999 and Hecht (PSR) *UNAIDS* 2000). Therefore, a public awareness campaign should be intensified to educate the masses on ways to prevent the spread of the epidemic.

One cannot over-emphasise the effects of social policy and cultural values and attitudes "as obstacles to or facilitators of progress" of nations. Thus some cultural values are fundamental obstacles to progress and this helps to explain the 'intractability' of the problems of poverty and injustice in parts of the *Third World* (Harrison 2000; Etounga-Manguelle 2000). For instance, the culture of *polygamy* (having more than one wife at a time) in Nigeria and some other *Third World Nations* is one of the major causes of poverty, corruption, illiteracy and even diseases in this part of the world (Taiwo and Kehinde Onalaja 1997). Very often, laws designed to protect the civil and human rights of the people witness zero implementation. Thus *'Culture Matters'* (Harrison and Huntington, 2000). Factors associated with mismanagement of national resources (depletion of resources by corrupt political office-holders),*'419 scam'* and rising crime rate would discourage investment in the economy, thereby exacerbating the poverty profile of Nigeria (*Daily Champion*, July 5 2002). The 2003 Index of Economic Freedom Report ranked Nigeria 140th out of 156 countries on the corruption index. Some of the factors that contributed to the poor ranking are familiar, such as "pockets of violence, frequent executive-legislative face-off, inability to implement reform agenda and excessive government intervention in the economy" (*ThisDay*, Feb 25, 2003). Thus the economic 'unfreedom' of a society means the poverty of the people.

Table H: 2003 Index of Economic Freedom (Ranking of 156 nations)+*

Country	Score	Rank	Country	Rank	Score
Hong Kong	1.45	1	Botswana	2.50	35
Singapore	1.5	2	Japan	2.50	35
Luxembourg	1.70	3	Uruguay	2.50	35
New Zealand	1.70	4	Czech Republic	2.50	35
United States	1.80	5	Cambodia	2.50	35
United Kingdom	1.85	6	South Africa	2.65	44
Canada	N/A	18	Madagascar	2.65	44
Germany	N/A	19	**Nigeria**	**3.85**	**140****
Italy	N/A	29	Uganda	2.85	62
Brazil	N/A	72	Morocco	2.95	68
India	N/A	119	Tunisia	2.95	68
Russia	N/A	135	Mali	3.00	72
Botswana	2.50	35	Mauritius	3.00	72

Sources: Compiled by the author, from: *ThisDay*: "Nigeria Rated Low in Economic Freedom," Feb 25, 2003; *Daily Independent*: "Nigeria raked world's 16th loweat economy," Feb 26, 2003
+The Heritage Foundation and Wall Street Journal (USA) endorsed the report
*Not all countries in study are shown on the table
N/A: Not available
**Nigeria ranked 125 (3.60) out of 155 countries in 2002; 97 (3.35) out of 155 countries in 2001; 94 (3.30) out of 161 countries in 2000; and ranked 95 (3.20) out of 160 countries in 1999

At a European Commission (EC) meeting to support Nigeria's anti-poverty programme, Nicholas Costello stated the obvious: 'Nigeria has enough money to tackle its poverty challenges. If the government can win this battle against corruption and mismanagement, the money will start to turn into functioning schools, health services and water supply, thus laying the foundation to eradicate poverty' (Nov-Dec 2001). Globalisation and the *World Trade Organization* (WTO) liberalisation policy have been noted as modern day colonialism, which accentuated the poverty of the *Third World* countries. Some writers have suggested that Nigeria should boycott the WTO agreement, because the treaty leads to goods being dumped in the country, leading to the closure of local industries. And some have argued that the quality of goods made in Nigeria would not compete effectively in the global market (*Vanguard*, July 5, 2002 and *The Guardian*, April 2, 2002). Therefore, Nigeria's oil and import-dependent economy lead to rising unemployment and the poverty of the people.

Discrimination, ethnicity and poverty are closely related. They affect peoples' ability to secure employment and earn a living. Entrenched ethnic prejudices and nepotism sometimes determines a person's chances of securing employment in Nigeria. The *de facto* 'state of origin' prerequisite for securing employment in the state and local government areas in Nigeria is a case in point. Often, those who relocate to states other than their 'state of origin' are treated as *non-indigenes* and thus discriminated against. This practice is not, however, peculiar to Nigeria. In the United States race is a factor in employment. "Nonwhites are often prevented from reaching certain occupational or managerial levels" irrespective of their qualification (Mansfield 1977). There are laws against such practices in the United States. And any person can relocate to any state of his or her choice, secure employment, and participate in the affairs of the community. Inept leadership, bad social policies and reliance on traditional methods of productions are impediments to prosperity.

Other causes of poverty include corruption, unproductive university-private sector relationships, and failure to take risks and make tough choices. It has been noted that many nations that are not creating wealth at a high rate are over-reliant on natural resources, including cheap labour. And they believe in the simple advantages of climate, location, and government favour (Sachs and Warner, Dec.1995). One would not fail to mention the unhealthy state of Nigeria's educational institutions and hospitals, lack of economic opportunities for the citizens, and lack of skills in computers and information technology for mass production are among the causes of the nation's low productivity and the poverty of the country. Any individual from a poverty-ridden society is, undoubtedly, familiar with the effects of poverty on the poor and the society in general.

Effects of Poverty

Perhaps, due to its complexity and its corrosive effects on humanity, many journal articles and books have addressed the issue of poverty (Schiller June 6, 2000; and Sen 1999; Harrison and Huntington, 2000). Poverty destroys aspirations, hope and happiness. In Nigeria, as in other poverty-stricken nations, this is the poverty one can feel. Poverty affects tolerance of others, support of civil liberties and openness toward foreigners. It affects positive relationships with subordinates, self-esteem and sense of personal competence. And it also affects one's disposition to participate in community affairs, interpersonal trust, and self-satisfaction (Inglehart 1997; and Fairbanks 2000).

Deprivation of basic things of life can result in premature mortality, significant under- nourishment (especially among children), persistent morbidity and illiteracy, among other problems. Life expectancy and literacy are correlated with the productivity and prosperity of a nation (Fairbanks 2000). As it relates to Nigeria and other poverty-ridden African and Asian countries, high level of poverty could lead to brain drain - the emigration of many of the most highly educated workers to rich countries, where these workers can enjoy a higher standard of living (Mankiw 2001). The poverty of a nation can also lead to human trafficking, prostitution, the spread of *HIV/AIDS*, child labour and human and civil rights abuse. As *The Guardian* (June 24, 2002) noted, "poverty leads to corruption, increase in crime rate and the disruption of family relations and social life, among other vices".

In *Development as Freedom*, Sen (1999) argues persuasively that an individual's advantage (or otherwise) in a society should not be judged solely on his or her *income*. Poverty must also be measured in "terms of substantive freedoms he or she enjoys to lead the kind of life he or she has reason to value." Thus poverty is a *deprivation* of *basic capabilities* (such as *undernourishment* and *illiteracy*) rather than merely as lowness of income that is the standard criterion for identifying poverty. Sen adds that the "capability-poverty" perspective "does not involve any denial" of the fact that low income is clearly one of the major causes of poverty, since lack of income can be a principal reason for a person's capability deprivation (Sen 1999, p.87). He equally noted that poverty, as "capability inadequacy" and "lowness of income" are related, because "income is such an important means to capabilities." And because "enhanced capabilities" tend to expand a person's ability to be more productive and earn a higher income" it is also normal for people to "expect a connection going from capability improvement to greater earning power."

The role of productivity in determining living standards is important for nations, as it is for individuals. A nation can enjoy a higher standard of living if it can produce a large quantity of goods and services needed by the people. The productivity of a society is determined by many factors, including *physical capital, human capital, natural resources,* and *technological knowledge* (Mankiw 2001). With the havoc caused by bad leadership and corruption, good *leadership* is among the determinants of a nation's productivity. These factors complement each other. A country will remain poor, in spite of its resources, if its leaders cannot organise the resources at their disposal for efficient and effective productive purposes. Unfortunately, this is one of the most deep-rooted impediments to higher productivity in Nigeria and the deteriorating poverty profile of the nation. In summary, poverty is degrading to human beings, and the life of the person afflicted by it is comparatively miserable and brief. Consequently, poverty, destitution, indigence and scarcity are words that show images of economic disadvantage and lack of financial resources. Previous poverty alleviation programmes in the society have not improved the poverty profile of this group, as they were not religiously implemented.

Previous Poverty Reduction Programmes (PPRP)

The problem with Nigeria is lack of consistency and non-implementation of government policies to the letter. Different administrations in Nigeria (civil and military) adopted their own poverty alleviation programme, instead of continuing with, and improving on the previous poverty programmes. This is the crux of the matter with poverty alleviation programmes in Nigeria. The first known poverty programme in Nigeria was the *National Accelerated Food Production Programme* and the *Nigerian Agricultural and Co-operative Bank* set up by General Yakubu Gowon in 1972. Nothing was shown for the huge sums sunk into the programmes, as they only served as conduits to transfer money to his cronies. In 1976 General Olusegun Obasanjo came in with his *Operation Feed the Nation*. The programme delegated university students to the rural areas to teach the rural farmers how to use modern farming tools that were not available. The civilian administration of Alhaji Shehu Shagari had the *Green Revolution Programme of 1979*. The objectives of the programme were to reduce food importation while boosting local food production. In theory, the programme was a noble one, but like others before it, the programme had nothing to show after gulping billions of *Naira*. The programme ended when General M. Buhari chased Shagari out of office in 1983. After that General Buhari introduced the *Go Back to Land Programme*. But this programme was as bad as the previous ones.

When General Babangida took over power in 1986, he established the *Directorate of Food, Roads and Rural Infrastructure* (DFRRI). The *Peoples Bank of Nigeria and the Community Bank, of Nigeria*, which were part of the programme, were set up to give out small loans to the rural poor. Even Babangida's wife came up with her own poverty reduction programme -*Better Life Programme*. It was designed apparently to improve the lives of rural women. However, the programme turned into a goldmine for the well-connected and powerful women entrusted with its implementation. General Sani Abacha, who wrestled power from the interim administration of Chief Shonekan in 1993, set up the Family Support Programme and the Family Economic Advancement Programme. After spending several billions of *Naira* to reduce poverty, poverty instead blossomed, because Abacha took delight in dismissing civil servants with impunity. And with Chief Olusegun Obasanjo's Second Coming in May 29, 1999, he promised to improve the lots of the masses. But he quickly transformed himself into a 'roving ambassador' instead of tackling the deteriorating living standards of Nigerians. Reports show that more than *N10 billion* (ten billion Naira) went into his poverty alleviation programmes in fiscal year 2000, but Nigeria is still the 26th poorest country in the world. Given the resources at her disposal, Nigeria should not have been so poor. But the inept and corrupt political leadership seems only interested in chasing shadows, raising the question of whether they can ever find any remedies to the poverty problem in Nigeria.

Remedies of Poverty Challenges

There is no *'quick-fix'* to reducing poverty in any society. If not, the streets of the United States could have been free of beggars. This is not to say that poverty should be tolerated. As Alfred Marshall observed, "there is no moral justification for extreme poverty side by side with great wealth." And James Madison was credited to have said that 'the happiest and most secure society was that in which most citizens are independent. [And that] No republic could remain untroubled [he believed], if large numbers of citizens were economically marginalized' (see Schwarz, Oct 1998). This is true, but many people are poor in the *oil* rich Nigeria. And this has generated a lot of social conflicts lately, but the leaders seem not to care. One writer notes: "It is not solely the lack of resources that generates conflicts [and social instability] in a polity, but corruption and lack of fairness in the distribution of resources". Thus, groups in the deprived areas of the world must never be forgotten and underestimated, because "what generates bitterness, tension and conflicts is the brazen denial of distributive justice, equity, and more importantly the process, which allows this denial." This condition is particularly volatile when it is accompanied, as it is often the case in Nigeria, by blatant display of conspicuous consumption by a privileged few overwhelmingly in control of the reigns of power (Amoo, Jan 1997). Thus to improve the poverty profile of the country, its "political economy must be characterised by transparency, accountability and distributive justice" (Amoo Jan 1997).

It is fair to say that lack of distributive justice was the main cause of the recent uprising in the Niger-Delta, where a group of women seized some oil installations, demanding that the oil companies making billions of dollars from the land, should employ the youths from the community. They threatened to go stark naked should they be attacked. It is obvious that the lack of fairness, inequitable distribution of resources, lack of transparency and accountability in governance as well as lack of minority-rights protection, would bring about social and political instability, which would scare local and foreign investors. Fairbanks (2000) suggests that to create prosperity in any nation and alleviate poverty, the state should create "a stable macroeconomic environment" that will enable the "private sector entrepreneurs to create growth."

The political leadership should make efforts to restructure the polity and diversify the economy so as to avoid the continuous reliance on a mono-cultural oil economy, whose price is subject to the vagaries of world politics. The government can also reduce the poverty of the people by controlling corruption, paying the workers living wages as, and when due (*Vanguard*, March 28, 2002; and *Guardian*, April 29, 2002). Since one of the reasons a nation is poor is lack of, or low productivity (see the causes of poverty above), the simple logic then would be for the leaders of Nigeria to device ways and means to motivate their citizens for higher productivity. Therefore, the economic problems of Nigeria are also a productivity issue. Nigeria has perhaps one of the worst reward systems in the world, and this has affected the morale of the workers and their productivity (see the section on inflation).

Some of the previous poverty alleviation programmes involved small loan disbursement to the rural poor. But these programmes did not increase their productivity or improve the poverty profile of the nation, largely because they did not give them the needed education and skills to manage their lives and to remove the specific frustrations of the environment to which they are subjected. Modern poverty may not be eradicated by giving out small loans to the poor. And this method may not solve *Case* poverty, because the "specific individual inadequacy" that precludes them from participation in the loan programme has not been eliminated. And because of the self or environmental factors, those administering the programmes could not reach the targeted groups. Some of the banks involved in the programme were not even located in poor and rural communities where the majority of the group lives. The true remedy for poverty in Nigeria should begin with providing education and skill training to the needy, and assisting them to secure employment, either in their localities or elsewhere. Those entrapped in the 'homing instinct', which crowd them into areas of inadequate opportunity and frustration, should be educated to work against that. The spread or location of industries in these communities will have remedial effect on the poor.

A society can also alleviate poverty by guaranteeing a minimum income to the poor and the unemployed for decency and comfort (like the welfare, pension, and unemployment programmes in the United States and some other developed economies). Pension programmes should be well implemented, as the retired are known to constitute a bulk of the poor in many societies. A combination of medical treatment and individual therapy would go a long way to alleviating their problems, because a sick person is usually an unproductive worker. Corruption and bureaucratic bottleneck are known to have destroyed the pension programmes in the country.

There should also be unemployment benefits. Though there are concerns that unemployment insurance could be a disincentive to work, one way out is to ensure that the unemployed are actively looking for work and that any assistance to them is ceased as soon as the unemployed gets work. Securing this minimum standard would help ensure that the misfortunes of parents (deserved or otherwise) are not visited on their children. And it ensures that poverty would not be self-perpetuating. Any fairly rich, rational, and compassionate society could afford this prescription. In a rich but cruel Nigeria, any person without a job would starve, even if he or she has physical and mental disabilities. The remedy for poverty is a bit difficult to prescribe for alcoholics and those with mental problems.

The UNDP prescribed some poverty alleviation strategies, which we would like to underscore. The UNDP strategies include the adoption of a long-term process and to have a broad understanding of what poverty is; to adopt an inclusive process with women and minorities, and to utilise local expertise and have a better coordination within governments. Others are training and education of the public (within and outside formal educational establishments) in poverty issues, and to make sure the strategies are [well] funded (see UNDP: 15-17 March 2001).

Poverty could also be remedied by ensuring that investment in the children from families presently afflicted with poverty is increased. As Galbraith (1956 and 1958) notes, if the children of poor families have access to first-rate schools; and if school attendance is properly enforced; if the children (though, poorly fed at home), are well nourished at school; if the community has good health services and the physical well being of the children is vigilantly watched; if there is opportunity for advanced education for those who qualify regardless of means; and if law and order are well enforced and recreation is adequate, then there is a very good chance that the children of the very poor will come to maturity without grave disadvantage. Nigeria can turn things around by adopting 'pro-poor distribution' and 'pro-poor growth' policy actions by investing more in rural areas (Moore 1999; *IDS Working Paper*, 1999).

Thus, slum clearance, establishment and expansion of low and middle-income housing in rural areas, provision of non-interruptible electricity for cottage industries will be helpful in reducing poverty. Good roads will attract investment to neglected rural areas and improve distribution of goods and services.

The adoption of people-oriented and pro-poor social policies would assist in poverty alleviation. These would include investment in rural areas and in agriculture as well as an increased investment in information technology, healthcare, provision of non-interruptible electricity for cottage industries, good roads for the distribution of goods and services, investment in human capital and skills training (and re-training) for jobs. The leaders of Nigeria should develop a compelling vision that would create a sense of shared purpose among the citizens. The leaders should also teach the values of hard work and creativity, the need for the citizens to take pride in their country as well as encourage and reward them for honesty. These will serve as incentives for individuals to change their behaviour and action that are inimical to the nation's prosperity. Finally, no poverty alleviation programme will be successful in any society without controlling corruption and government waste, showing transparency, accountability, and effective leadership. We shall, in the next chapter discuss technology and how it affects productivity and the entire economy.

References

Amoo, Sam G; "The Challenges of Ethnicity and Conflicts in Africa: The Need for a New Paradigm." Emergency Response Division, United Nations Development Programme, New York, January 1997
Daily Champion: July 5, 2002
Daily Independent: "Nigeria raked world's 16th loweat economy," Feb 26, 2003
Dike, Victor E; "The Global Economy and Poverty in Nigeria." In NESG: Economic Indicators, Jan – March 2003, Vol. 9, No 1.
------------------; "Poverty in Nigeria." *The Daily Independent*, October 6, 2002
Etounga-Manguelle, Daniel; "Does Africa Need a Cultural Adjustment Program?" in *Culture Matters* Lawrence E. Harrison and Samuel P. Huntington, editors, (New York: Basic Books), 2000

Fairbanks, Michael; "Changing the Mind of a Nation: Elements in a Process for Creating Prosperity," in *Culture Matters*, Lawrence E. Harrison and Samuel P. Huntington, editors, (New York: Basic Books), 2000, pp.270-281

**Galbraith (1955)

Galbraith, John Kenneth; "Inequality in Agriculture-Problem and Program." J. J. Morrison Memorial Lecture, Ontario Agricultural College, Guelph, Canada, 1956

Galbraith, John Kenneth; *The Affluent Society*; [New York: Mentor Book, 1958]

Harrison, Lawrence; "Why Culture Matters;" in Culture Matters, Lawrence E. Harrison and Samuel P. Huntington (Editors), [New York: Basic Books, 2000]

Harrison, Lawrence E. and Samuel P. Huntington. *Culture Matters.* (Editors), [New York: Basic Books, 2000]

Hecht, Robert; "Poverty, Debt and AIDS- Mainstreaming the Epidemic and Mobilizing Additional Resources for the Response." UNAIDS Inter-Country Team for West and Central Africa

Inglehart, Ronald; Modernization and Post modernization: Cultural, Economic, and Political Change in forty-three Societies (Princeton: Princeton Univ. Press, 1997 (see Ch.1 in particular).

Ireland: *The National Anti-Poverty Strategy* (NAPS) report, "Sharing in Progress" (1997); see the 1997 Living in Ireland Survey.

IMF Report – Nigeria: Selected Issues and Statistical Appendix, August 1998

IDS Working Paper: 1999

Journal of Poverty; See "Statement of Purpose;" at www.journalofpoverty.org/joppurp/joppurp.htm.

Lindsay, Stace; "Culture, Mental Models, and National Prosperity." In *Culture Matters*, Lawrence E. Harrison and Samuel P. Huntington (editors) [New York: Basic Books, 2000], pp. 282-295

Mankiw, N. Gregory; Principles of Economics (2nd ed.). [Fort Worth: Harcourt College Pub, 2001, pp. 530-552]

Mansfield, Edwin; *Economics: Principles, Problems, Decisions*; (2nd ed.) [New York: W.W. Norton & Company, Inc,]

Marshall, Alfred; *Principles of Economics*; (8th ed.); [London: Macmillan, 1927]

Marshall, Alfred; *The Study of Poverty* (1927)

Moore, Mick; Jennifer Leavy; Peter Houtzager & Howard White; "Polity Qualities: How Governance Affects Poverty;" IDS Working Paper 1999. This paper is a new version of "Responsiveness of Political

Systems on Poverty Reduction;" presented at a meeting held at Castle Donnington, UK on 16-17 August 1999, by Governance Department for the UK Department for International Development.

Ndulo, Muna; "Democracy, Institution Building, and Poverty in Africa." Inclusion, Justice, and Poverty Reduction - Villa Borsig Workshop Series (DSE), 1999

Ray, Debraj. Development Economics (Princeton: Princeton Univ. Press), 1998, p.9

Sachs, Jeffrey and Andrew Warner; "Natural Resources Abundance and Economic Growth," National Bureau of Economic Research, Cambridge, Working Paper 5398, December 1995

Schiller, Bradley R. The Economics of Poverty and Discrimination (8th ed.). Prentice Hall College Div., June 6, 2000

Schwarz, John E. "The Hidden Side of the Clinton Economy;" *The Atlantic Monthly*, October 1998

Sen, Amartya; "The Concept of Wealth" In *The Wealth of Nations in the Twentieth Century: The Policies and Institutional Determinants of Economic Development;* Ramon Myers (ed.), (Stanford: Hover Institute Press) 1996.

Sen, Amartya; Development as Freedom (New York: Anchor Books, 1999), pp. 87-110

Taiwo, Onalaja and Kehinde Onalaja; How Polygamy Wrecks Nigeria; *CAPWONA* Books, UK, 1997

The Commonwealth Yearbook (2002)

The Guardian: "Nigerians Among The Poorest People In Commonwealth," March 17, 2002

------------------: "The horror of human trafficking," June 24, 2002)

------------------: "Nigeria and the IMF," April 29, 2002

------------------: "Again, Nigeria and the WTO," April 2, 2002

------------------: "UNDP report ranks Nigeria 26th poorest country," July 26, 2002

The U SAID: Nigeria: "The Development Challenge." www.usaid.gov/country/afr/ng, (May 29, 2002)

TheWashington Times. "Giving Credit where credit is due. People's Bank of Nigeria reaches out to empower the poor" Advertising Department, September 30, 1999

The World Bank Group. "Nigeria: Targeting communities for effective poverty alleviation." Findings: African Region, No 68, August 1996

The United Nations AIDS Program (UNAIDS) 1999

The United Nations Development Programme: Conference Report on "Poverty Reduction Strategies: What have we learned?" Bergen, Norway 15-17 March 2001

The United Nations Development Programmes and Poverty Eradication - Sustainable Livelihoods *(SL)*; see www.onusida-aoc.org/Eng/Publications/Poverty.htm. The document was accessed (6/29/2002).

ThisDay; "Nigeria Rated Low in Economic Freedom," Feb 25, 2003

-----------; See Andrew Ahiante on "Nigeria Rated Low on Economic Development;" July 30, 2003

USAID: 2002

Vanguard: "Whiter Nigeria," July 5, 2002

-------------: "Formula for Taming domestic conflicts and insecurity," June 25, 2002

-------------: March 28, 2002

Webster's New Twentieth Century Dictionary: See the definitions of poverty.

Chapter 6

The Nigerian Economy: Technology and Productivity

We saw in the preceding chapter the factors that affect the economy and some of the arguments on how to build a better economy. In this chapter we shall discuss the impacts of technology on productivity and the overall economy. Scholars have noted the relationship between a developed and healthy economy and political democracy (Lipset 1960, Friedman 1979, Mirsky 1994, Dike 2001). You cannot have political freedom without a free economy (Bartlett 1981) and some have pointed out that democracy is meaningless to a hungry person.

Former Chairman of the *National Economic Intelligence Committee* (NIEC), Prof Sam Aluko, noted at some point that "one major problem of ours [Nigeria] like any developing country is undue interference with the currency. He pointed out that once a nation's currency is interfered with "it affects everything..." (Akin 1998, and Lewis May/June, 1994). Others note that "When the Naira is devalued, it leads to increase in cost of imported inputs and machinery. This in turn leads to increase in production costs, increase in local product prices and rise in inflation. The devaluation of the currency also leads to increase in prices of imported finished goods and services; which in turn leads to inflation (Alabi and Nwachukwu, April 28, 1999, see also the section on inflation). A weak currency is good for countries that have industrial products to export, and local industries to protect from import competition because their goods would be competitive in world markets, *ceteris paribus*. Since Nigeria's economy depends on imports and has limited industries to protect from foreign competition, a weak *Naira* makes imports expensive and drives up inflation. Bruising the *Naira* is a bad policy judgment. Dependence largely on the unpredictable oil export means that the economic well being of the country hangs precariously on the state of the world oil markets. And this has been the problem with the Nigerian economy.

A Review of the Economy

In the 1980s the IMF offered prescriptions for economic regeneration in Africa (see IMF Conditionalities below). It prescribed or recommended financial and budgetary discipline, reduction in state interventions in local markets, the promotion of exports and price liberalisation such as through the abolition of the marketing boards. Despite its enormous resources, Nigeria has moved from a wealthy country to the position of Africa's biggest debtor nation (*Vanguard*, Nov 3, 1998). Statistics about Nigeria are conflicting on the actual amount the nation owes. For instance, Abuja reported recently that the nation's debt was $27 billion at the end of 1997, down from $28 billion at the end of 1996. The World Bank report on Nigeria in May 1997 put the country's debt at $31.4 billion at the end of 1996. But an IMF report in August 1998 shows that Nigeria's total debt is $28.7 billion down from $28.8 in 1996 (IMF, August 1998 Report on Nigeria). It was reported by *BBC News* in August 28, 2002 that Chief Obasanjo admitted that the nation could no longer service its $33 billion foreign debt. And the *Daily Trust* of August 1, 2003 (among other national dailies) reported that the new economic adviser to President Obasanjo, Prof. Charles Soludo, noted that Nigeria currently 'owes $32bn abroad.' With these confused and confusing statistics, the exact size of the debt remains a mystery. Is Nigeria's debt $28 billion, $32.3 billion, $33 billion or $31 billion? However, a look backward shows that at the end of 1982 Nigeria's total debt was $9.3 billion (Girling 1985). Irrespective of the real amount owed, the fact remains that Nigeria is currently staggering under a massive burden of foreign debt. Like other *Third World* nations, Nigeria's debt is firmly rooted in the misapplication of resources.

A big chunk of the nation's debt (about $22 billion), as has been noted earlier, is owed to the *Paris Club* (*Vanguard*, July 23, 2003). The *Paris Club* is the informal name for a consortium of

Western creditor countries that have made loans or have guaranteed export credits to developing nations. They meet in Paris to discuss borrowers' ability to repay debts. The organisation has no formal or institutional existence and no fixed membership. The French treasury manages the secretariat; and it has a close relationship with the World Bank, the International Monetary Fund, and the United Nations Conference on Trade and Development (Metz, June 1991).

Many 'political physicians' have prescribed varied 'medicines' for the Nigerian economy, including the nation's structural adjustment policy of the 1980s. In spite of the policies, the economy remained comatose while the nation has witnessed varying degrees of social instability. Some people have attributed the failures of those policies variously to corruption or the 'African or Nigerian factor'- whatever this might mean!

Whatever may be the reasons for those policy failures, the fact remains that the economy has been characterised by low productivity (Dike, May 15 and 22, 2003). By the mid-1970s Nigeria was in the mentality of the oil boom. During this period the Organisation of Petroleum Exporting Countries (OPEC), which was the first Third World commodity cartel to successfully set a price structure, forced up the world oil prices. The OPEC cartel was formed in 1960, but Nigeria became a member of the cartel in 1971. The society was on the verge of a miraculous socio-economic development or transformation during the oil-boom period. But the mood of optimism that started during the boom era suddenly turned to pessimism. By the late1980s, and with the decline in the world oil prices, the expectations of Nigerians to positively transform their standard of living became a giant tale of nightmare; the boom collapsed. Only those in the corridors of power benefited from the boom while the ordinary citizens remained in abject penury (Wiseman 1990).

Oil, which has remained the main source of government revenue, has been one of the problems with the economy. It contributes about 75% of government revenue, and typically, over 90% of export earnings. While the oil money was flowing in, little was done to diversify the nation's economic base. The impact of the reliance of Nigeria on the unreliable oil economy was manifested on the 1999 national budget. At the beginning of 1998, the average selling price of crude oil in the world market was about $16-17 per barrel. But by October 1998 the price had dropped to $12.8 per barrel. The price of oil for January 1999 deliveries was less than $11 per barrel. Because of this slump in the global oil market, the revenue for the 1999 budget was based on the price of $9 per barrel. This, according to Sobowale (Jan 1,1999,) was against the projected price of $16-17 used in planning the 1998 budget.

Despite the fact that Nigeria is the 6th largest oil-producing nation in the world, it still has a lot of problem supplying enough petroleum products to the local market. Some of the reasons for the shortage of fuel are lack of, or broken-down refineries, inadequate distribution channels (diversion and hoarding of fuel by distributors) and incessant strikes by oil workers. Nigeria supplements what the inefficient government refineries could produce with massive importation of fuel for local consumption. The government has been slow in granting licenses to private businesses to establish and operate refineries. That is the only way the problem of fuel shortages could permanently be solved. However, during the dark and brutal days of military rule in the 1980s and 1990s, motorists would spend many hours at petrol stations for petrol due to fuel shortages. At the early part of the civilian government of Obasanjo, the situation improved but towards the end of his first term in office (before the 2003 elections), long queues had returned in petrol stations. In March 2003 the situation deteriorated sharply, with motorists spending hours looking for fuel. The government, however, blamed the shortages on either its "political enemies" or on wilful sabotage. During this period a gallon of petrol was about N400 (about $3) in the black market – or roughly four times the official price. Frustration reigned, as many activities, including industrial production, were paralysed. One frustrated citizen encapsulated the feelings of many when he declared: "The truth is that the Government is completely a failure" (see The *BBC* of Feb 28, 2003).

Export instability clearly inhibits economic development. When export income falls, purchases in other sectors would decline, resulting in sharp reductions in investment, employment, and government revenue. It is particularly difficult to plan, and invest because of fluctuations in revenues. As economic conditions deteriorate, social conflicts often intensify.

Table I: **Nigerian Economic Growth Record (1979-2002)**

	Oil Price (p/b)	Economic Growth Index	
b/w1979-1983	$40 (Shehu Shagari era)	1999	2.80%=real; 3.00%= target
1986	$12	2000	3.80%=real; 3.00%= target
1990s	$35 (Gulf Crisis)	2001	3.80%=real; 5.00%=target
1997	$19.2		
Early 1998	about $16-17	Year	Inflation
Oct 1998	$12.80	1999	May -Dec ↓ (12.2 % - 6.6%)
1999	$18	2000	June =0.90%
2000	$28.60	2000	Dec=6.90%
2001	$26	2001	Jan=8.60%
2003	$35.77 (US light); London Brent $32.45	2001	Dec=18.9% ↑ (12% in 2001)
		2002	Nov 13.2%++
	Exchange Rate (per $)	Official	Parallel
1999	29 May	N94.88	N99.00
	b/w May '99 – Dec '99		
	Lost:	1.3%	0.2%
2000	December (closed)	N101.70	N111.10
		↓=5.8%	↓= 12%
2001	January	N110.05	N120.00
		↓= 12%	↓= 20.2%
2002	January (open)	N113.45	N/A
2002	February	N120.10	N/A
2002	June 3	N116.80	N/A
2002	June 14	N119.55	N/A

Sources: Compiled by the *Author* from, *ThisDay Sunday*: "Issues 2003" 19 May 2003;
Dike, Victor E. *Democracy and Political Life in Nigeria* [Zaria, Nigeria: *ABU* Press,

2001], p.117; *ThisDay:* "Bankers Express Concern over Naira Depreciation" Feb. 7, 2002

Daily Trust: "Oil prices jump again" Feb 13, 2003.

++Inflation rate still remains above single because of persistent excessive liquidity and increased fiscal surprises.

Broad money (M2) grew by 25.5 per cent, against permissible rate of 15.3 per cent for fiscal 2002. However, the

impact of good agricultural harvest on food prices moderated inflation rate of inflation at this period.

ThisDay: "CBN Gives Economy Thumbs Down," Feb 18, 2003

N/A: Not available

↓ = Down

↑ = Up

These factors would produce a fertile ground for crime. Nigeria has experienced both good and bad economic times. How can Nigeria achieve an economic turn-around and move from "mono-cultural" oil economy to a diversified economy? Nigeria's hardest period came during the General Sani Abacha years. He and his henchmen had difficulty distinguishing between the national treasury and their private bank accounts. The looting of the nation's resources during his reign has been well documented. The economy remained stunt throughout the 1990s. And the shortage of petroleum products (especially in 1998) worsened the social and economic life of the common man in Nigeria. This shortage was largely caused by the failure of the military governments (and the ineffective and corrupt managers), to carry out the scheduled *'Turn-Around Maintenance -TAM'* of the nation's four oil refineries. This problem, as Nwokoma, (Dec.7, 1998) noted, will persist unless creative planning and development programmes are instituted to ensure the maintenance of these refineries and efficient distribution of petroleum products. The usual economic penalty for falling behind in the race for increased efficiency is bankruptcy – for nations, companies, and individuals.

SAP and the Nigerian Economy

Nigeria's economy began to nose-dive with the drying up of the petro-dollars in the 1980s. This created an unprecedented shortage of foreign exchange, making it difficult for the country to finance her imports. The scourge of unemployment began to show up in the country as factories and industries were shut down for lack of raw materials in the early 1980s. Inflation began to rear its ugly head due to inadequate supply of essential goods and services (see the section on inflation). There was an under-utilisation of productive capacity due to lack of material inputs, machine tools, and spare parts (Attah, et al, 1987).

Because of the severe economic problems, Nigeria approached the International Monetary Fund (IMF), in 1983 for loan. To ensure a prudent use of the loan, the IMF characteristically gave Nigeria some conditions for the loan. Some of the conditions include:

Currency devaluation or deregulation, trade liberalisation, price and wage freeze and de-subsidisation (Ndebbio 1987). The massive cuts in public subsidies in Nigeria (e.g. gasoline) made life difficult for the people. The Shagari civilian government initiated the loan negotiations, but Gen. Ibrahim Babangida rejected the conditions for the loan when he came to power. In June 1986 he announced the *Structural Adjustment Programme* (SAP) for the period of July 1986-June 1988 for the country. The economic recovery programme, the austerity measures and the SAP were, however, within the policy frameworks recommended by the World Bank and the IMF. The SAP programme ended a long time ago, but the negative impacts on the economy are still visible.

The World Bank, which was initially called *IBRD*, was founded in July 1944 at the Bretton Woods Conference, New Hampshire but it commenced operation in 1946. The World Bank is the sister institution to the International Monetary Fund (IMF). It was one of the multinational institutions established after the First World War (1914-1918) "to rebuild, to provide a safety net for, and to structure the postwar world economy."

113

Victor E Dike

Other institutions set up at that conference are the International Monetary Fund (IMF) and the International Trade Organization (ITO) (Girling, 1985). These institutions are popularly known as the Bretton Woods institutions.

The (SAP) measures were intended "to correct the continued over-valuation of the Naira through the setting up of a viable and substantial *Second-Tier Foreign Exchange Market* (SFEM), simultaneously with further downward adjustment to the official rate..." *(Daily Times,* June 28, 1986). However, as noted by ThisDay (July 27, 2003), the SAP was an insincere variant dose of the remedy recommended by the *World Bank* and the IMF to the *Third World*. As noted earlier, the Naira was considered overvalued, and IMF recommended to the government of the time to devalue the local currency (Naira) to two to one (2-1) American dollars but instead the Babangida regime allowed the currency to depreciate three to one (3-1) dollar. As Caulcrick noted in the *ThisDay* (July 27, 2003) the SAP adversely impacted the life of most Nigerians. In fact the imposition of IMF policy guidelines (conditionalities) on Third World countries have, in virtually all the countries where they were introduced, adversely affected people's living standards and provoked violent reactions. Alfred Sauvy claimed that he invented the term the "Third World," in 1952, modelled on the *Third Estate* of the 1789 *French Revolution*. In 1956, a Paris journal, *Tiers Monde*, adopted the term. This term identified not just a group of "new states" (later joined by older states of Latin America), but it was seen as a political alternative to United States, Britain and the former Soviet Union (Russia) - the first and second worlds (Harris 1986). The Third World Countries are often referred to as the less developed, developing, underdeveloped, the non-industrialised, the poor, the backward, or the South. They are contrasted with the First World (see above), the more developed, the developed, the industrialised, the rich, the advanced market economies, or the North (Harris 1986).

An underdeveloped country, according to Mills (1982), is one in which the focus of life is necessarily upon economic subsistence. Its industrial equipment is not sufficient to meet

Western standards of minimum comfort. Its style of life and its system of 'power' are dominated by the struggle to accumulate the primary means of industrial production (Howard 1982). They lack the necessary advanced technologies that are available in developed nations. The policies of the IMF on loans to the *Third World* nations have often resulted in dramatic price rises for basic necessities without the corresponding real wage increases. There were riots in Egypt in 1977 when it was forced to end food subsidies; it also reduced clothing subsidies to meet the stipulations of the *IMF*. The story was much the same for Nigeria; there were riots in urban centres across the nation when the government removed subsidies on petroleum products to meet the stipulations of the *IMF* (Girling 1985 and Dike, May 28, 1999). It has been noted that expensive import leads to increase in general price level. For a *Third World* country such as Nigeria with a weak industrial base to benefit from the SAP policy, it should first overcome all the limitations of Import Substitution Industrialization (ISI) such as the lack of a good industrial environment for the rural society, good roads, electrification, water, good communication system, affordable and relevant education and basic health services and so forth (Ndebbio and Ekpo 1985). These basic needs are preconditions for meaningful growth and development in any society.

Boosting production and the enlargement of the 'economic pie' (by investing in the economy, technological development, fighting corruption, investment in human capital, privatising ill-managed state corporations, conducive political environment, among others) would help in solving Nigeria's economic problems. When General Sani Abacha came to power in 1993, he did not embrace the 'main elements of the Structural Adjustment Programme,' haphazardly undertaken by General Ibrahim Babangida. Instead, he outlawed the *Autonomous Foreign Exchange Market* (AFEM), which was in place, and imposed a "legally binding fixed official rate of 22 Naira to a dollar" on the country. This amount (22 Naira) was only a fraction of the rate obtained at free market transactions. He also suspended his once promised privatisation programme. Not surprisingly, this policy created a huge subterranean economy. By the end of 1994 the difference between the official and non-official exchange rates was roughly 300 percent. A boom on hard currency transaction, even among senior military generals and other senior government officials resulted. All these negatively affected the value of the Naira and life became more miserable for the ordinary Nigerians (Obadina 1998). The *Naira* is still struggling in 2003!

The IMF criticised Nigeria's dual-exchange rate system, which was in operation during the military regime. The federal government had an official exchange rate of 22 Naira to the dollar for government transactions, and the Autonomous Foreign Exchange Market (AFEM) rate of 86 Naira (or thereabout) to the dollar for the public. State and local governments received their allocation at the official rate of 22 Naira to the dollar. With this, some transactions were measured at N22, while others were measured at N86. The system was abolished during the 1999 budget because it caused a lot of confusion and 'distortion' in the economy. For the World Bank 'distortion' is any deviation in a nation's price structure from a perfectly competitive model, including those deviations that impede foreign competition in a domestic market. Thus economic distortions could be caused by tariff barriers (which result in a higher domestic price; and mismanagement by political elite (diversion of capital inflows that could be used for economic development to support conspicuous life-style (Girling 1985). The distortion in the Nigerian economy has continued with an attendant increase in the level and spread of poverty in the society.

In Nigeria, the very few (less than one percent of the population) that controlled about 90 percent of the nation's wealth save their money outside the country; and this does not create wealth and jobs for the nation, but for the nations where the monies are dumped. Nigerians must be persuaded through favourable social policy to bring their wealth back to the country (Caulcrick, July 27, 2003).

Since economic insecurity abounds in the country, Nigeria needs unemployment insurance. And a nation should make available the basic needs (food, clothing, water, decent shelter, and healthcare) for its citizens (JASPA, 1981; Sisk and Williams, 1981; and Maslow 1943). The lack of all these basic needs have negative impacts on workers' morale and productivity. Productivity can be broken down into three component parts: ability, opportunity, and motivation (Managers, Nov 1993). However, productivity is 'the relationship between the amount of one or more inputs and the amount of outputs from a clearly defined process' (Thor 1991). Thus, Nigeria should re-double its efforts to provide an enabling environment for its workers to improve their productivity. As Webster's New Collegiate Dictionary 1980 notes, morale, among other things, "is the mental and emotional condition (including enthusiasm, confidence, or loyalty) of an individual or group with regard to the function or task at hand."

Lack of Motivation and Low Productivity

With all the material resources available in Nigeria, it is unbelievable that the workers lack the necessary *motivation* to perform their duties. Many workers are owed arrears of wages and salaries. The fact is that the money looted by military generals (especially Abacha and his cronies) from our national treasury would have been enough to pay the workers for years. The country should be committed to combating fraud and to bringing criminals to justice. However, any action in this regard should be transparent, fair, just, and honest. For a worker to be productive he/she should be well motivated and corruption controlled. Without this, funds meant for the workers would end up in private pockets. Nigeria cannot effectively compete in the global market place with ill-motivated and hungry workers.

Motivation, among other definitions, 'is a person's inner state that energises, sustains, and directs behaviour to satisfy a person's need' (Milkovic and Glueck 1985). According to Donaldion (March 1992), motivation can stimulate "someone to action by creating a safe environment in which their motivation can be unleashed and through providing a reason or incentive for people to produce." Good employee motivation may cause one to abandon one's own goals for the goals of the organisation. Therefore, individual nations should develop novel solutions to the problems facing them. But for any solution to be effective, countries such as Nigeria should wage serious war on ethnicity, sectionalism, nepotism, and other negative '...isms' that is dividing and alienating the people in the society.

Resource mismanagement is a serious problem in Nigeria. And ineffective management of resources and lack of, or poor motivation of the workers, mostly causes low productivity. These are common occurrences in state-owned organisations because of state intervention in employment and management of these public organisations. Consequently, many managers in the public sector (when compared with the private sector) lack the skills necessary to lead a productive workforce. Nigeria should pursue the present privatisation programme with seriousness, but the process should be given a human face (refer to the chapter on privatisation). Thus the state should, as Lukman, (May/Dec 13, 1999) noted "de-emphasize undue interference in government parastatals so as to promote professionalism and efficiency" in this area.

Information Technology and Globalisation

Communication (verbal and written), telecommunication, and Transportation - Road network, Vehicles, Air and Sea transportation, have been noted as a central corollary of democracy. The issue of "free flow" of information boils down to the rights of individuals to freedom of opinion, and expression. Scholars such as Emerson (1969), Merrill (1981) and Ayish (1992) have written extensively on the area of communication. New technologies such as the Internet should be given the desired attention in the country so as to improve and increase the quality and volume of information available to Nigerians. Without freedom of information, the interest of the people, and that of the nation, is in jeopardy.

The role of the mass media in a democracy is to inform the electorate on public issues, enlarge their base of participation in the political process, and serve as a watchdog over government behaviour. A society is better served by free and open- reporting press. For the media to play these roles however, freedom of expression is a precondition. Robust debates usually lead to a better understanding of the issues facing a nation and its people. And out of a better understanding grows a greater chance for solutions (Ayish 1992). Thomas Emerson has noted that a system of freedom of expression embraces a set of rights, which includes the right to hold beliefs and opinions on any subject, and to communicate the same in speech, writing, music, art, or in other ways (Emerson 1969). Merrill maintains that freedom of expression is the continuation of, and practical manifestation of freedom of thought, which is the most fundamental human right (Merrill 1983). Without this right a country cannot meaningfully participate in the emerging computerised global economy.

It has been noted that democracy does not work in a vacuum. The availability of the necessary political and institutional structures makes democracy possible. The world, which is evolving into a global village, is being propelled by the revolution in information technology (IT). Information technology offers opportunities for developing countries to "leapfrog into the 21st century", and it "reduces the cost of doing business". It also removes the huge geographical barriers that have been impediments to development in Africa (including Nigeria). Thus, as Amoako has noted in *Africansource.com*, IT "offers opportunities to small-scale entrepreneurs, and opens opportunities in social sectors, such as long distance education."

Globalisation means the rapid integration of world economies, trade, financial services, etc, through information technology. Many scholars have argued that the economic globalisation process would lead to the widening of the gap between the rich and poor nations. Nevertheless, the process of globalisation and the new communication media (especially the Internet) have created the economic and technological foundations that make possible the existence of a transnational community (*Alvarez*, et. al, 1998). The pace of technological development is relatively slow in Nigeria. The fixed line public telephone system is still a novelty in the country and the use of computers; the Internet and fax machines are not yet common. But in the industrialised nations – the 'knowledge' societies – these are common. Thus, "a knowledge society", among other things, is "a society of mobility." It "is a society in which many more people than ever before can be successful." With this "people no longer stay where they were born, either in terms of geography or in terms of social position and status." And according to *Drucker*, (Nov 1994) "people no longer have a neighbourhood that controls what their home is like, what they do, and indeed, what their problems are allowed to be."

Globalisation has also its downside. For instance, it could wipe out many traditional jobs (though, it also usually creates new ones). With globalisation, you could have less "bookkeepers but more data-entry clerks" (Blinder and Quandt, Dec 1997). There might also be less office messengers, but more electronic mail technicians. And local farmers might wither away due to foreign competition. To reap the benefits of the global economy, Nigeria should bountifully invest in information technology and transform the nation into a mobile society. The society must therefore be serious with technological development, because, as *Drucker* (Nov.1994) notes, "developing countries can no longer base their development on their comparative labour advantage – that is, on cheap industrial labour." The earlier the leaders of Nigeria realise this, the better for the country.

Towards Improving Workers' Productivity

Employee motivation, which is a serious problem in Nigeria, can take many forms. Thus, any serious productivity improvement programmes in the country should include, among other things: the replacement of ineffective and obsolete technologies; the replacement of equipment in poor conditions; the establishment of good working conditions for workers (good payment system, incentives, good retirement benefits, and so forth) and the provision of appropriate training (skills) etc. Investment in human development (employee training) and technological modernisation are among the most efficient and effective methods of improving workers' productivity. Without the availability of necessary tools and modern technologies, workers productivity will remain dismal. It has been emphasised that "the only enduring competitive advantage [in this global economy] is a high quality, well-motivated workforce willing to work together as a team to increase productivity" (Greene, April 1991 and Dike, May 15, 2003). In addition, the workers should be paid living wages and they should be paid when it is due. Late payment or non-payment of workers, which is a serious problem in Nigeria, discourages workers and thus drives their productivity down.

Because managers are responsible for the day-to-day operation of their organisation, the work climate of any unit or organisation is determined, for good or bad, by the work habits of the manager (or managers) of a particular unit or organisation. If the managers were not concerned about the welfare of their organisation, how would they expect such from their workers? Many managers in Nigeria are corrupt and therefore will not see corruption among their subordinates as a vice. This partly explains why corruption is endemic in the country. Any motivational programme in organisations would only work if the employees feel confident in the management. Thus the Nigerian society should create the appropriate organisational environment and value system that would stimulate the morale and productivity of the workforce and leadership. And overtime, a culture of high productivity would be created.

In conclusion, Nigeria has a system that suffers from many deficiencies, one of the most glaring of which is lack of workers' motivation. Nigeria can survive only if persistent efforts are made to correct these anomalies. This is because as Bob Crandell, president of *American Airline*, was credited to have said, "If you always do what you always did, you will always get what you always got" (Sharman, Feb. 1991). Thus, for Nigeria to move forward in this 21st Century, it has to change and "understand and apply what works." Because as Daniel Chirot (1977) notes, "poverty or wealth in any one country is caused by its internal characteristics…[and] any efforts to help poor societies would have to start with internal reform." In the next chapter we shall extend our discussion of the economy to a discussion of inflation as well as workers' struggles for economic survival in the face of a malfunctioning economy.

References

Attah, et al; The Nigerian Economy Under (S) FEM: The Economics of the Foreign Exchange Market in A Developing Economy. [Zaria, Nigeria: ABU Press, 1987]
Alabi, Lanre and Obinna Nwachukwu; "Phillips criticizes devaluation of Naira." *Vanguard:* April 28, 1999
Alveraz, Sonia E; Evelina Daquino, and Arturo Escobar (eds.); Culture of Politics, Politics of Cultures: Revisioning Latin American Social Movements. [West View Press, 1998]
Akin, Soji; "A policeman for the Nigerian economy." Online posting: Africa Economic Analysis, 1998
Ayish, Muhammad I. "International Communication in the 1990s: Implications for the Third World." *International Affairs*, 68, 3, 1992
Amoako, K.Y; "Economic Development and Reform Issues in Africa: Lessons for Ghana." See *Africaresource.com*: Scholars-K.Y. Amoako, *African Educational Web Portal* (source June 20, 2002).
BBC News: "Nigerian fuel shortages worsen," Feb 28, 2003
BBC News: "Nigeria admits debt Crisis;" August 28, 2002
Bartlett, Bruce; Reaganomics: Supply Side economics in Action. [Westport, Connecticut: Arlington House Pub, 1981]
Blinder, Alan S. and Richard E. Quandt; "The Computer and the Economy." *The Atlantic Monthly*, Vol. 280, No. 6, Dec 1997
Camdessus, Michel; "The Challenges for the Arab World in the Global Economy: Stability and Structural Adjustment."(An address delivered at the Annual meeting of the Union of Arab Banks), New York, May 20, 1996.
Caulcrick, Samuel; "Keep Nigeria's Wealth Within;" *ThisDay*, July 27, 2003

Conabel, Barber; "Beyond Halifax" An article written shortly after the June 1995 meeting of the G7 at Halifax, Canada, (see www.cgg.ch/barber.htm)

Chirot, Daniel; Social Change in the Twentieth Century; [New York: Harcourt Brace Jovanovic, Inc., 1977]

Daily Trust: "Oil prices jump again" Feb 13, 2003.

---------------; See Rueben Yunana on "Nigeria now owes $31bn abroad;" August 1, 2003

Daniel, Isioma; see *ThisDay*, Nov 16, 2002 (for the article that was said to have caused the Miss World contest riot in Nigeria).

Donadio, Patrick J. "Capturing the Principles of Motivation." *Business Credit*, March 1992, p.40

Drucker, Peter F. "The Age of Social Transformation." *Atlantic Monthly*, Vol. 274, No. 5, Nov 1994

Dike, Victor E. "The Bretton Woods Institutions and the Third World: Impacts of Loan Conditionalities on Domestic Economy - with emphasis on Nigeria;" Online publication, *Nigeriaworld.com*, May 28, 1999

------------------. "The Global Economy and Poverty in Nigeria." In *NESG: Economic Indicators*, Jan – March 2003, Vol. 9, No. 1

------------------. "Nigerian Society at the dawn of the 21st century: Reward Systems, Workers Morale, and Productivity." *African Economic Analysis* Online (*www.afbis.com*), January 2000

------------------: "Reward system and labour productivity;" *Daily Independent*, May 15, 2003.

------------------; "Toward Labour Productivity;" *Daily Independent*, May 22, 2003

------------------; "To Sustain the Unity of Nigeria;" *Daily Independent*; Jan 30, 2003

-----------------. *Democracy and Political Life in Nigeria* [Zaria, Nigeria: *ABU* Press, 2001]

Emerson, Thomas; The System of Freedom of Expression; [New York: Vintage Books, 1969]

Friedman, Milton (1979); as cited by Chiichii Ashwe in "An Economic Agenda for Democracy," *The Nigerian Economist*, May 28, 1990, Vol. 3, No. 17

Girling, Robert H. Multinational Institutions and the Third World; [Praeger Pub, 1985]

Greene, Robert J. "A '90 Model for Performance Management." *HR Magazine*, April 1991, pp.62-63.

Harris, Nigle; The End of the Third World; [Penguin Books, 1986]

IMF Report – Nigeria: Selected Issues and Statistical Appendix, August 1998

Journal of Poverty; See "Statement of Purpose;" at www.journalofpoverty.org/joppurp/joppurp.htm.

JASPA: First things first: Meeting the basic needs of the people of Nigeria: Report to the Government of Nigeria by a JASPA Basic Needs Mission," Addis Ababa, JASPA (1981), p.22.

Lewis, Peter M. "The Politics of Economics." *Africa Report*, Vol. 39, no. 3, May/June, 1994

Lipset, Seymour; *Political Man.* [New York: Doubleday, 1960]

Lukman, Rilwanu; "Aspects Affecting Investment in African Energy." A speech delivered to the CWC Associates' Conference on Oil & Gas Investments in Africa, London, UK, 12-13 May 1999.

Lukman, Rilwanu; "Prospects for the Oil Market in the 21st Century and Consequences for Producers in West Africa." Financial Times Conference on Nigeria, London, UK, 4-5 May 1999.

Managers: "Improving productivity through motivation." *Managers*, Nov. 1993, p.29

Metz, Alex; "Improve productivity through delegation;" T&D, Jan.1992, p.25.

Milkovich, George T. and William F. Glueck.; Personnel/Human Resource Management: A Diagnostic Approach. 4th ed., *Business Publications*, Inc., Plano, Texas, 1985, p.136.

Mirsky, Yehudah; "Democratic Politics, Democratic Culture: Democratization and Civil Society." In *Current,* Jan 1994

Merrill, J. "A Growing Controversy: The Free Flow of News among Nations." in Richstad and Anderson (eds.) *Crisis in International News, Policies and Prospects*; [New York: Columbia University Press, 1981]

Metz, Helen Chaplin; "Nigeria: A Country Study" (editor), June 1991

Mills, C. Wright. "Culture and Politics." In Gerald Howard (editor), *Sixties.* [Washington Square Press, 1982]

Ndebbio, J.E; "….." In Attah, editor, The Nigerian Economy Under (S) FEM: The Economics of the Foreign Exchange Market in A Developing Economy. [Zaria, Nigeria: ABU Press, 1987]

Nwokoma, Ndubisi; "Big Country, No Fuel." *The Guardian*: December 7, 1998

Obadina, Tunde; "Nigeria's new leader faces tough job mending economy." Online: Africa Economic Analysis, 1998

Sharman, Paul; "Winning Techniques for productivity: The activity link." CMA Magazine, Feb. 1991, p.8; p.11.

Sisk, Henry L. and J. Clifton Williams; Management and Organization

(4th ed.) [Cincinnati: Southwestern Pub Co., 1981] p.317.
Soros, George; "Toward a Global Open Society." *The Atlantic Monthly,* Vol. 281, No 1, (Jan. 1998); pp. 20-32)
ThisDay: "Issues 2003" 19 May 2003
-----------: "Bankers Express Concern over Naira Depreciation" Feb. 7, 2002
-----------: "CBN Gives Economy Thumbs Down," Feb 18, 2003
Thor, Carl O. "How to measure organizational productivity." *CMA Magazine,* March 1991, pp.18-19).
Thurow, Lester; "Building Wealth" *The Atlantic Monthly,* June 1999, Vol. 283, No. 6; pp.57-69.
The Economist: August 21, 1993
Vanguard: "Foreign debt: Nigeria's mill stone;" July 23, 2003
Webster's New Twentieth Century Dictionary: See the definitions of poverty.
Wiseman, John; Democracy in Black Africa: Survival and Revival. [New York: Paragon House Pub Company, 1990]

Chapter 7

The Economy: Inflation and Economic Survival

We saw at the end of the preceding chapter that poverty or wealth in a society is caused by its internal characteristics and any efforts to help poor nations should begin with internal reform. In this chapter we shall consider the nature of inflation and its impacts on the society. The problems of inflation and unemployment, which have been difficult to remedy in the country, call for an urgent need for social safety nets.

The history of Nigeria's inflationary predicaments illustrates the problems that emerge when a government fails to make good social and economic judgments. It is a common belief that in life, unresolved problems have the unfortunate characteristic of reinforcing each other. Nigeria's inability to control the petroleum product shortages and the resultant skyrocketing of oil (energy) prices exacerbates the inflation problem. For this, rising energy costs pushes up price in other sectors of the economy. Wage earners attempt to keep up with prices by demanding large wage increases, which leads to greater inflation, because "...energy is used in the production and distribution of almost everything" (Thurow 1980).

Inflation has both economic and political ramifications. The political implication is mainly felt in organised democratic societies where politicians face the consequences of their actions at the ballot box. Since Nigerian politics is not issues-based, it is difficult for the country to hold the politicians responsible for anything.

What is Inflation?

Inflation is an increase in the volume of money and credit relative to available goods and services in a country, resulting in a substantial and continuing rise in the general price level. As J.K. Galbraith (1958) explains, inflation means "persistently rising prices." In *The Affluent Society,* he points out that inflation can occur "only" when the demands on the economy are somewhere near the "capacity of the plant and available labour force to supply them." Any further increase in demand at this point is capable of bringing price increase - the so-called 'demand-pull inflation.' Here he emphasised *capacity* use of plant and labour force. Galbraith (1958) defined capacity of use of plant as "that point where any further increase will incur abruptly rising short-run marginal costs," and notes that full labour force is the "point where... additional labour effort is forthcoming only at steeply rising marginal cost."

Lester C. Thurow puts it differently. He noted that whenever upward price shocks occur, inflation would set in unless other prices and incomes fall. Unfortunately, in modern economy prices and wages in other sectors do not easily fall. In the labour market money wages exhibit downward rigidity (they do not fall when surplus labour exists). According to Thurow (1980) relative wages are rigid and change only in the long run. As mentioned earlier, the increase in the cost of petroleum products (energy) in Nigeria has a multiplier effect on the economy. The distributive effects on the society are noted on the upward movement of transportation fares and consumer goods (particularly food items). Tremors in the energy sector (the rising cost of energy), would lead to rumblings in other part of the economy (*Domino Effect*); that is price increase in other goods and services in the country (Samuelson, Oct 12, 1998). The prices of transportation, foodstuffs and other services went up recently in Nigeria when the federal government increased the prices of petroleum products in the country (Dike, June 26, 2003)

Causes of Inflation in Nigeria

Numerous studies have been conducted on the causes of inflation in Nigeria. Most of the studies seem to agree that the key factors influencing the rate of inflation in the country are money growth, income growth, and exchange rate movements. The impact of the high domestic interest rate seems to have received only a passing mention in most of the studies. Some however argue that the impact of exchange rates movements on inflation is less clear. Moser for instance emphasised the role of agro-climatic conditions (rainfall and drought in particular) in causing inflation in Nigeria (Moser 1995).

The studies by Darrat (1985), Ojameruaye (1988), Ekpo (1992) and the World Bank (1993) concluded that excess domestic demand generated by expansionary fiscal and monetary policies, has been the major cause of rising inflation in Nigeria. Other studies such as Adamson (1988), and Aigbokhan (1991) emphasised cost-push inflation emanating from excessive Naira devaluation and wage increases as underlying causes of inflation in the country. The perennial shortage of petroleum products is another factor. This is because energy is used in the production and distribution of almost everything (see increase in gasoline price above). Enwere Dike (1990) notes that 'the transmission belt of inflation in most of the Less Developed Countries (LCDs) is the low supply elasticity in agriculture and industry as well as the chaotic nature of the distribution channels."

There is also the impact of foreign exchange control on inflation. High duties and anti-growth policies such as the ban on the importation of certain groups of *Tokumbo* (used cars), at various times have in many cases served only to encourage smuggling. This reduces the revenue of the customs (assuming the collected duties are properly accounted for). For any modern economy to function well, roads, bridges, railways and airports should be in good operating conditions. In Nigeria, all these infrastructures are in dilapidated conditions. Storage and marketing facilities, communications systems and power (electricity) must also be built and maintained for the economy to function well. Lack of spare parts for plants and production inputs are among other factors hampering productivity in the country as plants close down due to lack of, or expensive spare parts. These factors contribute to low industrial productivity and inflation in Nigeria.

Spontaneous salary increases also tend to fuel inflation in Nigeria. During the 1999 salary increase, some of the civilian governors were financially incapable of paying the new minimum wage. And in 2003 the Nigeria Labour Congress (NLC) and the federal government were again talking about a 25 increase in workers pay. The Chief Olusegun Obasanjo administration recently accepted to give Federal workers a - 12.5% salary increase (excluding employees of the state and local government and the private sector; see *Vanguard*, May 2, 2003; Dike, May 15, 2003). Not long after, the federal government increased the prices of petroleum products, which caused the Nigeria Labour Congress (NLC) to call out the workers for mass protest. The increase in fuel price and resultant strike action, as widely noted by many writers including Dike (June 26, 2003) and Mohammed (July 5, 2003), contributed to the inflationary pressures on the economy and concomitantly to the worsening of misery and poverty in the country. Nigeria should adopt a *cost of living adjustment (COLA)* system whereby workers' salaries/wages are adjusted periodically according to the rate of inflation in the country. This would do away with the current system of the spontaneous salary and wage increases, which fuel inflationary pressures.

A situation where more money is pumped into an economy without a proportional increase in the production of essential commodities can only lead to inflation. Thus, the economic crisis in Nigeria is also partly a crisis of production and leadership ineptitude. What Nigeria needs at the moment is not an increase in workers' nominal wages, but an increase in productivity and the appreciation of the value of the Naira. In the inflation drama it remains only to introduce *Hamlet*. And this, by common consent, is the Labour Union. Labour union is, as Galbraith 1958 puts it, is the instigator of the familiar economic phenomenon of "wage-price." Nigel Harris (1986) puts it this way:

"...Without a relaxation of the repressive conditions governing labour and society at large, it will prove increasingly difficult to make the transition to a modern economy. The growth of capital will be punctuated by explosions of the frustrated fury of the workers, [who are] simultaneously called upon to play an increasingly responsible role [in the economy] but denied the legal means to do so."

And Nigeria's unending labour disputes – usually involving the ASUU, NLC, the police, schoolteachers, medical doctors, nurses, Judges, and so forth have contributed to the continued hiccup in the economy. This affects workers' morale, productivity and leads to relentless upward movement of inflation in the country. Despite the policies to tackle inflation and unemployment, the economy is still riddled with high inflation and unemployment in 2003. How can Nigeria get out of the economic and sociopolitical stagnation? While we await answers to this question, let's discuss the effects of inflation.

The effects of inflation on a country are numerous. Galbraith (1955) has noted that inflation has different effects on different groups – teachers, preachers, public servants (the salaried professionals) -white [and blue] collar and the retired. Nevertheless, inflation reduces peoples' purchasing power by reducing the purchasing power of the local currency. As Thurow (1980) notes, it also negatively impacts peoples' standard of living, which leads to a fall in demand. In addition, inflation increases the cost of production by making material inputs expensive, which usually leads to low capacity utilisation. Inflation equally increases the prices of foodstuffs and transportation costs. It leads to unemployment, as industries close down for lack of material input (spare parts, raw materials, and so forth). The youth - young secondary and university graduates are especially vulnerable.

Control of inflation in Nigeria

We shall here discuss some of the strategies that are used to control inflation and discuss their relevance to Nigeria. Inflation could be controlled through appropriate m*onetary* and *fiscal policies* (*Monetary* -control of money circulation through interest rate, etc; and *Fiscal* - price and wage control spending). Unlike monetary policy, fiscal policy makes its initial contact with the economy by reducing consumer expenditure (Thurow 1980). Below are some of the instruments traditionally used to fight inflation in other countries:

◊ *Appreciation in the value of the local currency*: The theoretical assumption here is that the price of imports would fall with moderate inflationary shocks. An increase in currency value is good during inflationary times because with a depreciating currency import prices go up (Thurow 1980). Instead of striving to strengthen the Naira, Nigeria's policy makers seem to be in the habit of perpetually devaluing it or allowing its value to depreciate.

◊ *The government could control inflation by balancing upward price shocks with downward price shocks:* According to Lester Thurow (1980), if the price of energy rises, the government should look around the economy to see where it has some leverage to reduce prices. Industries such as the airlines, telecommunication and postal service could be deregulated and subjected to private competition.

◊ *Efficient and effective distribution systems:* Good roads, regular electricity supply, fuel, water supply and other infrastructures should be improved for large-scale production and distribution of food items. The reliance on rainfall makes food production seasonal and scarce. As Enwere Dike (1990) notes, 'the transmission belt of inflation in most *Less Developed Countries* (LCD's), is the low supply elasticity in agriculture and industry, as well as the chaotic nature of the distribution channels.'

◊ *Realistic single exchange rate:* A realistic exchange rate would prevent economic distortion and bring discipline in financial management and bring down the cost of imported materials. The Central Bank of Nigeria (CBN) has to work hard on this.

◊ *Increase in food production and improved food processing and storage:* Policymakers should address the measures that could increase food output. In other words, agricultural production must be enhanced, and industrial base strengthened to tame inflation. Low interest loans, fertilisers, and other farming equipment should be made available to farmers for large-scale food production. Food processing and storage facilities are also important, as farming in Nigeria is mostly seasonal. The development of the agricultural sector would help to absorb the local labour force, and thus check migration to the cities (Ifode, Jan.13, 1997).

◊ *Efficient financial system and regulatory infrastructure:* One of the strengths of the United State's financial and economic system is the regulatory excellence of the *Federal Reserve Bank System*. Numerous teams of bank examiners and regulators are at work to detect any flaws in the financial system that could paralyse the U.S economy. Nigeria's regulatory system is poor, perhaps among the poorest in the world. The CBN and other regulatory financial institutions should be strengthened and made to emulate the system that works in other countries (Uzonwanne 1998).

Workers and Economic Survival

Nigerian workers have been subjected to numerous inhumane treatments, ranging from non-payment (or late payment) of salaries and wages to lack of welfare packages such as unemployment and retirement benefits. When employers complain about the low productivity of the Nigerian worker, they seem to forget that the ill treatment of the workers affects their morale and productivity. Thus, for workers to be more productive they should be well-trained and motivated. When they are treated humanely, they are bound to reciprocate this with higher productivity and critical thinking, which in turn would enable them to better organise their daily activities. It has been noted that organisations and nations that lack creative and critical minds may not compete well in the 'transitional' and global world economy of today (see Soro Jan 1998).

The psychology of 'creative' and 'critical' thinking is beyond the scope of this book. Nonetheless, Ennis (1985) has defined critical thinking as "reasonable, reflective thinking that is focused on deciding what to believe or do." Thus thinking is "reasonable" when the thinker strives to analyse arguments carefully, looks for valid evidence, and reaches sound conclusions. And critical thinking helps individuals to become fair-minded and objectives and to commit to clarity and accuracy. Contributing to the issue of 'creative thinking', Perkins (1984) notes that "creative thinking is thinking patterned in a way that tends to lead to creative results." For that, "we call a person creative when that person consistently gets creative results, meaning, roughly speaking, original and otherwise appropriate results by the criteria of the domain in question." However, Halpern (1984) states, "creativity can be thought of as the ability to form new contributions of ideas to fulfil a need." In addition, creativity involves re-framing ideas; and it is often facilitated when one gets away from intensive engagement for a while to permit free-flow of thoughts (Marzano, et. al, 1988). As this seems to suggest, the ultimate purpose of creativity is increased productivity.

Managers in organisations must recognise each worker's needs and reward and motivate that individual for increase in productivity. They should strive to identify what motivates individual workers because what motivates one person may not motivate the other. Why is this book concerned about creativity and critical thinking? This is simply because the ability to solve problems is a prerequisite for human survival (Rowe 1985). Nigerian workers who have been dehumanised for so long have the right to demand to be treated as humans; they should be re-humanised and encouraged to be more creative because, as Sherman, (Feb 1991) notes, "in the face of intense global competition...businesses are scrambling to introduce a number of new techniques aimed at improving quality and productivity." Toward this end, employers of labour in Nigeria should assist their workers to behave well by treating them like the human beings they really are. It is simply a fact that organisations with good reward systems often attract and retain the best employees a society can offer. As Weber (April 1991) testifies, valuable employees, *ceteris paribus*, are normally indispensable.

Restructuring and reforms have been drummed in the political circle in Nigeria for so long, but nothing concrete has happened; the workers are still being treated harshly. Does it mean that the leaders of Nigeria are not sure of what to do or that they do not think it necessary to do the right thing? It may be both. As Barber Conable, former President of the World Bank (1986-1991) notes, "when governments aren't sure what to do about a problem they readily resort to talk about institutional reform" (www.cgg.ch/barber.htm). This is probably true of Nigeria! However, when it comes to managing complex social challenges, such as productivity, corruption, ethnicity, and workers' welfare in a volatile and complex polity such as Nigeria, institutional restructuring could in some cases be appropriate. But positive changes seem to take many years to come. That is why late payment and non-payment of workers persist. Remi Oyo (May 14, 1999) noted that workers in Nigeria work for the love of work and not for "money" because they do not get paid regularly. Up till 2003, non-payment and late payment of workers have remained serious issues in the country.

Bad labour relations and reward systems in Nigeria, as Dike (May 15, 2003) rightly noted, have negatively impacted the workers morale, productivity and the general health of the economy. If one may ask, how long can the workers in Nigeria work for the 'love of work and not for 'money'? Have the workers other sources of income? How can a worker who has not been paid for months fulfil his or her family obligations? How does a manager expect his or her employees to improve on their productivity if they have not been paid for many months? We cannot ask enough questions here! And how does an organisation expect its workers to become productive, or produce good quality products and services, if they are not appreciated or motivated? How is an organisation going to make profits if the workers cannot produce due to lack of motivation? Something is definitely wrong with any organisation or society that threats its workers with disdain. How can a society develop if the workers are poor? If workers are generally poor, they will find it difficult to be well fed such that maintaining public infrastructures will not be their priority. Kapur (Dec 1999) in fact noted that a "people's social and economic circumstances dictate what goes onto their plates."

It is appropriate to underscore the remarkable benefits a society would receive from workers' increased productivity. As earlier noted, if workers are well motivated, there is the tendency for their morale to increase, with the resultant increase in productivity, *ceteris paribus*. But if they are under-appreciated, their morale is bound to go down, and their productivity is bound to plummet. In addition, inefficient firms and unproductive nations (individuals) will wither or cease to exist, as increased productivity enables everyone in a society to enjoy a higher standard of living (Sisk and Williams, 1980). If poor and hungry people populate a society, money will not circulate in that society. And when money is not changing hands in an economy, economic gridlock would result, with its attendant socio-political and economic problems.

One of the many challenges facing Nigeria is to establish the necessary social programmes that people will lean on during economic downturn. Presently, any person who is sick or unemployed in Nigeria is on his or her own (if the person does not have a well-off family) even if one is old or disabled. In well-organised societies, the old, sick and disabled are not left on their own to struggle for survival, without assistance. The leaders of Nigeria should design a system whereby workers could contribute towards their retirement in the form of social security when they are young and healthy. And they would fall back on this saving when they are old and unfit to work. Since, many of the old and sick live in desperate poverty, this could help to reduce the level of poverty in the country. This is how it is done in the United States, a country whose political system we have elected to copy. Here, social security is the longest and most successful anti-poverty programme (Baker & Weisbrot 1999). A worker with family responsibilities is likely to resort to an illegal and corrupt means to make ends meet if he/she is not paid for months. This is probably one of the causes of low productivity, inefficiency and massive corruption in Nigeria.

The Economy and Privatisation

Discussions regarding the privatisation of state-owned enterprises in Nigeria gathered momentum soon after the inauguration of the civilian administration of Chief Olusegun Obasanjo on May 29, 1999. Privatisation, which is "the transfer of state-owned enterprises to the private sector," could play a vital role in the economic growth of developing countries, as it could help to transform state-controlled economies to market economies. Privatisation is now a growing trend, changing the public sector worldwide, from developed countries (such as Britain, France and Italy), to developing nations (such as Mexico, Argentina, and Bangladesh). The programme is also becoming popular in the newly formed market economies of Eastern European nations (Campo-Flores 1994). The pace of privatisation is however slow in many African countries, including Nigeria. The *Vanguard* (July 18, 2003) rightly noted that those who have been feeding fat on the corruption and inefficiency of the public corporations are understandably resisting changes.

There are many other reasons why governments sell off state-owned corporations. Some of these include:

◊   Government-owned companies tend to be poorly managed, and often managed by managers who are not well motivated, and not sufficiently monitored;

◊   Availability of government subsidies gives them little, if any incentive, to maintain efficiency.

◊   3) Since state-owned enterprises are considered public properties, and unscrupulous politicians meddle in their affairs; also unions tend to be very powerful (Hemming and Mansoor, 1988).

◊   4) State-owned corporations are quasi-monopolies, there is little pressure to improve their performance (Goodman & Loveman 1990).

Countries could also privatise public corporations for reasons such as to abolish subsidies to inefficient and poorly managed public enterprises; to create more productive corporations to induce economic growth; to improve the quality of products and services in the firms; to increase the tax base with profitable companies and acquire additional funds from the sale of the firms etc. (Campo-Flores 1994).

The concept of privatisation, as Udueni, (Jan. 13, 1997) noted, is relatively new (less than 30 years) with United Kingdom and France having more experience in the business. Strangely, but not surprising, few countries in Africa have privatised state-owned corporations, because their corrupt and "authoritarian rulers...resist the loss of valuable patronage resources" from these industries (Lewis, May/June, 1994). Despite the apparent consensus on the need for privatisation in Nigeria, those with vested interests in state enterprises – the powerful military Generals, workers and other powerful groups are opposing it. This is because privatisation will mean an end to the easy and cheap money from these firms. Cruz (1990) and Cowan (1990) have noted that *Argentina* and *Mexico* are among the many countries where a reduction of state's role in the economy has helped to turn the economy around.

Nigeria, like many other African nations, is very slow in the privatisation of its inefficient and ill-managed, and corruption-ridden state-owned enterprises, despite the claims that its costs the federal government some 200 billion Naira annually to subsidise those industries.

The General M. Buhari coup of 1983 disrupted Shagari's privatisation programme although Buhari later reconstituted the Onosode Study Group in Sept 1984. The Group recommended the privatisation of the Nigerian Airways, Nigerian External Telecommunications (NET), the Nigerian National Shipping Lines (NNSL) and the Nigerian Ports Authority (NPA). Other facilities listed for privatisation included the National Electric Power Authority (NEPA), Nigerian Railways, Post and Telegraphs (P&T), and the Nigerian Airports Authority (NAA). The programme was however abandoned after General Ibrahim Babangida toppled the General Buhari regime in August 1985 (Dike 1990). When General Sani Abacha came to power he promised to privatise the state-owned telecommunications corporation (NITEL). However, until his death on June 8, 1998, nothing was heard about it (Corry 1998). When General Abdulsalami Abubakar took over power (after the death of Abacha) he promised to complete the privatisation programme before the May 29, 1999 handover date to the elected civilian government of Chief Olusegun Obasanjo. That time came and went and nothing serious was accomplished in the privatisation programme.

With the passage of the Public Enterprise (Privatisation and Commercialisation) Act of 1999, the Chief Obasanjo civilian administration gave the privatisation programme a new push by setting up the National Council on Privatisation (NCP), the agency that handles the privatisation programme. The NCP however performs its functions through its secretariat - the Bureau of Public Sector Enterprises (BPE). The BPE issues public notices inviting the public for 'expression of interest' in state-owned enterprises that would be privatised. The government has to retain a stake in any of the state-owned enterprises that is put up for privatisation. The privatisation policy allows the government to retain up to 40% equity share (and a 'golden share') in the companies slated for privatisation; 40% of the shares would be open to local and foreign investors, while the remaining 20% share would be sold to the Nigerian public through the stock exchange (*African News Agency*, Oct 6, 1998).

The origin of the 'golden shares' that are sometimes acquired by states in privatised but strategic state-owned corporations is the United Kingdom during the administration of Margaret Thatcher. The government acquired 'golden shares' in privatised British Telecom, British Airport Authority, Britoil, Electricity, Water and Gas Boards, Jaguar, Rolls Royce, British Aerospace, to mention but a few organisations (Udueni 1997). Citizens of countries, including those of Nigeria, have always protested and argued against the privatisation of public enterprises. Some protestors argue that privatisation of state-owned corporations will hurt the poor and often back up their argument by referring to experiences from Argentina, Russia, Sri Lanka, and so forth. Others say that privatisation "has enriched the few at the expense of the many, increased consumer prices, and reduced jobs." These groups even complain that privatisation "hasn't delivered on the promise to boost production and growth" (Birdsall and Nellis, Sept 26, 2002).

Some writers have argued against privatisation in Nigeria. For example, Idachaba noted (*Post Express*, April 16, 1999) that privatisation: 1) may replace one public monopoly with a private monopoly. 2); that private monopolies may not have a 'human face' compared to public monopolies; that the pricing policies of a private monopoly may be more harmful than that of public monopoly. 3) There is also the fear that some well-connected 'geo-political and ethnic groups' might use essential privatised enterprises to victimise other less privileged groups [that is, given the ethnic prejudices prevalent in the society]. 4) It is also feared that privatisation with its focus on profits might neglect some areas and groups that do not have the market. In other words, the companies might avoid areas that are economically disadvantaged. For instance, telephone and electricity companies might neglect the depressed rural areas, and concentrate on urban and industrial areas. This would "create new inequalities and inequities" in the nation. 5) Opponents of privatisation also see it as a way to transfer national assets created with public resources to private individuals. They regard this as an unfair transfer. 6) Opponents also argue that only a few well-connected individuals could corner and dominate the privatised industries, given the fact that most Nigerians are poor.

I will argue that the benefits of privatisation to the broader population outweigh these disadvantages, if the process is transparent. The benefits to consumers may be small in the short-run, but in the long run it may accomplish the following: **1)** It may secure efficiency gains – quality products. **2)** It will make more funds available to government, as it eliminates subsidies to state-run firms, and increases the taxes paid by the privatised profit-oriented companies. **3)** Money from the privatised companies could be used to increase funding to social services. **4)** The money could also be used to expand utility coverage (Birdstall & Neills, Sept 26, 2002).

How can the industrial world invest in a society with dilapidating infrastructure? Since NEPA, NNPC, NITEL and the refineries are crippled, the economy will remain comatose. But with the monopoly of *NITEL* broken, and with the coming of the Global System for Mobile Communications (GSM), many telephone lines are now available to the public despite its interconnectivity problems, inefficient billing system (billed per minute instead of in seconds) and poor quality service (QoS) as reported recently by *ThisDay*, (July 30 and July 31, 2003), *Vanguard*, (July 30, 2003) and *Daily Independent*, (July 30, 2003). This has drastically changed the economic and social environment of Nigeria, and improved to a certain level the standard of living of the majority of the people. The subjection of the National Electric Power Authority (NEPA) to competition will improve its performance and could help ensure efficient distribution of power to the consumers.

The same applies to NNPC, which is thought to be an epitome of corruption. Its privatisation could ensure a more efficient distribution of fuel. The presence of private refineries will ensure the availability of more petroleum products, thereby bringing down prices and queues in fuel stations. In fact, liberalising the Nigerian economy, will, according to Mallam Nasir El-Rufai (former Director- General of BPE), "enhance the efficient performance of our utilities and align [them] with global economic realism." As has been noted, the benefits of this to the Nigerian economy are "clearly visible and cannot be over-emphasised" (*Daily Champion*, Jan 22, 2003). However, these benefits will depend "heavily on the quality of policy, the enforcement of contracts, and the competence of regulators" Birdstall and Neills (Sept 26, 2002). It is therefore apropos to say that bad governance or government policy, poor management and leadership, complacency, poor industrial relations, inefficient financial institutions, and bad labour relations have all contributed to the current poor state of the Nigerian economy. Therefore, the leaders of the nation must take drastic measures to remove all political and institutional bottlenecks for effective privatisation. In the next chapter we shall examine the state of education in the nation, as education plays a vital role in the overall economic health of any society.

References

Adamson, Yahya K. " Structural Disequilibrium and Inflation in Nigeria: A Theoretical and Empirical Analysis of the Causes and Effects of Inflation in a Developing Economy." *Centre for Economic Research on Africa Research Publication*, No. 89.5 (Upper Montclair, New Jersey: Montclair State College, Centre for Economic Research on Africa, 1989.
African News Agency, Oct. 6, 1998
Aigbokhan, Ben E. "The Naira Exchange Rate Depreciation and Domestic Inflation." *The Indian Journal of Economics,* Vol.71, April 1991, pp. 507-17
Baker, Dean and Mark Weisbrot; Social Security-The Phoney Crisis; 1999
Birdstall, Nancy, and John Neills; "Privatisation's bad name isn't totally deserved." *The Christian Science Monitor,* Sept 26, 2002
BusinessDay News: "Privatisation Implementation Falls Behind Schedule." December 2, 2002
Central Bank of Nigeria: *Annual Report and Statement of Account* 1997.
Campo-Flores, Filemon; "Lessons from Privatisation of Argentina's National Telephone Company." *Policy Review*, 13:3/4, 1994

Corry, John; "Investigation: In Nigeria, an election, a failed coup, rising social tensions. What next for this embattled African nation?" *The Earth Times,* Jan. 27, 1998, p.3.

Cowan, G. *Privatisation in the Developing World.* [New York: Praeger Publication, 1990], pp.1-3.

Conabel, Barber; "Beyond Halifax" An article written shortly after the June 1995 meeting of the G7 at Halifax, Canada, (see www.cgg.ch/barber.htm)

Cruz Jr., A. "Glory past but not forgotten" *Insight,* 6(32), 1990, pp.8-17.

Darrat, Ali F. "Monetary Explanation of Inflation: The Experience of Three Major OPEC Economies;" *Journal of Economics and Business,* Vol. 37, Aug. 1985, pp. 209-221.

Diamond, Larry. "The Political Economy of Corruption in Nigeria." Paper presented to the 27th annual meeting of the *African Studies Association;* Los Angeles, California, Oct. 1984, pp.25-28.

Daily Champion: 'NEPA sale crucial to power sector reform,' vol. 15, No. 211, January 22, 2003

Daily Independent: See Emma Okonji on "Hiccups in GSM networks;" July 30, 2003

Dike, Enwere; "Nigeria: The Political Economy of Buhari Regime." *Nigeria Journal Of International Affairs,* Vol. 16, No.2, 1990.

Dike, Victor E.; "Reward system and labour productivity." *Daily Independent,* May 15, 2003

-------------------; " Fuel price increases and distributive consequences;" *Daily Trust,* June 26, 2003

Ennis, R.H. "Goals for critical thinking curriculum." In A. Costa (ed.), Developing Minds: A Resource Book for Teaching. [Alexandria, VA: Association for Supervision and Curriculum Development, 1985]

Ekpo, Akpan H; "Unemployment and Inflation under Structural Adjustment: The Nigerian Experience." East Africa Economic Review, Vol.8, Dec. 1992, pp.102-113.

**Galbraith, John Kenneth. (1955)

Galbraith, John Kenneth; *The Affluent Society.* [New York: A Mentor Book, 1958].

Goodman, J.B. and Loveman, G.W. "Does Privatisation Serve the Public interest?" *Harvard Business Rev. 69* (6), 1990, pp.26-38

Halpern, D.F. Thought and Knowledge: An introduction to Critical Thinking. [Hillsdale, NJ: Erlbaum, 1981]

Harris, Nigle; *The End of the Third World.* [Penguin Books, 1986]

Hemming, R. and Mansoor, A.M. "Is Privatization the Answer?" *Finance and Development,* 25 (3), 1988, pp.31-33.

Idachaba, F.S. "The Political Economy of Privatisation 1 & 2:" see The Guardian, April 16, 1999.

Ifode, Abraham; Business Concord: January 13, 1997

International Telecommunication Union: "Telecommunication Development Situation in Democratic Nigeria." *World Telecommunication Development Conference* (WTDC-02), Istanbul, Turkey, 18-27, March 2002

Kapur, Akas; "A Third Way for the Third World." *The Atlantic Monthly*, Vol. 284, No. 6, 1999, pp.124-129

Lewis, Peter M. "The Politics of Economics." *Africa Report*, vol. 39, no.3, May/June, 1994, pp.47-49.

Marzano, et al. *Dimensions of Thinking: A Framework for Curriculum and Instruction.* [Alexandria, Virginia: Association for Supervision and Curriculum Development, 1988] p. 6.

Mohammed, Aminu; "Mass protest at last;" *Daily Trust*, July 6, 2003

Moser, Gary G. "The Main Determinants of Inflation in Nigeria." *International Monetary Fund*, Vol.42, No. 2, June 1995

Ndebbio, J.E. and A.H. Ekpo; "Ideology, Basic Needs, and Nigeria's Planning Experience," in *The Fifth National Development Plan and The Restructuring Of the Nigerian Economy*, Nigeria Economic Society (NES), Lagos, 1985.

Ojameruaye, E.O. "Analysis of the Determinants of the General Price Level in Nigeria." *Research for Development*, Vol. 5, Jan. 1988, pp.80-96

Oyo, Remi; "Nigerian Workers do it for love, not money." *The Daily Mail and Guardian*, May 14, 1999

Perkins, D.N; "Creativity by Design." *Educational Leadership*, 42, 1984, pp. 18-19

Post Express: "FG Woos Foreign Investors on Privatization Programme," Oct. 12, 1998.

--------------: "The Minimum Wage Bungle," Nov. 18, 1998.

Reuters: "Nigerian workers vow general strike to go ahead," June 7, 2000

Rowe, H; Problem Solving and Intelligence; [Hillsdale, NJ: Erlbaum, 1985]

Samuelson, Robert J. "The Crash of '99?" *Newsweek*, October 12, 1998, pp.26-31.

Sharman, Paul; "Winning Techniques for productivity: The activity link." CMA Magazine, Feb. 1991, p.8; p.11.

Sisk, Henry L. & J. Clifton Williams; Management and Organization; 4th (ed.), Southwestern Pub Co., Cincinnati 1981, p.317.

Soros, George; "Toward a Global Open Society." *The Atlantic Monthly,* Vol. 281, No 1, Jan. 1998

The World Bank Report; 1993.

ThisDay: See Tayo Ajakaye on "Telecom Act: NCC Begins Enforcement;" July 31, 2003

-----------; See Kola Ologbondiyan on "Wabara Wants MTN to Adopt Per Second Billing;" July 31, 2003

-----------; See Onyebuchi Ezigbo on "M-tel Moves to Resolve Interconnectivity Crisis;" July 30, 2003

Thurow, Lester C; *The Zero-Sum Society;* [Penguin Books, 1980]

Udueni, Henry; "In Defense of Golden Shares." *Business Concord,* Jan.13, 1997

Uzonwanne, Jude; "Positioning Africa's Economies in the Era of Opportunity: Lessons from the Global Financial Markets." Online: *Africa Economic Analysis,* 1998

Vanguard: January 1, 1999.

-------------: "Phillips criticizes devaluation of Naira," April 28, 1999.

-------------: "Another controversy over pay rise," April12, 2000

-------------: "FG confirms 12.5% pay rise for workers;" May 2, 2003

-------------; See Rueben Mouka on "What Kind of GSM services are these?" July 30, 2003

Weber, Eric; *The Indispensable Employee: A Survival Manual.* [New York: Berkley Books, April 1991]

Chapter 8

The State of Education and the Health of the Nation

In the preceding three chapters, we have discussed the economy, but we cannot build a 'completely rounded system' without a sound educational system. So, this chapter is devoted to this great task of reforming the nation's schools. Reform and restructuring of Nigeria's educational system have been burning national issues for sometime now. But all the 'talks and no actions' have lately resulted in an educational system that is ill-equipped to prepare the nation's students to function well in the emerging highly competitive global economy, and sustain the country's democratic experiment. The general educational attainment of the citizens of a nation is an important factor in sustaining democracy in that society. Education "...means simply teaching and forming values, attitudes, behaviours, knowledge and skills" (Wagaw and Oxenham 1989). Richard Paul (1986b) envisions the product of education as an inquiring mind. He points out that education is:

"a passionate drive for clarity, accuracy, and fair-mindedness, a fervour for getting to the bottom of things, to the deepest root issues, for listening sympathetically to opposite points of view, a compelling drive to seek out evidence, and intense aversion to contradiction, sloppy thinking, inconsistent application of standards, a devotion to truth as against self-interest - these are essential components of a rational person..."

The emphasis here is on those forms of education deliberately organised and sustained, rather than casual and incidental. However, we are not discounting the importance of the informal education given by parents to their children. No matter the form it takes, education is a tool or means to achieve a goal. A tool, by definition, is an instrument for doing something. It is a means to an end; a process or an agent employed to reach a goal. It is a device to which one has recourse to realise a purpose. It can be physical, material, or mechanical means. Education, as The *Guardian* (May 6, 1999) noted, transforms or refines a person's personality by modifying, changing, developing and re-orientating it from its original crude or natural state.

There appears to be a relationship between literacy, general educational standard, and democracy. While this relationship is not always easy to establish some studies of democracy as a political system seem to indicate that sustainable democracy is the product of strong and highly trained minds. Some studies have in fact found that the degree of success of democracy in a society increases in proportion to the intellectual capability of those called upon to interpret, and apply its basic assumptions (see for instance Lipset, 1960 and Raymond, 1978).

Democratic values are nurtured on the fertile ground of basic education – a functional education with the right focus and correct scope. Democracy, it has been argued, thrives on the productivity of its diverse constituency - a productivity fostered by free, critical, and creative thought on issues of common interest (Marzano, et. al, 1988). Downs (1957) identified the features of democratic regimes, including the election of a single party (or coalition of parties) to run the governing apparatus. Such elections are held within periodic intervals, the duration of which cannot be altered by the party in power acting alone. All adults, who are permanent residents of the country and who are sane and abide by the laws of the land, are eligible to vote during such elections. Each voter may cast one and only one vote in each election.

In a mature democracy, the losing parties in an election never try by force or any other illegal means to prevent the winning party (or parties) from taking office. The party in power never attempts to restrict the political activities of any citizen or other parties as long as they make no attempt to overthrow the government by force. There are two or more parties competing for control of the government apparatus in any election (Downs 1957).

The above features of democracy cannot be achieved or sustained if the people operate in a thick cloud of ignorance. It will be wrong to argue that education at the post-secondary level is needed from the masses for genuine democracy to take hold in a society. However, some degree of literacy and enlightened education is a *sine qua non* for democracy in this era. And as Anele (October 13, 1998) observed, if the masses are educated, they will be less vulnerable to the fraudulent exploitations and manipulations of the 'political gold-diggers.'

Undoubtedly, democracy is hampered by ignorance, especially, if the leaders are uneducated and operate without an ideological compass. We are not arguing that education would turn a political vulture into a political dove. But one could argue that extremely poor, traditional societies characterised by illiterate, rural populations in which inter-group communication is barely developed and national identifications and institutions barely in existence, will have considerable difficulty in establishing and maintaining political democracy (Neubauer 1967). This is probably one of the reasons why democracy has for long eluded Nigeria. One of the major domestic challenges facing Nigeria, as the world moves into the next millennium, is how to sustain democracy and good governance.

For many years, Nigeria has allowed her educational institutions, socio-economic infrastructures and social services to deteriorate to the point of total collapse. Yet these are prerequisites for creating the enabling environment for sustainable development and democracy. The facilities in the three levels of the nation's educational systems (elementary, secondary and tertiary) institutions are insufficient and dilapidated. And because of the many years of neglect, the nation's 36 universities, 46 polytechnics and 64 Colleges of Education are in serious need of funds. As a result the standard of education in the country is declining rapidly.

A brief history of tertiary education in Nigeria is apropos here. The University of Nigeria, Nsukka, was established in 1960, and the University College, Ibadan, was granted autonomy in 1962. It was the implementation of the Lord Eric Ashby Commission's report on higher education in 1962 that led to the granting of a full-fledged University status to the University

College, Ibadan. According to Hassan (June 25, 1999), the same report necessitated the establishment of the University of Ife, Ahmadu Bello University, Zaria, and the University of Lagos. It is for this that these 'first generation Universities' are referred to as "Ashby Babies."

Although Nigeria's educational institutions in general are in dire need of funds, the most troubled of the three tiers is the primary education sector. According to the executive secretary of the National Primary Education Commission (NPEC), Dr. Ali Adamu, there are about 2,015 primary schools in Nigeria with no buildings of any type. Classes are held under trees. The UNICEF in its 'state of the world's children' report for 1999' (as noted in Akhaine, Jan 10, 1999), pointed out that about four million Nigerian children have no access to basic education, and that majority of those that are 'lucky' to enter schools are given sub-standard education.

Presently, there are about 48,242 primary schools with 16,796,078 students in public schools and 1,965,517 in private schools. In addition, Nigeria has 7,104 secondary schools with 4,448,981 students (The *Guardian*, May 6, 1999). What are the reasons for the establishment of the National Primary Education Commission? The federal minister of education in the General Abubakar regime, Mr. Samuel Oni, announced before he left office that a National Commission for Secondary Education (NCSE) would also be established. The question remains: how can a commission located at Abuja determine the type of education a child in *Umuaka,* Imo State, *Ogoni* or *Ijaw* in the Niger Delta, Sokoto, or *Ota* in Ogun State would have? And how can this commission solve the problems facing elementary and secondary schools in communities, for instance, in Njaba Local Government of Imo State and other schools in many remote localities? For these schools to be properly supervised and taken care of, local and state ministries of education should play major roles.

The ministries should be adequately financed and staffed to enable them perform their traditional functions of supervising and monitoring of schools. The NPEC and similar commissions should be scrapped. Nigerian schools are overcrowded, and the structures are not maintained. With education as an important variable for the survival of democracy in any society, it is practically impossible for citizens to achieve their highest potentials in a thick fog of ignorance. The late Chief Bola Ige, one of the founding fathers of NADECO, once noted that some schools built for 320 students were admitting 3,500 students. He lamented that teachers were often not paid their salaries on time, and as a result, schools were sometimes closed for months. If the trend were allowed to continue, Nigerian schools would never keep pace with the rest of the world (Obafemi, Sept. 21, 1998). Professor Ojetunji Aboyade, in a lecture in Ilorin in 1982, pointed out that the development of human capital has long been established "historically and analytically as the real foundation of economic growth and social transformation" in a nation. Because of the importance of education in the overall national economic and political development, even the most advanced countries of America and Europe relentlessly increase their budgetary allocation to education (particularly higher education). But in Nigeria, the issue of education is relegated to the background, with the physical structures of every institution of higher learning in Nigeria in sorry conditions.

The former vice-chancellor of the University of Ilorin, the late Prof. Afolabi Toye in the 1980s lamented the deplorable condition of universities in the country. He believed that universities had been reduced to 'glorified secondary schools' (Obafemi, Sept. 21, 1998). Prof. Abdullahi Mahdi, the vice-chancellor of Ahmadu Bello University, joined the many critics of Nigeria's educational system, when he noted that the type of education Nigerians pursue (in Nigeria) "is not education for empowerment and development but education for exploitation, suppression and oppression." He wondered why, in spite of the rich natural resources and the avalanche of professors, doctors, lawyers, engineers, and other specialists being churned out in numbers every year from Nigerian universities and polytechnics, the country cannot move forward (*Today*, Nov 8-14, 1998)

It is proper to emphasise that the nation's current education system is incapable of engendering and sustaining national development and prosperity. These are signs of fundamental defects within the system. In fact, it is easy to measure the quality of education in any country from the state of things in that society (their homes and roads, the quality of service in their public sector - offices, ports, schools and hospitals). The state of the economy, the type of politics that is practiced, the quality of productivity and the management of its human and natural resources are other indices. Eke-Okoro, in "The Vanishing Ivory Tower" lamented the "embarrassing condition of services of Nigerian University teachers and the non-academic staff who work with them. The poor state of university teachers are re-echoed in the fact that: "For the Nigerian University teacher, a car is a luxury, a good salary is an anathema, research grant which is a very important ingredient for development at all levels, is not in the dictionary of the government." According to Eke-Okoro (Dec14, 1998), young university graduates in Nigeria are discouraged from the academic profession after seeing the poor conditions of service of their teachers.

To say the least, their conditions of service are discouraging, disappointing and unfortunate. To revive the present epileptic Nigeria, the academicians should be well motivated and encouraged to put in their best in the classroom. We must understand that they are entrusted with the important responsibility of training the nation's labour force. The review of their conditions of service should be realistic and not cosmetic, because they are the drive train of prosperity of any nation. The Nigerian University system should also be restructured, deregulated, and given the necessary financial support. Like their counterparts in the United States and Britain, tertiary institutions in Nigeria should be allowed unfettered hands to operate and compete with one another (raise funds, and so forth.), with the government setting up laws and regulations (standards) for them to follow. Those institutions that are unviable should whither or be swallowed by the viable ones. With competition, higher standard of education with better quality of graduates will resurface, as it were when the schools were not under the proprietorship of the federal government. It is appropriate to note here that there was a nation-wide government take-over of schools in Nigeria in 1975.

The federal government should introduce a student loan programme at the university level, to enable qualified indigent students to finance their tertiary education. Appropriate methods of loan repayment should be devised and effectively implemented. The crucial question is how can Nigeria achieve technological breakthrough comparable to the advanced countries? Is it by importing technology, or by developing it locally? First and foremost, the government should revisit and redesign the educational system, and have a clear-cut plan and discipline in the implementation of its educational programmes. Critics such as Ozoemena (Oct 7-13, 1998) have rightly argued that the transfer of technology from the West alone will not be enough for Nigeria to be a giant technologically.

However, borrowing technology can be useful, but it is often better for an economy to build a relatively inefficient plant, for instance, than simply purchasing one. Local efforts begin the whole process of internally generated technological advance, which may be hampered by continued reliance on imports. The ideal is to follow the example set by Japan in the late 19th century and early 20th century (Chirot 1977). Japan has since become one of the world's industrial giants. Investment in human development is a critical area Nigeria has neglected for too long. As Anya (April 26, 1999) noted and as was re-echoed by Dike (May 28, 1999), "National competitive advantage is no longer conferred merely by the nation's natural resources but by the pool of skilled technical manpower and innovative technical processes in manufactures and industries."

Without any doubt, one of the effects of the continued neglect of the educational sector in Nigeria will be a continued political and economic paralysis, and an upsurge in the wave of 'brain drain' from the country. Many Nigerian academics have emigrated to Europe, the United States and southern African countries where conditions in the teaching profession are

151

relatively better. Meanwhile, Nigeria has a literacy rate of only about 30-40 percent (U.S. Dept. of States, April 1991; Wiseman 1990). There is a need for Nigeria to break away from its traditional theoretical method of teaching and adopt a more practical and progressive method of education, where children learn by doing, and where self-expression is encouraged. What are the socio-political and economic implications of low literacy rate in Nigeria? What should the country do to increase the literacy rate of its population? Are the educational institutions in Nigeria arming their students with the necessary tools that will enable them to consistently and effectively take intelligent ethical actions to accomplish the tasks a democratic society expects of all its members? Nigeria can attain great heights if her educational system is overhauled and properly managed.

UBE Programme: Educating the Educators

Nigeria has toyed with different educational programmes, most of which have only served as conduits to transfer money to the corrupt political leaders and their cronies. For instance, the nation launched the Universal Primary Education (UPE) in 1976, but as noted, the programme failed due to lack of funds caused by corruption, among other factors. Nigeria has again launched another mass-oriented education programme, this time branding it the Universal Basic Education *(UBE)*. The President, Olusegun Obasanjo, declared during the launching of the programme in Sokoto that the nation "cannot afford to fail this time around." However, not long after that, the federal government reported that the falling standard of education in Nigeria was caused by the "acute shortage of qualified teachers in the primary school level." Ogbeifum and Olisa (July 1, 2001) reported that about 23% of the 400,000 teachers in Nigeria's primary schools do not have even the Teachers' Grade Two Certificate. This is discouraging, given that the National Certificate of Education (NCE), which is much higher than the Teachers' Grade Two Certificate, is the minimum educational requirement one should posses to teach in the nation's primary schools.

In the 1970s, there was the Universal Primary Education (UPE), which had similar goals as the UBE but which failed because of lack of funds, shortage of trained teachers and lack of school buildings. Despite this, the Obasanjo regime launched two educational programmes - the Universal Basic Education (UBE) and the Mass Literacy Programme (MLP), without apparently trying to incorporate the lessons learnt from the earlier programmes that failed. This therefore raises the question of whether these programmes were established for the sake of nomenclature. Or is it a way to channel money to certain groups? In what ways are they different from the UPE? How are we sure that what destroyed UPE will not hamper the effectiveness of UBE and MLP? What Nigeria needs is an educational programme that works - one that would give the youths good quality education – not an unnecessary duplication or changes in the nomenclatures of existing programmes?

If one may ask: with the troubling revelations of the shortage of teachers and "half-baked" teachers employed to teach in the nation's schools, how are we certain the current *UBE* programme will succeed? Has the government trained the required number and quality of teachers needed to successfully implement the programme? Are the teachers going to be motivated to perform their duties well? Have the classrooms and seats been built or are the pupils going to sit on bare floor? Are the books and other teaching materials ready? As I noted elsewhere (Dike, July 14, 2000), to improve the standard of education in Nigeria, the country has to first educate the educators, and motivate them to perform their duties well. But the leaders do not seem to want to listen!

Education in Nigeria: A public health issue?

At the dawn of the year 2003, Nigeria is still uncertain where it is headed. In other words, her destination is still unknown. The country is being rocked by much labour unrest caused mainly by the non-payment of salaries. The police even went on strike, which the federal government branded 'an act of mutiny' (*The*

Guardian, Feb 2, 2002; *Reuters,* Feb 2, 2002). Nigerians often blame the woes of the country, in particular that of the educational sector, on the many years of military misrule. There is the common feeling that the military neglected the universities because of their opposition to military rule. The inauguration of another civilian rule has unfortunately not improved the situation. University professors are still not being paid on time. There are however some that believe there are signs of improvement but this remains to be seen.

If, strictly speaking, there is no such thing as democracy in Nigeria, it is because its past and present histories are synonymous with crises. The role of the ordinary person in Nigeria in the making and sustaining of democracy is, generally speaking, not appreciated - after casting his or her vote. Also, the positive contributions of others who struggled, and are still struggling, for the sustenance of democracy in the country have not been appreciated by the politicians, who have been elected (or selected/rigged into) public offices.

The sordid state of education in Nigeria affects the entire polity. It could in fact be argued that the survival of Nigeria as a viable society will depend on the health of her educational institutions, and how well the professors and support staff are treated. The role of education in the development of a society has been so well documented in the literature that we do not intend to revisit it here. Nigerian leaders should pay close attention to the needs of the educational sector, and treat it as a public-health issue, because the socio-political and economic development of a nation and (or her health) is, in many ways, determined by the quality and level of educational attainment of the population. Political leaders should take politics out of education, as the continued neglect of this sector would lead to social paralysis. The youth should be given the appropriate quality academic training and an environment that would enable them to reach their full potential. *UNICEF* underlined the sorry state of education in the country when it observed in its 'state of the world's children' report for 1999' that about four million Nigerian children had no access to basic education, and that majority of those that were 'lucky' to enter schools were given sub-standard education (*Akhaine*, Jan 10, 1999).

Most of the schools in the country are in dilapidating states. This shows that Nigeria has a weird value system: it is a country where priorities are turned on their heads. For instance, salaries of local government councillors are higher than those of University professors - despite the fact that they are usually much less educated and far less experienced. Nigeria is a place where known rogues (the perpetrators of the *419* scam) are applauded for donating huge sums of money to local communities and churches. It is a place where nobody cares about how one makes his/her money. It is also a place where the roads leading to million dollar homes are filled with potholes. And the country is a place where the streets in capital cities are littered with heaps of thrash. The irony is that nobody seems to care. Something is obviously wrong with any society that does not take her educational institutions seriously.

Nevertheless, the increased need for higher education during the oil boom of the 1970s in Nigeria, coupled with political pressure, led to the establishment of many universities in the country. And "an explosive expansion in enrolments" during this period marked the beginning of 'the decline in quality' of education in the society. In two decades, the number of university students increased eightfold, from about 55,000 in 1980 to more than 400,000 today (*Bollag*, Feb 1, 2002, A40). Presently, Nigeria has about 36 public universities, 46 polytechnics and 64 colleges of education (Dike 1999). In addition, some private universities have been approved and registered by the federal government. They are *Bowen University*, Iwo, Osun State; *Babcock University*; *Igbinedion University*, Okada; and *Madonna University* (*Oladeji*, August 2, 2001). Others are the *Covenant University*, Ota (Ogun State), *Benson Idahosa University*, Benin, and *Pan African University*, Lagos (*ThisDay*, Oct 16, 2002). Many more private universities are likely to be given approval by the National University Commission.

It has been noted that the primary function of a University is "to push back the frontiers of ignorance, carry out research, transmit learning and culture" (Maduekwe, May 26, 2002). But as the ugly tradition of corruption persists, the public tertiary institutions have been left to rot away. Some of the loans received from the World Bank toward education during the 1990s were used to purchase unnecessary and "expensive equipment" that "could not be properly installed or maintained, and many institutions received irrelevant and useless books and journals" (*Bollag*, Feb 1, 2002, A40). This contributed to "the collapse of university bookshops" in many campuses. All these, including the ubiquitous corruption, have contributed to the decline in the quality of instruction in Nigeria's educational institutions, which were once, highly regarded. With the news of corruption still filling the pages of Nigeria's newspapers and magazines, the apparent war on corruption in the society seems an uphill task since those waging the war on corruption are themselves as corrupt as corruption could be.

Although Nigeria's educational institutions in general are in dire need, the most troubled of the three tiers is the primary education sector. The recent statistics on primary education available to this writer shows that there are about *2,015* primary schools in Nigeria with no buildings of any type. Classes are held under trees. The quality of teaching under such an inhumane condition could only be imagined. Despite this dismal statistics, the government is still in the habit of allocating less money to the educational sector (see Table: M). If Nigeria's allocation to education is contrasted with those of other less affluent societies in Africa, the picture becomes more discouraging (see Table: N). Nigeria's educational system is so bad that its candidates cannot compete favourably in public examinations with students from even war-ravaged countries such as Liberia and Sierra-Leone.

For instance, a report by Shelter Rights Initiative (an NGO) shows that candidates from Nigeria in WAEC exams (1992-1999) were behind those from Ghana, Gambia, Sierra-Leone, and Liberia in Mathematics, English Language, Physics and

Chemistry. The situation, as the *Vanguard (Feb* 13, 2003) noted, is not likely to get better in the nearest future, given the incessant strike actions in schools across the nation, necessitated by the non-payment of teachers salaries and other bad working conditions. The disheartening statistics show how insufficient Nigeria's allocation to the educational sector has been. One can only get what he or she has ordered! Nigeria has to change her value system and invest on education, which is the intellectual laboratory of any nation and the engine that propels the economy. As *Anya (June* 19, 2001) pointed out, "without a formidable intellectual base" it is not likely that any society would move forward.

The current crisis in education, as noted earlier, also has implications for democracy since democratic values are nurtured on the fertile ground of basic education - a functional education with the right focus and correct scope (Marzano, et. al, 1988). With everybody chasing the shadow of money, and with the pittance sum invested yearly on education, how could the system produce the critical and creative minds Nigeria needs to guide and manage its democracy and survive as a viable nation? If the society continues to neglect her schools, it could not educate her citizens.

Table J: **Federal Government Budgetary Allocation to Education, and Spending on Education (%GNP) Compared to those of some African Countries**

Year	Allocation (%)	Country	% GNP
1995	7.2	Angola	4.9
1996	12.32	Cote d' Ivoria	5
1997	17.59	Ghana	4.4
1998	10.27	Kenya	6.5
1999	11.12	Malawi	5.4
2000	8.36	Mozambique	4.1
2001	7.00	Nigeria	**0.76**
2002	5.6*	South Africa	7.9
2003	1.8**	Tanzania	3.4

Sources: Compiled by the author from, *The African Dept as* reported by Jubilee 2000.

See Alifa Daniel, 'Intrigues in FG-ASUU *Face-off,' The Guardian, June 17, 2001.*
Also see 'Still A Bleak Future for Education,' The Guardian, Jan 5, 2003*.
Vanguard, Feb 13, 2003, Education & Manpower: 'Nigeria's performance in
WAEC exams poorest in W-Africa'**

Consequently, the political landscape would be littered with illiterate politicians, and the society would be incapable of gathering and maintaining a reasonable database for national planning and other development programmes. To avoid this, the political leaders should begin now to re-order their priorities, as their priorities have so far been, for the most part, dictated by how much they will gain from any policy decision (by way of contracts), and not how the policies will benefit the society as a whole.

Lack of qualitative education and the associated unemployment help to worsen the numerous social ills in the society, including crime, prostitution, and the breakdown in law and order. For this, the society should invest more on the youth, and educate them to differentiate right from wrong before they become adults. As Jean-Jacques Rousseau noted: "People, like men [and women] are amenable only when they are young; in old age they become incorrigible." And "once [bad habit] and customs are established and prejudices ingrained, it is a dangerous and futile enterprise to try to reform them." Betts (1994) also notes that "the people cannot bear to have the diseases treated, even in order to destroy it, like those stupid and fearful patients who tremble at the sight of the physician."

To move the nation forward, the leadership should adopt necessary policies to destroy the current bad value system in the society. They should create a healthy environment that would enable the educational institutions to engage in healthy competition, raise funds through private donations and grants, and attract and retain qualified students. Higher education in Nigeria should not be free. If one would pay for any service, one could afford to complain, or move to an institution where he/she could get the money's worth of service. This, however, does not mean that degrees should be sold to the highest bidder. Also the universities should develop a system whereby students could transfer to schools of their choice (and change their major) if they are qualified, without it adversely impacting their studies. And university admissions should be based strictly on merit, without ethnically and state-based criteria, which have unfortunately coloured the system.

If these suggestions are implemented they will assist the institutions to prepare for intense academic competition. They will also be able to attract better quality teachers by "rebuild [ing] a culture of scholarship which has been eroded by under funding" (*Bollag*, Feb 1, 2002, A40).

It is known (at least in the developed world) that education determines, not only earning capacity, but also the very quality of human life (even longevity has relationship to education). In a society that appreciates education, those with good education tend to earn higher incomes; they are also healthier and live more quality life. Higher education gives one a greater sense of how to reduce risks in life and change their behaviour. As Davies (Nov 30, 2001) noted, confidence, self-reliance, and adaptability are all hallmarks of advanced education.

Education and Basic Needs

Building good schools for the education of the population does not guarantee automatic good health to the people. The political leadership must take care of the basic needs of the people – portable water, food, good roads and habitable environment (the streets are filled with garbage). The voiceless - the unemployed, the old and disabled – should be taken care of. Corrupt politicians currently divert the fund for this service to individual purses. The society should offer education that provides adults with the skills and knowledge they need to secure a job and to compete in the technologically advanced world economy. And it should find a way to reward those (teachers and others outside academia) who have contributed positively in creating new ideas and jobs in the society. Nigeria can sustain economic growth based on technology if a good number of the adult working population can read and write well, and be able to make productive use of computers and information technologies. According to a recent World Bank study (cited in Bollag, Feb 1, 2002, A41; see also BBC July 22, 2002) employers complain that the quality of university graduates and secondary school graduates especially their communication skills, has fallen continually for two decades.

Improvement in their communication skill and the use of computers and information technologies will increase their productivity, and in the long run translate into lasting, durable and participatory democracy. All these mean the need to positively transform the society, especially the educational sector, into a viable sector. The need to improve higher education should begin with giving greater attention to our preschool, elementary, secondary, and vocational schools. These areas are the building blocks of society's educational foundation, as not everyone needs a university education. Thus, the society must make meaningful use of the current Universal Basic Education (UBE) programme, which is expected to provide free education to children between the ages of seven and seventeen (Umar and Adoba, June 12, 2001). In addition to the free primary education, the government should guarantee free lunch for needy students, as no child can learn while hungry. To supplement the efforts of the government, the private sector should assist in the form of financial and material donations, and collaborate with institutions of higher learning to help the primary and secondary schools to improve their teaching standards, governance, and community relations.

If Nigeria cannot give adequate and qualitative education to students at the elementary and secondary school level, tertiary institutions would continue to be populated by those who are least prepared to face the rigours of university education. And 'cultism,' intimidation of professors into awarding better grades, cheating in examinations and other vices will continue to blossom on the campuses across the nation. The government should also device ways and means of helping indigent students in higher institutions such as by making available affordable financial loans to enable them to complete their education. A 'merit-based' and 'need-based' approaches should be used in putting the loan policy in place (King, March 1999). An effective machinery should also be put in place to ensure that the loan is repaid as soon as the borrowers find employment. Nigeria has the resources to implement a good student loan programme, but as always, her problems have been corruption and implementation (the old student-loan programme in the country died because of this).

Private financing of higher education could contribute immensely in improving both the financial situations of the institutions and the quality of the education they offer. Poor schooling, ignorance, poverty, and unemployment or underemployment among the youths could lead to their being easily manipulated by the political elite for selfish purposes. That will spell danger for the society, as the youths are the nation's future leaders. How can Nigeria manage a complex democratic process without educated, critical and creative minds?

President Olusegun Obasanjo has taken pride in punching and kicking ASUU with verbal assaults (The *Guardian*, Dec 9, 2001). His attack on the university professors seems to suggest that the teachers are the cause of the present poor state of the nation's educational institutions. It is appropriate to note that the face-off between ASUU and the government has been an ongoing struggle, with the under-funding of the universities being the major issue. It was the same issue when Festus Iyayi was the leader of ASUU, and during the leadership of Atahiru Jega, Asisi Asobie, and under the current leadership of Dipo Fasina (*ThisDay*, March 1, 2003). The face-off leads to frequent strikes and closure of the nation's tertiary institutions.

Though it is possible there could be some bad eggs among the lecturers, in general, it is difficult to believe that the lecturers, who work extremely hard under appalling conditions, could be the ones wanting to pull down the education sector they work in, and for. The president's outbursts are sometimes insensitive and unbecoming of a leader. A good example was his outburst at the scene of the explosion in Ikeja, in front of relatives who lost their dear ones in the explosion: Concluding that the mourning crowd was unruly, the president insensitively retorted: "Shut up. I took the opportunity of being here to see what could be done. I don't need to be here... after all, the governor of the state is here, the General Officer Commanding Two Division and the Brigade Commander as well as the Police Commissioner were all here. These sets of people could between them do what needs to be done. I really don't need to be here" (*The Guardian*, Jan 31, 2002). The President has increasingly become known for this type of rude remarks, raising questions in some quarters about his skills and suitability for the exulted position he occupies. Leaders should show good examples, as our children learn more from what they see us do than from what we say. Yes, the youth deserve something better! This does not mean that we would create utopian society for them. As Albert Camus notes: "Perhaps we cannot make this a world in which children do not suffer...But we can lessen the number of suffering children. And if you and I do not do this, who will?"

Without treating education as a public-health issue that requires serious attention, the youth will continue to receive inferior education. They will continue to suffer mass unemployment and armed banditry will continue to rise; the society will continue to have illiterates and non-leaders as political leaders; the society will continue to have political parties without ideology, and Nigeria will continue to fall behind economically, socially and politically.

Information and Educational Technologies

It is pertinent to note the role of modern information and educational technologies in the educational development of the nation. Development-conscious societies are constantly restructuring, updating and equipping their educational institutions with modern technologies, but Nigeria is still lagging too far behind in acquiring the basic technologies for its educational institutions. The engineering departments of the nation's tertiary institutions are sorely lacking the basic tools for effective teaching and learning. Thus the problems facing the nation today emanate from the paucity of information and educational technologies in the nation's citadel of learning, from where ideas for national development emanate. There is need for modern information and educational technologies at all levels in Nigeria's educational institutions.

In 'knowledge' societies –"a knowledge society is a society of mobility" and one "in which many more people than ever before can be successful" (Drucker, Nov 1994), students begin to build up their technology skills from primary and secondary schools, but this is not the case in Nigeria. Information and educational technologies would empower teachers and enable students to acquire the skills they need to become productive citizens and compete effectively in the emerging computerised global marketplace. But how could the educational institutions catch up with other institutions in the world without adequate funding?

Many devices provide multiple ways to connect an educational institution to the 'learning community.' The 'learning community' begins with students, teaching staff and administrative staff; it extends to parents and families, states, regional and local community members, educational offices and agencies and professional associations. According to the *American Association of School Libraries, and Association for Education Communication and Technology* (1998), the 'learning community' encompasses international institutions. However, it requires money, skill and dedication to link up to this group. In retrospect, the devices to link up to the group include computers, local area networks, electronic mail, cable and satellite hook-ups, TV and "electronic whiteboards and presenter stations" (Barrett, May 1999). The two-way audio and video communication equipment is among the important teaching tools that would enable schools in Nigeria to be connected and get valuable information from renowned educational institutions, all over the world. Without the necessary technology, Nigeria's much-lauded long distant educational programme would be unattainable, because a baby would crawl first before walking. The society should acquire the basic technological infrastructures before venturing into the *Space*.

At this time of information revolution, no school or nation could survive in isolation. To avoid its teachers from being cut off completely from the global academic community, Nigeria should begin to invest in modern information and educational technologies for the future. With the provision of modern information and education technologies and commitment from the stakeholders (as well as cooperation from scholars across the world) the nation's educational institutions could turn around, for good. Modern technologies would "provide a foundation for an innovative learning environment where students and teachers could reach beyond the confines of a school building for information, interaction and enrichment." They would also ensure that teachers and students are current with the latest technological developments around the world and respond with changes in their educational programmes at home and disseminate current knowledge and research works to the public. Research conducted at a distance institution could be used to solve local problems if the necessary tools are provided. Thus to thrive in today's modern workplace, students in Nigeria must have the necessary skills and "good understanding of how technology works, and what it can do."

Appropriate technologies could assist to determine the authenticity of personal IDs and create instant new IDs for those who need them; it could help to verify fingerprints, addresses and other personal information. It could expedite voting, collation of votes and announcement of winners or losers, thereby reducing election frauds. In addition, modern technologies could dramatically enhance the ability of the educational institutions to prepare students for the realities of modern workplace and help to design and manage databases (such as on birth and death), control crime and collect revenue. Economic planning, population projection and resource management are among other benefits of modern technologies. With the necessary tools, schools would "produce bold and innovative solutions" to solve the problems that confront a nation (Carlin, Nov 5,1999). The creative and 'innovative' steps could enlarge a nation's *economic pie*, create more jobs and reduce poverty and crime, because poverty could lead to fraudulent and criminal activities.

An appropriate environment in schools facilitates learning. To fully restore sanity to the nation's institutions of higher learning, academic research should be encouraged with the necessary funding and improved working conditions for teachers. If teachers are properly motivated, students will equally be motivated to learn and participate in national development programmes, as the condition in one area often affects the other. This was amply demonstrated in the recent face-off between the federal government and the Academic Staff Union of Universities (ASUU) which kept students at home for many months. Technology, education and training have vital roles to play in any sustainable economic development process of a nation. According to the United Nations' World Commission on Environmental Development *sustainability* means "meeting the needs of the present without compromising the ability of the future generations to meet their own needs" (Scully, Jan 28, 2000). This means that a society should not deplete its natural resources for short-term benefits. This, unfortunately, has been the trend in Nigeria - a place where the leaders often embezzle the funds budgeted for community development projects without minding the effects of their actions on the people. Thus one of the problems with Nigeria is that the leaders are often insensitive to the peoples' sufferings.

The perennial problem of fuel scarcity could be solved by the private sector being allowed to build modern refineries to refine enough crude oil; and good network of roads and railroads being built to distribute the petroleum products. This means introducing true competition into the oil sector to make petroleum products available and drive down the price of fuel. Resorting to frequent and irrational increases in the price of fuel means applying wrong economic 'medicine' to the problem. The nation's obsolete technologies would also need to be updated. According to Albert Einstein, '"the specific problems we face today cannot be solved at the same level of thinking we were at when we created them" (cited in Dike, Fall 2000; and *Online: nigeriaworld.com*, Feb 1, 2000).

The mere provision of information and educational technologies would not solve all of Nigeria's socioeconomic, political and educational problems. For the technologies to serve their purpose the users should be continually and properly trained in their use. More importantly, well-trained and on-site support technicians should be made available to assist the users in taking care of their day-to-day technology problems because without technical support the technologies would become cog in the wheel to teaching, learning and national planning.

Given Nigeria's poor maintenance culture, preventive maintenance is likely to pose a serious problem. It is in fact possible to imagine a situation where servers will go down, and remain down for months. In such a situation, technology will become a hindrance to learning rather than the facilitator it was meant to be.

References

Ajayi, Rotimi, Kingsley Omonobi and Kenneth Ehigiator; *"Obasanjo apologises, cancels US trip. Ogohi allays fears over Naval Base, Ojo. "* The *Guardian*: Jan 31, 2002.
American Association School Libraries, and Association for Education Communication and Technology, 1998: See Information Power Building Partnerships for Learning, p. 54
Anele, Douglas; "Government of the rich, by the rich, and for the rich." *Vanguard:* Nov. 25, 2001
--------------------; "An Essay on the presuppositions of Democracy." *Vanguard*, Sept. 13, 1998
Anya, Anya O. "Preparing Nigeria for Competition in the 21st Century." *The Guardian*, April 26, 1999
--------------------; "The dreams, vision and myth of Nigerian reality" *The Guardian*, June 19, 2001
Aristotle: Politics. (Trans. by J.S. Sinclair) [England: Penguin Books, 1962]
Awosika, Kofo. *"Destination unknown," The Guardian*, July 5, 2001

Babasola, Sina. "FG freezes March salaries of striking varsity lecturers," *Vanguard,* March 30, 2002.

Barrett, Brad; "A New Approach to Collabourative Learning;" The *Journal,* Vol. 26, No. 10, May 1999

BBC News: *"Nigeria's graduate problem,"* July 22, 2002.

Bollag, Burton. "Nigerian Universities Start to Recover From Years of Violence, Corruption, and Neglect" *The Chronicle of Higher Education,* Feb 1, 2002, A40-A42.

Callan, Patrick M. and Joni E. Finney with Kathy Reeves Bracco and William R. Doyle (Ed), October 1997: *Public and Private Financing of Higher Education: Shaping Public Policy for the Future. American Council on Higher Education, Series in Higher Education/Oryx Press*

Carlin, James F.; "Restoring Sanity to an Academic World Gone Mad;" *The Chronicle of Higher Education,* Nov 5, 1999, p. A76

Chiahemen, John; *"Nigeria Orders Army Deployment as Police Mutiny."* Reuters: Lagos, Feb 2, 2002.

Chirot, Daniel; Social Change in the Twentieth Century, [New York: Harcourt Bruce Javanovic, Inc, 1977]

CNN: (Buenos Aires, Argentina): "Argentina Presidential Elections set for March 3," Dec 21, 2001.

Daniel, Alifa; 'Intrigues in FG-ASUU *Face-off;* ' *The Guardian,* June 17, 2001.

Daily Trust: "The public and Nigeria's universities," July 18, 2002.

Davies, Gordon K: *The Chronicle Review,* Nov 30, 2001, ppB16-B17

Dike, Victor; *Democracy and Political Life in Nigeria,* [Zaria, Nigeria: ABU Press, Dec. 2001].

----------------; *Leadership, Democracy, and the Nigerian Economy: Lessons from the Past and Directions for the Future* [Sacramento:
            The Lightning Press, 1999].

--------------. 'The Universal Basic Education Program: Educating the Educators in Nigeria' www.Nigeriaworld.com, July 14, 2000

--------------. "The State of Education in Nigeria and the Health of the Nation." In NESG Economic Indicators, Jan – March, Vol. 8, No. 1, 2000

--------------; "The Bretton Woods Institutions and the Third World: Impacts of Loan 'Conditionalities' on Domestic Economy – with
            emphasis on Nigeria." *Online publication: Nigeriaworld.com,* May 28, 1999.

--------------; "The Emerging Computerized Global Economy: A Challenge for Nigeria;" In *Dark Matter,* New York: Blacklines of Architecture Inc., Vol. No. 2; Fall 2000, pp. 13-16

Drucker, Peter; "The Age of Social Transformation;" *The Atlantic Monthly*, Nov 1994, Vol. 274, No. 5, pp. 53-80

Downs, Anthony; An Economic Theory of Democracy, [NY: Harper and Row, 1957]

Djebah, Oma *"Return to the Wild, Wild West?"* *ThisDay*: Dec 25, 2001

Eghagha, Hope; "University Students and Cheating," *The Guardian*, July 21, 2002.

Eke-Okoro, S. T; "The Vanishing Ivory Tower." The Guardian, Dec 14, 1998

Hassan, Tajudeen; "Private varsities and mode of entry." *Vanguard*, June 25, 1999

King, Jacqueline E. *"Financing a College Education: How It Works, How It's Changing;"* March 1999, Oryx Press).

Lipset, Seymour; *Political Man*. [New York: Doubleday, 1960].

Madu, Emeka; *"More Than 200 Reportedly Die in Nigeria Religious Riots."* *Reuters*: October 4, 2001.

Maduekwe, Ojo; "Corruption and the Nigerian Project." *ThisDay (Sunday)*: May 26, 2002.

Marzano, et al; *Dimensions of Thinking: A Framework for Curriculum an Instruction*. Association for Supervision and Curriculum Development, Virginia (1988), p.2

Maeroff, Gene I., Patrick; M. Callan and Michael D. Usdan (editors) *The Learning Connection: New Partnerships Between Schools and Colleges* [Teachers College, Columbia Univ/Teacher College Press, Jan 2001

Neubaner, Deane E. "Some Conditions of Democracy." *The American Political Science Review*, No. 1007, Dec, 1967

Obafemi, Olu; "Reviving Academia and the Academic." *Post Express*, Sept. 21, 1998.

Ogbeifum, Sam & Evelyn Olisa; "Half-baked teachers bane of education woes." *Vanguard*, July 1, 2001

Oladeji, Bayo; *"More private varsities coming – FG."* The Nigerian Tribune online, August 2, 2001.

Onuorah, Madu and Aniete Ben-Akpan; *"Govt. Releases N1b To Pay Police." The Guardian*: Feb 2, 2002.

Ozoemena, Emman; "How Nigeria can achieve technological Development." *Abuja Mirror*, Oct. 7-13, 1998

Paul, R.W. "Program for the Fourth International Conference on Critical Thinking and Educational Reform." Rohnert Park, CA: Sonoma State University, Centre for Critical Thinking and Moral Critique, 1986b.

Rousseau, Jean-Jacques; The Social Contract. (Translated by Betts) [Oxford Univ. Press, 1994]

Reuters: February 2, 2002

Today: November 8-14, 1998.

The African Dept: Reported by *Jubilee* 2000.

The Guardian: "Money and politics of bitterness." August 2, 2001

------------------: May 6, 1999

------------------: 'Still a Bleak Future for Education,' Jan 5, 2003.

------------------: "A System in Chaos," July 28, 2002.

------------------: 'Still A Bleak Future for Education.' Jan 5, 2003

Umar, Bature and Iyefu Adoba: "Senate Passes UBE Bill" *ThisDay*: June 12, 2001

US Dept of States: April 1991

Scully, Malcolm G.; "The Rhetoric and the Reality of Sustainability;" *The Chronicle of Higher Education*, Jan 28, 2000, p. B9

ThisDay: "All Lecture Rooms Remain Closed," March 1, 2003

-----------: "Cultism in Higher Institutions, Externally Influenced – Minister," July 14, 2002

-----------: "No Half Measures As Covenant Varsity Opens Its Doors," Oct 16, 2002

Vanguard: "Education & Manpower: *"Nigeria's performance in WAEC exams poorest in W-Africa."* Feb 13, 2003,

-------------: March 30, 2002

Wagaw, Teshome & Oxenham, John; "Educational Determinants of Modernization and Their Dilemmas: To Trans-form the Indigenous or to adapt the Exogenous?" In *Education and Values in Developing Nations*, (ed.) John Oxenham) [New York: Paragon House, 1989], p.64.

William, Alabi; "Unending Feud between Government and ASSU." *The Guardian*: Dec 9, 2001

Wiseman, John; *Democracy in Black Africa: Survival and Revival.* [New York: Paragon House Publishing Company, 1990]

Chapter 9

Political Instability and Insecurity

In the preceding chapter we considered the state and place of education in the socio-political and economic health of the nation. Political instability and insecurity are no less important than education, because political instability and social insecurity affect the educational activities of nations. The leaders talk too much about what needs to be done to improve the situation of things in Nigeria, without actually implementing them. They have been drumming the need to improve the state of education, tackle corruption, reduce poverty, improve social infrastructures and security situation, but evidence on the ground shows that the society is yet to begin to solve these problems.

Review of the insecurity situation in Nigeria

Insecurity is a serious issue, which needs to be addressed urgently. This is because every other activity in the nation (from political governance, private business, education and so forth) depends on the security situation on the ground. Nigeria, as we all know, is strewn with cases of religious, ethnic and political assassination and intimidation. Given what happened during the 2003 elections and the recent attempted civilian coup in Anambra state (see Dike, Gamji.com July 2003 and August 5, 2003) political violence is assuming an alarming and dangerous proportion. Violence and insecurity threaten not only the poor, but also the political leaders. The leaders have, until the Anambra mess, wrongly assumed that their security gadgets and plethora of special political assistants could shield them from the criminals (some of whom they may have created as part of their militia). The insecurity in the country affects every facets of life in the country. Under this circumstance, it will be an uphill task to attract foreign, and even local investors. It also negatively affects education because no one would learn effectively in an insecure and unhealthy environment.

Admittedly, it is difficult to maintain stability in an ethnically heterogeneous society. With each ethnic group identifying with, and emotionally tied up with individuals in their groups, they often see "us" and "them" (see Dahl 1998) in virtually every situation. "The problem of managing or limiting violence" according to Anthony Giddens (1999), "ranks as one of the most difficult and demanding in human affairs..." And this has particularly been a serious problem in Nigeria since the inception of the Fourth Republic, because some individuals embraced violence as a tool for achieving their political objectives. The country has witnessed a series of religious (*Shariah*), ethnic and political violence resulting in killings, looting, and destruction of properties.

For instance, there were religious riots across the country following an article on the Miss World contest in *ThisDay* by Miss Isioma Daniel. The deputy governor of Zamfara State, Mamuda Aliyu Shinkaf passed a *fatwa* (a death sentence or penalty) on Isioma, as result (see the section on *Ethno-Religious Crises* below). During this period many felt insecure, as the police was ill- equipped to deal with the magnitude of violence that was unleashed. Consequently, some states resorted to *ethnic militia* and *vigilante* groups for security. But this type of security outfits later became a public nuisance, often intimidating and killing innocent citizens.

The issue of ethnicity or 'tribalism' is complex, and it is more cumbersome in a complex society such as Nigeria. Ethnic group is a social group that, within a larger cultural and social system, claims, or is accorded, a special status in terms of a complex of traits (ethnic traits), which it exhibits, or is believed to exhibit. Such traits are diverse. And prominent among them are those drawn from religious and linguistic characteristic of the social group, the distinctive skin-pigmentation of its members, their national or geographic origins or those of their forebears (Tumin 1964 and Sithole 1985). For Yinger (1976), an ethnic group is "a segment of a larger society whose members are thought, by themselves and/or others, to have a common origin and to share important parts of a common culture. They also share activities in which the common origin and culture are common ingredients.' Nnoli (1978), in apparent agreement with Tumin (1964) in the definition of an ethnic group, stressed that the relevant factors may be language, culture, or both. He noted however, that "language is clearly the most significant defining variable of ethnicity in Nigeria." These features make individuals to develop a distinct cultural behaviour from the society as a whole.

There are some misunderstandings between *race* and *ethnic* groupings. Clyde Kluckhohn (1949) notes that though "the concept of race is genuine enough, there is perhaps no field of science in which the misunderstandings among educated people are so frequent and so serious" as in racial and ethnic groupings of mankind. Allport (1979) notes that "race refers to hereditary ties," while "ethnicity refers to social and cultural ties." And for Yinger (1976), a racial group is a kind of ethnic group, one that is set apart by some combination of inherited biological traits, which include skin colour, facial features, and stature (Smelser 1981). Thus, people of one race could belong to different ethnic groups. For instance, black people all over the globe are members of the black race, but they do not belong to the same ethnic group. The descendants of each race carry with them their racial propensities, even if their heredities were mixed. Ethnic and religious crises seem common in multi-ethnic and multi-religious societies, thereby making commitment to democratic norms or national identity problematic.

Ethno-Religious Crises

There are intractable ethnic conflicts in Nigeria, resulting in socio-political instability. It is difficult to enumerate all the numerous incidents of ethnic violence in the country. Suffice it to say that they undermine political stability and the nation-building project. There are also distrust between Muslims and Christians, with blunt ethnocentric rhetoric in Nigerian politics.

In the 1959 federal election campaign for instance, Chief Obafemi Awolowo, a Yoruba from the western part of the country, was reportedly prevented from campaigning in the north on rumours that he was 'contemptuous of Islam', and that he would ban it if elected to office (Schwarz 1967). Similarly, as the *Sharia* issue raged in the North, General Muhammadu Buhari, a former military head of state, was reported to have urged Muslims to protect their faith by voting only for Muslims in the 2003 elections.

In July 1999 there were ethnically-motivated riots in Sagamu, Lagos State, and Kano in Kano State. There were reports that some "army boys" from the north who were retired by Chief Olusegun Obasanjo might have incited the riots (*BBC,* July 28, 1999). But, as noted earlier, ethnic problems have been with Nigeria before the riots. The killing of the *Ibos* in the late 1960s, which resulted in the Nigeria/Biafra war, has been for now (anything seems possible in Nigeria) the greatest history-making ethnic crisis in Nigeria.

The issue of religion again polarised the country when the case of Federal Sharia Court of Appeal came up for debate in the 1978 Constituent Assembly. However, instead of the Federal status, which the Muslim proponents of Sharia demanded, the *1979* Constitution provided for State Sharia Courts of Appeal. In 1987 religious zealots went on rampage in Kaduna, with loss of life and property. The issue of Sharia Court heated up again in 1988, when another *Constituent Assembly* gathered to discuss the Constitution for the abortive Third Republic of 1993 (*West Africa,* Dec.18, 1988 and *Newswatch,* Oct 24, 1988). On May 17, 1992, Kaduna erupted again, with religious fanatics having a field day. Alhaji Shehu Shagari's attempt to establish a Department of Islamic Affair in 1983 provoked a hostile reaction from the Christian population. There was another religious rancour in 1986 when General Ibrahim Babangida secretly made Nigeria a member of the Organisation of Islamic Conference (OIC).

The *Shariah* issue has been a recurring theme in Nigeria for sometime now, but it took another dimension when the civilian governor of Zamfara State, Ahmed Sani Yerima, introduced

Sharia legal system in the state, making the state effectively an Islamic state. Consequently, Kaduna erupted again in February 2000, as the State readied to imitate Zamfara, state. Many lives were once again lost in the fracas, not to talk of the wanton destruction of property (*BBC,* February 25, 2000).

Ethnicity and religion are emotionally charged issues in Nigeria; and many activities in the country have ethnic and/or religious undertones. Ethnicity has even been blamed by some for the hanging of Ken Saro Wiwa (the leader of the Movement for the Survival of Ogoni People) and eight others, on November 10, 1995, by the military administration of General Sani Abacha. As *The Economist* (Nov 4, 1995) and Africa Political Review (1995) noted, Ken Saro Wiwa and his followers were killed by the military administration of General Sani Abacha only because Ogoni is a minority ethnic group of about 500,000 people in Nigeria's oil-rich Niger/Delta area. In Nigeria, even serious issues such as the perjury scandal of the former Speaker of the House of Representatives, Alhaji Ibrahim Buhari, who pleaded guilty for certificate forgery, as was reported in *TheNEWs* (July 11, 1999), was ethnicised.

The annulment of the June 12, 1993 presidential election, by General Ibrahim Babangida, believed to have been won by Chief Moshood Abiola, a Yoruba, was also ethnicised. Recently, there was a religious riot across the land following an article on the botched *Miss World* contest in Nigeria in the newspaper *ThisDay,* by Miss Isioma Daniel, which the Muslims claimed was offensive to their faith. As a result, the deputy governor of Zamfara State, *Mamuda Aliyu Shinkaf* passed a *Fatwa* (a death sentence or penalty) on Isioma. In fact, the *Daily Independent* (July 22, 2003) and a letter by the *International Press Centre* (IPC) published in the *Daily Independent* (July 29, 2003) in condemnation of the action noted that a *fatwa* was also passed on another journalist, Nduka Obiagbena, publisher of the newspaper, *ThisDay,* during this period. This was indicated in the *Jama'atul Nasril Islam* (JNI) – a Nigerian influential Islamic body's yearly report of July 21, 2003. Also the bombing of Afghanistan by the United States allegedly in pursuit of the

Taliban and Osama bin Laden caused religious riots and deaths in Nigeria.

These riots worsen the problem of sociopolitical instability in Nigeria. There is also the problem of ethnicity as has already been mentioned. During the 1999 elections for instance, ethnic issues were at the forefront, as many ethnic groups complained of 'marginalisation.' Ethnicity more than any other factor, seems to determine the outcome of the primaries and the final elections, as the retired generals who supported Chief Obasanjo did so to appease the *Yoruba* ethnic group that was angry over the annulment of the June 12, 1993 presidential elections. The clamour for a 'power shift' from the *North* to the *South* was another clear indication of the ethnicisation of politics in Nigeria. During the 2003 elections, the *Ibos* (and other groups) claimed it was their turn to produce the president of the country.

Political Behaviour: Ethno-Religious Factors

Students of ethnic politics have often asked, 'why do ethnics...vote as ethnics...?' (Parenti 1967) And why does ethnicity feature prominently in Nigerian politics, with ethnic divisions strewn all over the country? Some of the reasons for the persistence of ethnic voting behaviour in Nigerian politics include i) *the political system of a society.* Political candidates tend to rely on ethnic strategies in ethnically plural societies, more so, in a system that accommodates and propagates narrow ethnic, instead of broad national interests (Wolfinger, Dec 1965); *ii) Family-political identification.* Many voters tend to belong to the same party, as did their fathers. And many would continue to vote along the same party lines long after their parents are gone (Hyman 1959); *iii) Critical Election Theory.* The emergence of highly salient ethnic candidates, or what is branded "ethnic political entrepreneurs," may make ethnicity relevant in politics. Sensitive issues that touch the political nerves of some ethnic groups may also influence people's voting behaviour (Stone 1996; Esman 1996). *iv) Historical after-effects;* political affiliations persist long after the reasons for their emergence have ceased to be politically relevant (Key and Munger 1959); and *v) Militant core-city residue.* An ethnic community may retain an ethnic awareness despite a growing diversity of the population. Because the "assimilationist-minded" individuals would move to the suburbs, while those who choose to stay in the ethnic city settlements are more likely to be the most strongly in-group oriented (Wolfinger 1959 and Parenti 1967). For Nigerians to feel safe and secure, the polity has to be made stable because the ethnically assertive ethnic groups and individuals often stir ethnic conflicts, resulting in feelings of insecurity.

Human Rights Violations and Personal Security

The *Universal Declaration of Human Rights,* prepared by the *UN Commission on Human Rights* (endorsed by the *UN General Assembly* on Dec 10,1948), stands as the cornerstone document of human rights. Therefore, the laws of countries should be designed to protect the basic human rights - the right to life and security, to personal property, right to a certain liberty of conscience and freedom of association, and the right to emigration. This means that human rights should be recognised and secured everywhere (Rawls 1999). With this, any action that infringes on those rights constitutes human rights violation. Nigeria's political landscape is strewn with cases of human rights violations. These include genocide (against Biafra for instance), torture (in military regime), arbitrary incarceration (military and civilian), and public execution (military regime). There was nothing like basic human rights during periods of military governance because people were killed, maimed, and incarcerated for speaking up against the military.

The hanging of Ken Saro Wiwa, a human rights activists and eight others on Nov 19, 1995 under General Sani Abacha epitomised the lack of respect for basic human rights in Nigeria, under General Abacha. Ken Saro Wiwa was held in jail, denied access to his family, medical treatment and legal counsel for eight months before being hanged (*The Economist*: Nov 4, 1995 and *African Political Review,* 1995). And Chief Moshood Abiola, the apparent winner of the June 12, 1993 presidential election, was arrested and charged with treason under the Abacha regime for declaring himself president of Nigeria (*Current History*, Sept. 1994). Chief Abiola, who was the leader of the opposition National Democratic Coalition (NADECO), slumped and died while meeting with delegates from the United States in 1998. General Shehu Yar'Adua also died in detention in 1998, and one of Abiola's wives, Kudirat, was killed in the streets of Lagos in June 1996. The brutal dictatorship of the Abacha era forced many Nigerians into exile, including Brig. David Mark, Prof. Wole Soyinka, and Anthony Enahoro.

General Babangida and his regime were also involved in human rights abuses. General Babangida for instance banned the Nigerian Labour Congress (NLC), the Academic Staff Union of Universities (ASUU), and the National Association of Nigerian Students (Beckman and Jega, 1995; and ILO, 1994). And during the regime of General Babangida, Dele Giwa, the founding editor of the Newswatch magazine was killed with a letter bomb in October 1986.

After his inauguration as a civilian president in 1999, Chief Obasanjo set up a panel (Human Rights Violations and Investigation Commission) under the chairmanship of Justice Chukwudifu Oputa, to investigate the human rights violations that took place during the long period of military rule. However, as Newswatch (June 24, 2002) noted, General Ibrahim Babangida and some other accused retired generals refused to appear before the panel and even went to the court to stop the implementations of the commission's recommendations.

Another form of human rights violation rampant in Nigeria is 'human trafficking.' Some unscrupulous individuals have lately been involved in the business of trafficking young girls to some European countries as prostitutes. Because of poverty and unemployment, many of these young girls are lured into this dehumanising business to make ends meet. It was reported by some Nigerian dailies that about "500 Nigerian girls were deported from Italy in 1999" as prostitutes (*The Guardian*, Jan 24, 2003). There persists human rights violations under the present

Fourth Republic, led by Chief Obasanjo. Nigerians for instance still suffer unlawful detentions in the hands of the police, and not many people have the courage or the resources to take their case to the court (*ThisDay*, June 13, 2002). As noted in Teriba et al (May 19, 2002) and Jason (Oct 30, 2001), the military raided a small oil community of Odi in Bayelsa State and Zaki Biam (and other villages in Benue State) on the order of President Olusegun Obasanjo.

During the 2003 electioneering campaign, there were many cases of politically motivated assassinations. Chief Bola Ige was murdered in his home in December 2001 in Oyo State, and his assassins remained at large (*ThisDay*, Dec 25, 2001). In Plateau State, Alhaji Yusuf Doma, Senior Assistant on Political Affairs to the Governor, and a former local council chairman, Aliyu Maigari were beheaded (*The Guardian*, Nov 6, 2002). A Judge in Calabar (Cross River State), Maria Theresa Nsa was murdered, and her body mutilated (*BBC*, June 14, 2002). The local chairman of the Nigerian Bar Association, Barnabas Igwe, who was a government critic and his wife, Abigail Amaka Igwe, were killed in Onitsha (SouthEast). Barnabas Igwe was reported to have condemned Gov. Mbadinuju some months back for "allegedly trying to bribe judges and punishing those who ruled against the state government in court cases" (*CNN*, Sept 3, 2002). And as many news organisations reported, including the *AP* (August 17, 2002), the chairman of the Peoples Democratic Party, Ahmad Ahman Pategi (Kwara State) was killed as he was travelling to Abuja.

The more disturbing case of political assassinations was the murder of Nigeria's Attorney General and Minister of Justice, Bola Ige, in the presence of his police guards and the government has been unable to solve the murder case. The reaction of the country, as *ThisDay* (Dec 25, 2001) reported was: "if a minister can be gunned down in his house, what is the fate of the ordinary citizens?" This shows that the common person in the street could be killed by anyone and get away with it. Any government that cannot perform its basic function of protecting the lives and properties of the citizens has definitely failed.

We cannot document all the cases of politically motivated murders that took place in the 2003 elections, but it is fair to say that no section of the country was spared of this. In relative terms, Nigeria's response to emergencies has been substandard. This was demonstrated in the Ikeja Military Cantonment bomb explosion of January 27, 2002, and the explosion that rocked Idumagbo - a crowded commercial area in Central Lagos on Feb 2, 2003. News reports indicated that it took emergency response teams in Lagos many hours (about 24 hours) before reasonable activities to rescue lives were carried out in the two instances. And many of the victims who lost homes, family members, and livelihood had nothing to do than to lament in frustration (*Vanguard*, Feb 17, 2003). Because of lack of planning, people are allowed to live in business zones in the country. It was for instance reported that banks and other businesses were located in the building, which also served as homes to many individuals –something that would be unacceptable in many countries.

Cities in Nigeria should follow normal city and urban planning conventions with businesses and residential zones clearly defined. And laws should be made against people living in business zones (or businesses locating in residential zones) with stringent enforcement to discourage these kinds of behaviours. An agency, such as the National Orientation Agency (NOA), should undertake the function of enlightening the public on the dangers or hazards of living in business zones, because one of the problems bedevilling Nigeria is lack of proper information to the illiterate masses. When the people are properly educated, they will begin to change some of their irrational and negative behaviours and attitudes. The government should also prepare for disasters before they occur, by equipping the National Emergency Management Agency (NEMA) and Fire Service or Brigade for effective rescue operations in time of emergencies. In more advanced societies, the public depends heavily on these agencies when disaster occurs.

With the introduction of the full shariah law in Zamfara State on October 27, 1999, by Alhaji Ahmed Sani Yerima, cases of human rights violations in the Shariah States reportedly doubled. The federal government thought that the Sharia issue would 'fizzle out' but it did not. The federal government through the Attorney General and Minister of Justice, Kanu Agabi, later declared that the "discriminatory punishment prescribed under Sharia was unconstitutional" (*Vanguard*, March 22, 2002). There was for instance Safiya Husseini, who was convicted of adultery by an Islamic Court and sentenced to death by stoning (*BBC*, March 21, 2002). In 2000, Buba Bello Garke Jangebe made history as the first person in Nigeria to have his hands amputated under Islamic law for stealing a cow (Dike 2001 and *BBC*, Dec 19, 2002). The hand of Lawali Isa, a firewood seller was amputated for stealing two bicycles, and Alhaji Abba Ajiya, a traditional ruler, was given "40 strokes of the cane for keeping at home a housewife, Faiza Bala, who was not his legal wife" (*ThisDay*, March 22, 2002). Amina Lawal made headlines when she was sentenced to death by stoning for having a baby out of wedlock (BBC, July 8, 2002).

The relative weakness of the police adds to feelings of insecurity in the country. Those in power, in their unrelenting scramble for immediate financial gain, become intolerant of individuals who have contrary opinion about how the nation should be governed. This was rampant during the military era, but the politicians are equally guilty of the offence, hence the spate of politically motivated assassinations during the 2003 elections. A peep into the history of Nigeria reveals a furious storm. General Abacha's security personnel turned the state into an instrument of plunder and terror. Ekoriko (1996) has noted that some of "the motives for the killings [during the period] include settling political scores, business deals that have gone sour, and ruthless competition for positions in private and public institutions." Chief Olusegun Obasanjo's civilian administration has perhaps witnessed more crises and human rights violations than any other administration in Nigeria.

Threats to the nation's internal security have been enormous. For instance, violence erupted in June 1999 between the Urhobos and Itsekiris (*Warri* in Delta State) shortly after the inception of the Fourth Republic in May 1999. The Umuleri and Aguleri communities in Anambra State were also killing each other (*ThisDay*, Feb 22, 2003); Ife v Modakeke; and Zango and Kataf were also on each other's neck (*ThisDay*, 29, 2003). In February 2002, a little "misunderstanding between an *Hausa* man and a *Yoruba*" in Lagos turned into an *Hausa/OPC* conflict (Ahemba, Feb 4, 2002). When conflicts like these erupt, and follow ethnic or religious fault lines, people normally scamper back to their respective ethnic enclaves for refuge, giving ethnically assertive politicians and individuals an opportunity to exploit the situation for their own gain. Unfortunately, the nation does not have an effective judicial system to tackle such criminal activities. And the police are not much help either. The average Nigerian police officer is unfriendly and hardly the one to run to in time of danger. A good number of them are crude, rude and insensitive to people's problems; the police seem to treat every citizen as a suspect.

Security of property is also a problem in the country (though this is not peculiar to Nigeria). Some uniformed officers (military and police officers) are known to have snatched people's properties. As mentioned earlier, armed robbery (highway robbery) has been rampant. There have been cases of the involvement of the armed forces and police personnel in corruption, extortion, illegal roadblocks and high-handedness by some officers. And some 5,000 police officers have reportedly been dismissed from the service after being caught by anti-corruption squads at various roadblocks. The recent recruitment of new police officers increased the numerical strength of the police from 125,000 in 1999 to about 187,000 as at December 2002 (*ThisDay*, Feb 22, 2003). Yet, lives and properties are still being lost to "armed robbers, ethnic militias, hired assassins or the police" (*Vanguard*, June 21, 2002). This situation has been blamed largely on the low morale of the officers; and because of their obsolete weapons, the police have often been out-gunned by the bandits, as armed robbers operate with more sophisticated guns. It is therefore expected that an increase in pay, better training and more modern equipment could make the police more efficient.

Because of the pervasive feeling of insecurity in the country and the repressive military government, some ethnic groups began to feel, and rightly too, that they were being excluded from the scheme of things by the dominant Hausa/Fulani in the country. From that, the cry of marginalisation started to fill the air; the groups that felt they were being discriminated against resorted to establishing ethnic militia for apparent group-protection. And with the reprise of civilian rule in May 1999, riots and conflicts escalated in the country; and the political elite started to manipulate them for selfish political gain. This has transformed into what is recently branded *godfatherism* (See the section on 'political godfatherism and threat to the polity' in chapter 4 and 'security policies and procedures,' below). This political *godfatherism*, in my own opinion, is as dangerous as the ethnic militias, which often take the law into their hands.

The Emergence of Ethnic Militias

The emergence of ethnic militias is one of the ways ethnic groups that feel marginalized try to express their discontent, feeling of injustice, and insecurity. The aggrieved groups started to set up "militant organs as expression of defiance against the oppressive rule of the Nigerian State" (Babawale, 2001). Some of the controversial militant ethnic groups include the Movement for the Actualisation of the Sovereign State of *Biafra* (MASSOB); Egbesu Boys of Africa; Bakassi Boys; and Oodua Peoples' Congress (OPC). The Ibo People's Congress (IPC) and Arewa Peoples' Congress (APC) are regarded as being largely non-violent groups.

In the South East, the *Bakassi Boys* became a parallel security apparatus used by the traders in Aba to fight the menace of armed robbers who looted them and made life unbearable in Anambra and Abia States. The traders, originally funded the Bakassi Boys, but the government and some rich individuals in the states later assisted in funding the group. In fact, at some point, the Governor of Anambra State, Chinwoke Mbadinuju, incorporated the Bakassi Boys into the state's security apparatus, after which the name was changed to 'Anambra Vigilante Service.' The group, which was initially accepted as the answer to the severe threat posed by armed robbers in the area, became controversial, because of its indiscriminate killing of suspected criminals, and innocent civilians. The Movement for the Actualisation of the Sovereign State of Biafra (MOSSOB), led by Chief Ralph Uwazurike, is one of the controversial ethnic organisations. The main purpose of MOSSOB is to re-establish the State of Biafra. The group has been having a running battle with the federal government, with the members frequently arrested and detained by the government.

The Egbesu Boys of Africa is the militant (some will say military) wing of the Ijaw Youth Congress, which has been in frequent battles with the oil companies in the Niger Delta area. They have vandalised oil installations, kidnapped oil workers, and attacked and killed some police officers in their bid to stop oil exploration and environmental degradation of the Niger Delta area. Their confrontation with federal troops caused the military to destroy the community of Odi.

There is also the Oodua Peoples' Congress (OPC), a faction of which is led by Dr. Frederick Fasehun. It was formed in 1994 to 'defend' and protect "the rights of every Yoruba person on earth" (Newswatch, Dec 31, 1999 and 2000; Babawale, 2001). According to Frederick Fasehun, the group was "an offshoot of the June 12 crisis." As Newswatch (December 31, 1999) noted, the controversial OPC was specifically formed "to join the struggle to actualise the June 12, 1993 presidential election mandate, believed to have been won by Moshood Abiola..."

The OPC has been in some violent clashes with the authorities and the Hausa community in the Southwest. In early July 1999, a violent and deadly clash ensued between the OPC and the Hausa community in Shagamu, Ogun State, resulting in about 50 deaths; a retaliatory attack was carried out by the Hausas against the Yorubas in Kano with over 100 people killed. There was another clash between the OPC and Hausa in the Mile 12 area of

Lagos, leaving about 114 people dead. As a result of the Ketu and Mile 12 riots, Chief Olusegun Obasanjo gave the Police a 'shoot-at-sight order' on any OPC member in the area (*Newswatch*, Dec 31, 1999; and *ThisDay*, Oct 28, 2002). In October 2000, another clash between the OPC and the *Hausa* community was reported in Apapa, Agege and other parts of Lagos, resulting in the death of over 100 innocent citizens.

In October 1999, clashes were reported between OPC and the Police in Ilesha, Osun State. And in January 2000, there was a clash between the OPC and the Police leading to the death of Divisional Police Officer (DPO) for Bariga area in Lagos, Mr. Afolabi Amoo (Babawale, 2001). The OPC clashed with the Ijaw in July 1999 over a shrine built by the Arogbo-Ijaw at Apata, near a church owned by the Ileja, in Ilaje local government of Ondo State; but an unknown person set the shrine ablaze (*Newswatch,* Dec 31, 1999). The OPC has been known for unleashing terror on innocent citizens from other parts of the country (*TheNEWS*, 2000). Despite this, the Lagos State Governor, Bola Ahmed Tunubu, in June 2001, expressed his preparedness to invite the OPC to assist the State in its arduous task of crime control.

The Arewa Peoples' Congress (APC) is another ethnic militia; but relatively speaking, the group is not violent. It has been noted that the organisation was formed in response to the activities of the OPC in the Southwest (Babawale, 2001). The objectives of the APC, just like the OPC, "is safeguarding and protection of the Northern interest, wherever it is..."(*TheNEWS*, 2000). The Igbo Peoples' Congress (IPC) is a passive organisation; not much is known about this group. Like the APC, the IPC is formed in response to the activities of the OPC in the *Southwest* (Babawale, 2001).

The Nigerian public seems to hold the view that the Police are ill-equipped to protect lives and properties, which is another reason for the seeming popularity of the ethnic militias in some quarters. Some of the militias however, have ended up doing more harm than good to the society. This has led to calls by some Nigerians to disband all the ethnic militias.

Ethnic Problems and Solutions

I do not know of any 'medicine' that could 'cure' every society of its ethnic problems. Each society has to custom-design the solutions to meet its own peculiar situation. For this, Dahl (1998) notes that "there are no general solutions to the problems of culturally [and ethnically] divided countries." Every solution would be 'custom tailored' to the features of each country. Nevertheless, some of the measures likely to be effective in tackling Nigeria's ethnic problems include, **1)** *establishing a true federalism*: This will give the state and local governments the power (authority) and resources to tackle their own problems. **2)** *True democratic government*: A true democratic system, if honestly practiced under a non-corrupt leadership, is a major solution. In fact, it is one of the ultimate solutions for Nigeria's national question; **3)** *Durable and peoples' Constitution*: Crafting of a durable constitution, one, which every ethnic group should accept, could help to strengthen the nation-state; and **4)** *A good political culture*: This will give the society a sense of oneness, which it needs in forging a common national identity. This is an essential ingredient for successful governance and stability. As some writers, including Ake (1967) have noted, the problem of national unity entails developing a political culture, which the people would identify with.

Other measures to solve some of the ethnic problems in Nigeria are **5)** *Good educational system:* The system should be funded; and the youths should be given proper attention and encouraged to be of good behaviour, because they are the future of every society (Udogu 1994). It has been noted that 'good' education increases people's understanding and makes for broad-mindedness. **6)** *Good Policy Process:* Some of the problems with Nigeria are policy inconsistency, unclear direction, poor conception, and non-implementations of policies (*Vision 2010 Report*). **7)** *Restructure Nigeria into a true Mobile Society*: The nation should be a place where one could live in any state of his choice, secure employment at the state and local levels without limitations, contest elections, and participate meaningfully in the affairs of the community of his abode. And 'hard work, good skill and intelligence' should be rewarded strictly on merits, without regard to ethnicity and religion. The system whereby people are made to move back to their states of origins for employment at the creation of new States should be discouraged. Nobody should be discriminated against in Nigeria based on state of origin, ethnicity and religion (Umez, June 11, 1999; Dike July 8, 1999); **8)** *To develop a sense of 'Humanism:'* This is a way of life anchored on *human interests* and *good values*. This should be sincere efforts, and not opportunistic noise about *humanism*. **9)** *Leadership should eschew corruption, selfishness, nepotism, and opportunism*: These traits are regrettably common among Nigerian leaders. As long as these are allowed to thrive, ethnic, religious, and other differences would always be exploited for personal gain (Toyo, November 15 and 18,1998; and Dike, January 30, 2003); **10)** *To make Nigeria a true Nation:* One of the reasons why Nigerians refer to themselves as Ibos, Yorubas, Hausa/Fulani and so on, is because Nigeria has not evolved into a true nation. It is at best still a country made up of different nationalities.

A nation is a group of individuals, who feel that they have so much in common (interest, habits, ways of thinking, and the like), that they should all become a nation-state. Nation-states can count on much greater loyalty from their citizens. However, a Country is only a well-defined geographical area (different nations occupying an area). According to Chirot (1977), the term simply refers to a spatial concept. **11)** *True Power Sharing:* This will integrate the various ethnic groups into a single political structure, and give each a true sense of belonging (Lijphard 1991), and **12)** *To discourage injustice*: Social injustice breeds discontent and conflicts. The leadership must strive to discourage social injustice at all times.

To bring peace and security in the country, the political leaders must device ways to ensure distributive social justice, which includes equitable distribution of the nation's resources and wealth. It must ensure that the security apparatuses in the seat of government are not manipulated by those entrusted to administer them, as was done in Anambra State where a sitting governor was abducted on July 10, 2003.

Tackling the Insecurity Problem in Nigeria

Governance is a serious business. To ensure the security of any organisation or a nation, security policies must ensure that those given access to 'technology and information assets must abide' by the rules. Thus, policies and procedures concerning security breaches must be addressed and made known only to those who should know them. This was apparently lacking in Anambra State House as demonstrated by the ease with which those who abducted the governor on July 10, 2003, gained access to the security apparatus in his office.

The insecurity problems in Nigeria's sociopolitical environment could be tackled in the same manner with which security designs for various types of computer networks are handled. A lot of work has been done in this area, but I am taken in by the work of Subramanian (2000). Some of the policy procedures cited in his work include identifying what you are trying to protect and what you are trying to protect it from. Others are determining how likely the threats are, how to implement the measures that would protect your assets [including human beings] in a cost-effective manner, and reviewing the security process continuously to make improvements if weaknesses are found. But with everyone chasing the shadow of money in Nigeria, it is doubtful if such security procedure exists in the country. However, the nation's sensitive areas should be equipped with security alarms (connected to the operation's centre of the nation's security agencies) that could be triggered off in time of emergency. Although, there is no fully secured system in the real world, there are systems that 'are hard and time-consuming to break into.' Surely those in Nigeria are not among them!

Security breach could occur in many ways, which includes manipulation and disclosure of information by those in charge, allowing access to unauthorised persons to secured areas, and a breach caused by disgruntled employees. In the case of Anambra State in which the police abducted the sitting governor after the security gadgets were disconnected, the security breach was caused by a combination of forces. This includes the disgruntled Deputy Governor (now impeached) who wanted to replace the governor at all costs, and the *godfather*, Chief Chris Uba, who had unlimited access to information on the activities of the governor. The governor, Dr. Chris Ngige, had his own shortcomings. He should have changed his security plans when he discovered that many forces were against him. The security breach in Anambra State should serve as a lesson to the present and future political leaders in the country.

Security experts have noted that one of the main objectives (if not the only objective) in building security gadgets in both business and public establishments is to secure the human and material resources of the organisation. With appropriate security gadgets in place, privacy of information, authorisation and access controls are addressed and monitored. But without these, there might be threats to lives and properties and to the management of information in the form of interception and modification by unauthorised individuals. Lack of security could also enable unauthorised persons to send out information to the public by assuming the identity of an authorised person; the problem of forgery of documents (certificates, and so forth), bank and election frauds; and disclosure of management information to the outside world. As I noted elsewhere (Dike, August 5, 2003) all these could compromise governance and lead to disruption and denial of services to the citizens.

To tackle the insecurity problems in Nigeria, those in charge of security issues should resolve the security questions that could lead to security breaches. Thus in any serious organisation or nation, security policies must ensure that those given access to its database are monitored to ensure that they abide by the rules governing security policies to avoid any security breach. In addition, policies and procedures concerning security breach must be addressed and communicated only to those who should know them, to ensure effective security control and accountability. However, a security breach could occur in many ways, including manipulation and disclosure of information by those in charge; and allowing access to unauthorized persons to secured areas. Disgruntled employees could also cause security breaches as the situation in Anambra state demonstrated -, where a disgruntled and over-ambitious Deputy Governor revealed inside information to those that carried out the foiled abduction of the Governor, Dr. Chris Ngige.

To tackle the insecurity situation in Nigeria, there is a need for intelligence gathering and analysis. More importantly, additional police officers should be recruited and equipped properly for their job. They should be motivated to perform their duties; and the corrupt officers among them should be fired without any hesitation. Community policing (a policing system with the common interests of those living in particular areas in mind) could assist in tackling the insecurity situation in the country because the police would become more community-oriented if officers were deployed to the localities they were familiar with. This will also enable the people to trust the police because one tends to trust his or her own person more. There is the general feeling that the Nigerian police are crude, rude and insensitive to people's problems and are therefore part of the security problem in the country. There have been allegations that some of them connive with criminals to rob and kill the people they are supposed to protect. To tackle the security problems in the country, the military should be made to assist in the internal security of the society when it could afford to do so.

Nigeria's weird value system is among the causes of the worsening security situation in the country because many of those charged with enforcing the laws of the land (such as judges and the police) are themselves corrupt, and defer a lot to the rich, irrespective of the sources of their wealth. Thus to tackle its security problem, the country must also root out corruption. Closely related to corruption is poverty, which could also lead some individuals into behaviours unbecoming of good citizens, such as prostitution and human trafficking. Therefore, the government should work harder to fight poverty by providing assistance to the needy, improving the quality of education and creating employment opportunities for the youths (school graduates). This would refocus the mind of the youths on education because many have been discouraged by the extremely high level of unemployment in the country. Youth unemployment contributes to many social vices such as touting (passport touting, Motor Park touting, licence touting, courts and document touting, and so forth), prostitution, increase in incidents of *HIV/AIDS,* armed robbery or joining other criminal gangs such as the menacing *area boys,* among others. This situation is getting worse by the day but the government does not seem to care. We should remember that 'an idle mind is a playground for the devil.' The government should also improve the people's human and civil rights conditions by dismantling the forces that lead to rampant intra and inter-ethnic and communal clashes in the society. This is because the general feeling of insecurity increases with rising youth unemployment, hardship, poverty, human rights violation, rising uncertainty and corruption in the society.

The pervasive atmosphere of insecurity, as I noted somewhere, (Dike, August 5, 2003) is a problem of its own because it curtails social activities and makes people almost paranoid. To tackle the insecurity problems and the prevailing bad socio-cultural environment, the government should adopt pro-people social policies. The leaders should show the general public how to develop unflinching love for their country by espousing good moral character, because Nigeria, as presently governed, is like a society that belongs only to the few in the corridors of power who benefit from the nation's oil wealth. This has forced most people to recoil into their ethnic enclaves. But the love for one's country is engendered when the people believe that the government is taking care of their needs. The people, on their part, should learn not to worship money and the so-called *godfathers* (see chapter 10) in their communities who conspicuously display their ill-acquired wealth. Thus Nigerians should learn to respect the laws of the land and take the nation's security problems seriously because business and social activities in the nation depend on well managed judicial and security systems. Until this happens, and until the country devices effective sanctions for the 'big and corrupt politicians' and the criminals', security will remain a problem in the country.

In conclusion, riots, protests, political assassinations, armed robbery, human rights abuses, the abduction of a sitting governor in Anambra State, are all manifestations of deep-rooted problems facing the nation. Nigeria is a country where corrupt political *godfathers* and corrupt politicians use religious/ethnic and group sentiments to create tension and riots to win elections. This was demonstrated in Nigeria during the 2003 elections where the INEC declared "somebody who did not contest the election a winner" (*The Guardian*, July 27, 2003). Nigeria is a country where journalists collude with corrupt politicians to report incorrect election results for monetary gains. It is a country where judges pass bad judgement apparently for monetary gains. This was demonstrated in the apparently 'frivolous ex parte orders' granted by Justice Wilson Egbo-Egbo in the case of Senator Adolphus Wabara (PDP) and Elder Dan Imo (ANPP) and the mess between the Governor of Anambra State, Dr Chris Ngige and his political godfather, Chief Chris Uba (*The Guardian*, July 27, 2003).

The problems enumerated above cannot be cured without first eliminating the conditions that generated them. Nigeria needs a virtuous leader, 'a new man' with the necessary political muscle to tackle corruption, illiteracy and ethnic problems bedevilling the nation. The people should be made to understand that it is only peace and stability that can bring progress. Without this, stability, peace, unity and true democracy will continue to elude Nigeria.

References

Abdulsalami, Isa and Julius Alabi; "Governor's aide, beheaded in Plateau, six feared dead in Ondo;" *The Guardian,* Nov 6, 2002.

Abramson, Harold J; "Religion." In S. Thernstrom, A. Orlov, and O. Handlin (ed.) *Harvard Encyclopaedia of American Ethnic Groups.* [Cambridge, MA: Harvard University Press, 1980]

Ahemba, Tume; "Troops Join Police to Battle Nigerian Ethnic Riot." *Reuters:* Feb 4, 2002.

Akinola, Anthony A; "A Critique of Nigeria's Proposed two-party System;" Journal of Modern African Studies, 27, 1, 1989

Allport, Gordon W; The Nature of Prejudice (25th Anniv. ed.). [Addison-Wesley Pub Comp, 1979]

Babawale, Tunde; "The Rise of Ethnic Militias, De-legitimisation of the State, and the threat to Nigerian Federalism." *West Africa Review,* Vol. 3, 1, 2001

BBC: "Nigerian leaders condemns Sharia;" Feb. 25, 2000

------: See report on 'Sharia' amputation; March 23, 2000

------: "Eyewitness: Nigeria's Sharia amputees," December 19, 2002

------: "Nigeria Sharia architect defends law" March 21, 2002

------: "Nigerian appeals Sharia sentence," October 19, 2001

------: "Nigerian Judges strike after murder," June 14, 2002

------: "Nigerian Woman fights stoning," July 8, 2002

Beckman, Bjorn and Attahiru Jega; "Scholars and Democratic Politics in Nigeria." *Review of African Political Economy,* No. 64, 1995.

Bienen, Henry; "Leaders, Violence, and the Absence of Change in Africa." *Political Science Quarterly,* Vol. 108, Number 2, 1993

Chirot, Daniel; Social Change in the Twentieth Century; [N.Y, Chicago, San Fran, Atlanta: Harcourt Brace Jovanovich, Inc., 1977]

CNN/World: "Government critic killed in Nigeria," Sept 3, 2002

Daily Independent: see the July 22, 2003 report on the affirmation of the *Fatwa* by a Committee of the Jama'atul Nasril Islam (JNI)

------------------------: *"Fatwa* on Nigerian journalists and other assaults on media;" July 29, 2003

Dike, Victor E; "Leadership, Politics, and Social Change: Nigeria and the Struggle for Survival;" Online pub; - *Africa Economic Analysis,* July 8, 1999

------------------; "To Sustain the Unity of Nigeria." *Daily Independent,* January 30, 2003

------------------; *Democracy and Political Life in Nigeria.* [Zaria, Nigeria: ABU Press, 2001, p.87]

------------------; "Security Threat as a Lesson from the Anambra Imbroglio;" Online: Gamji.com, July 2003

----------------; "Tackling the insecurity problem in Nigeria;" *Daily Trust,* August 5, 2003

Esman, M; "Ethnic Politics." Kuper and Kuper (ed.), *The Social Science Encyclopedia* (2nd ed.). [New York, 1996], pp.259-262.

Giddens, Anthony; "Political Theory and the Problem of Violence." In *The Politics of Human Rights,* (ed.) Obrad Savic for The Belgrade Circle Journal, [London and New York –Verso, 1999].

Hyman, Hubert; Political Socialization; [The Free Press of Glencoe, 1959]

International Labour Organization: "Reports of Committee on Freedom of Association." (295th Report) Vol. LXXVII, 1994, pp.191-201

Jason, Pini; "The gathering storm." *Vanguard,* October 30, 2001

Key, V.O. and Munger, Frank; "Social Determinism and Electoral Decision: The Case of Indians;" In Eugene Burdick & Arthur J. Brodbeck (ed.), American Voting Behaviour. [IL: The Free Press of Glencoe, 1959]

Kluckhohn, C. M; Mirror of Man. [New York: McGraw-Hill, 1949]

Lewis, Peter M; "Endgame in Nigeria? The Politics of a Failed Democratic Transition." *Africa Affairs,* 1994, 93, pp.323-340.

Lijphart, Arend; "The Power-Sharing Approach;" In Montville, J.V. (ed.), Conflict and Peacemaking in Multiethnic Societies. [New York: Lexington Books, 1991]

Lipset, Seymour Martin, & Earl Raab; The Politics of Unreason (2nd ed.,). [Chicago & London: The Univ of Chicago Press, 1970]

Madu, Emeka; "More Than 200 Reportedly Die in Nigeria Religious Riots." *Reuters:* Oct 14, 2002

Maier, Karl; See article on Nigeria: *Africa Report,* July/Aug. 1992, pp.47-48.

Newwatch; (Lagos): *see* October 24, 1988, pp.9-16.

------------: (Lagos): see January 10, 2000.

------------: (Lagos): "War Against Nigeria;" December 31, 1999

Nigeria: *The Vision 2010 Report.*

Nkwocha, Jossy; "An All-out War." *Newswatch:* June 24, 2002

Nnoli, O; Ethnic Politics in Nigeria; [Enugu, Nigeria: Fourth Dimension, 1978]

Obinor, Francis; "Nigeria's republics, a recurring vicious circle," *The Guardian,* August 26, 2002

Odivwri, Eddy; "The Governors, Their Godfathers;" *ThisDay,* July 19, 2003

Okenwa, Lillian; "Man, 72, Awarded N2.1m for Illegal Detention," *ThisDay News,* June 13, 2002

Parenti, Michael; "Ethnic Politics and the Persistence of Ethnic identification." *The American Political Science Review,* 1967

Rawls, John; "The Law of Peoples." In *The Politics of Human Rights,* (ed.) Obrad Savic for The Belgrade Circle Journal, [London and New York –Verso, 1999].

Review of African Political Economy: 1995, pp.472-479.

Schwarz, F.A.O; Nigeria: The Tribes, the Nation, or the Politics of Independence. [Cambridge, Mass. & London, 1965]

Sithole, Masipula; "The Salience of Ethnicity in African Politics: The Case Study of Zimbabwe." *Journal of Asian and African Studies,* XX, 3-4, 1985, pp.181-192.

Smelser, Neil J; Sociology; [Englewood Cliffs, New Jersey: Prentice-Hall, Inc. 1981]

--------------------; The Theory of Collective Behaviour [New York: The Free Press, 1963]

Stone, John; "Ethnicity;" In Kuper and Kuper (eds.); *The Social Science Encyclopedia* (2nd ed.), 1996, NY, pp. 260-262.

Subramanian, Mani; Network Management: Principle and Practice [Addison-Wesley, Longman, Inc, 2000]

Teriba, Ayo, et al; "Issues 2003," *ThisDay,* May 19, 2002.

The Associated Press (AP); "Gunmen kill Nigerian ruling party official" August 17, 2002

The Guardian; "30 Policemen On Trial For Extortion In Lagos," Jan 25, 2003

------------------: "Reflection on human trafficking;" Jan 24, 2003

------------------; "The Judiciary As a Threat To Democracy;" *The Guardian,* July 27, 2003

The News; (Lagos); January 10, 2001

ThisDay; "How It All Began," March 22, 2002

-----------; "Return to Wild, Wild West?" Dec 25, 2001

-----------; "A Searchlight on Ethnic Militias;" October 28, 2002

-----------; "April Polls: Are the Police Ready," Feb 22, 2003

-----------; See Abimbola Akosile on "Security: Any Need for Reform?" July 29, 2003

Toyo, Eskor; "The National question in Nigeria (1);" *The Guardian,* Nov. 15 & 18, 1998

Tumin, M.M; "Ethnic groups" in Julius Gould and William L. Kob (eds.), *A Dictionary of the Social Sciences* [New York: Free Press, 1964], p.243.

Udogu, E. Ike; "The Military, Civil Society and the Issue of Democratic Governance Toward Nigeria's Fourth Republic." *Journal Of Developing Societies,* Vol. XI, 2, 1995, pp.216-218.

Umez, Bedford; "Urgent Appeal to President Obasanjo: Repeal the Separatist Law." Online: *Nigeriaworld.com*, June 11, 1999.

Vanguard: "Between a military and human face democracy," June 21, 2002

------------; "Response to emergencies," February 17, 2003

------------; "Sharia: Zamfara Gov. lambastes Agabi" March 22, 2002

West Africa; 12-18 Dec 1988, pp.23-53.

--------------: Feb 14-20, 1994, p.25.

Wolfinger, Raymond E; "The Development and Persistence of Ethnic Voting." *American Political Science Review*, 59, 1965

World Press Review; Jan 1988, pp.3-4.

Yinger, Milton J; "Ethnicity in Complex Societies: Structural, Cultural, and Characteriological Factors." In Lewis A (ed.), [New York: John Oxenham, Paragon House, 1989]

Yusuf, Razak & Tanyo Ajakaye; "Why Ige Was in Ibadan, By Elayo" *ThisDay*, Dec 25, 2001

Chapter 10

Political Godfatherism and Nigerian Politics: A Case Study of Anambra State

Conceptual Framework

The *godfather* phenomenon was said to have started in Sicily (Italy) with a group called *Cosa Nostra* – the *Mafia*. The *Mafia* is powerful and feared because of a belief that it is very connected to people in influential positions of authority. It is believed that the *mafia* could effectively challenge a constituted government or stall government operations because those linked to it are often treated as 'sacred cows.' (Sen 1999). During the early days of the group, it traded, as Ushigiale noted (see *ThisDay*, July 21, 2003) on prostitution and illicit liquor, cigarettes and debt collection. The political power and influence of the group is believed to extend beyond the shores of Italy; presently the *Mafia* constitutes a powerful political force in the United States with concentration around Chicago. Mario Puzo in the fictional novel, *The Godfather* (1995) appropriately portrays the role, influence and power of the *godfathers* within the *Mafia*.

The crude form of political *godfatherism* in Nigeria has similar characteristics with the Italian Mafia. The Nigerian political *godfathers* influence government policies, or try to hold the state hostage, because they control the decision-making apparatuses of the area in which they have installed their *godson*. They control the award of government contracts and high-ranking political appointments. They usually have no qualms about killing, or engineering assassinations to achieve their goal. Like the Italian Mafia, the Nigerian public also believe that the *godfathers* are well connected with the people in influential positions of authority, making them *untouchables* or *sacred cows*. Edwin Madunagu, in a recent article (Guardian July 31, 2003) called Nigerian *political godfathers* political *contractors* because they perform their political function with the sole purpose of making money like business contractors.

The recent foiled abduction of Governor Chris Ngige of Anambra state, allegedly masterminded by Chief Chris Uba, his so-called political *godfather,* is a case in point. It got many people shaking their heads in puzzlement over why anyone could do such a thing.

Political *Godfatherism* in Nigeria

The political *godfather* phenomenon is not new in Nigeria. It started during the First Republic when the influence and political power of Nnamdi Azikiwe, Obafemi Awolowo, Ahmadu Bello, Ladoke Akintola and Aminu Kano (among others) controlled political activities and shaped the political landscape of Nigeria. They all had (and still have) many political followers because they provided the needed political leadership for the people by espousing 'value-driven' political ideologies. In other words, their purpose for mentoring younger politicians was not to accumulate material wealth or to become what Chimaroke Nnamani called "settlement-seeking" *godfathers* (*nigerdeltacongress.com,* July 2003). Political *godfatherism* has recently acquired a negative connotation in Nigerian politics because those with ulterior motives now sponsor political candidates with the sole intention of holding sway, calling the shots and determining who gets what, when and how in the state governed by their political *godson.* Thus ideology does not seem to play any role in their choice of who becomes the political *godson.* Often, they find it easier to *godfather* candidates who do not have the resources, vision, and political will or charisma to contest and win a political office on their own. As *ThisDay* (July 19, 2003) noted, the *moneybags,* which could sometimes be a synonym for *godfatherism,* perceive any sponsorship as a business investment and expect to recoup their investment by controlling the treasury of the state and the political activities of the political *godson.* For that, an undertaken or *a contract* is signed between the *godfather* and the *godson,* which means that

197

the latter would 'worship' the former, or in the case of Ngige, *would not do anything without the permission* of his godfather, Chief Chris Uba. They often employ unorthodox and illegal means to ensure that the political *godson* keeps his own part of the bargain.

The Second Republic under the presidency of Alhaji Shehu Shagari also had its fair share of political *godfathers*. As the *Weekly Trust* (July 26, 2003) noted, Dr Olusola Saraki was the undoubted kingmaker in Kwara state. Dr. Olusola Saraki, who was also the Senate Leader in the Second Republic, imposed the late Adamu Attah on the people of Kwara State as their governor between 1979-1983. And it is not a secret that Dr. Olusola Saraki single-handedly made his son, Bukola, the Governor of Kwara State during the 2003 elections (Mohammed, July 26, 2003). Other *godfathers* in Nigerian politics are known to have sponsored other political candidates. Reports have it that without the sponsorship of S.M Afolabi of Osun State, Olagunsoye Oyinlola could not have become the governor of the State. The same was said of Lucky Igbinedion in his second term bid as Governor of Edo State as he was blessed by the sponsorship of Chief Tony Anenih. And Dr. Iyorchia Ayu was said to have sponsored George Akume to become the governor of Benue State.

There is perhaps nothing wrong in an elderly statesman providing an ideological support to novices seeking political office, as was the case in the days of Zik and Awo. In fact, in real life everyone needs a mentor. However, it is something else when the intention of *godfatherism* is to destroy a society, as demonstrated in Anambra State.

The Case of Anambra State

There are lots of differences between the ideologically driven *godfatherism* of the First Republic and the crude form of political *godfatherism* that prevails in many states of Nigeria today as typified by the Chris Uba saga in Anambra State. This form of political bravado was said to have started during the era of

General Sani Abacha, when Chief Arthur Eze became the *thin-god* of the land. He (Chief Arthur Eze) was said to have had many followers of whom Chief Chris Uba was one. As a staunch Abacha supporter, he was said to have influenced who would be posted to Anambra State as the military administrator. In return, Abacha and his junta awarded him "juicy contracts" some of which were uncompleted (Odili, July 13, 2003). The emergence of Dr. Chinwoke Mbadinuju as the Governor of Anambra State in 1999 was also said to have been made possible by the sponsorship of Chief Emeka Offor and A.B.C Ojiakor (Ajani, July 21, 2003). Chief Emeka Offor allegedly made his tenure as Governor a nightmare because of disagreements between them 'over patronage.' Chief Emeka Offor was said to have frustrated every policy-move made by Mbadinuju, who, in turn wasted a lot of his time and the state's limited resources either battling with Ofor or struggling to repay his IOUs to him. The situation was so bad that Chief Emeka Offor angrily "withdrew his nominees from serving in Mbadinuju's" administration and set up a political pressure group, *Anambra People's Forum* (APF) simply to fight the Mbadinuju government (Odili, July 13, 2003). Consequently, the state was in constant crisis and governance suffered; public schools were closed for about a year and public servants were not paid for about 10 months.

Political *godfatherism* took a more dangerous turn in Anambra State on July10, 2003 when Chief Chris Uba (a young man of between 37 years and 38 years old), decided to abduct the Governor in Awka due to disagreement over political patronage. He was said to have hired the Assistant Inspector General of Police, Mr. Raphael Ige and 200 other police officers to execute the planned abduction. But his small army of *coup executioners were* unsuccessful (see *ThisDay*, July 19, 2003, *Vanguard*, July 15, 2003 and *The Guardian*, July 15, 2003). As is often the case with modern political *godfatherism* in Nigeria, an agreement was apparently signed between Dr. Chris Ngige and Chief Chris Uba as to how they would share their bounty, should Ngige become the governor. As Rasheed, (July 23, 2003) noted, when Chief Chris Uba (popularly called *Eselu*), suspected that his *political godson* (Chris Ngige) would not keep their agreement, he forced him to sign an undertaking that in part stated:

"Whereas I was sponsored by the group headed and led by Chief Chris Uba, who made it possible for me to be Governor of Anambra State; therefore, I will be a true loyalist and a committed member of Chief Chris Uba's group in PDP, Anambra State"

In fact, during his inauguration speech in Awka on May 29, 2003, it was reported that Dr. Chris Ngige devoted a good portion of the address to praising his political *godfather* – Chief Chris Uba (Igboanugo, July 15, 2003). However, at some point Chief Chris Uba was not satisfied with the behaviour of Dr. Chris Ngige and therefore made him to swear on a 'shrine' to prove his allegiance. He was also forced to sign undated 'resignation letters' on different occasions that he hoped would work in his favour because all he had to do would be to put a date on any of those letters and forward it to the state legislature. Chief Chris Uba allegedly drew inspirations from Chief Arthur Eze and Chief Emeka Offor, said to be his own mentors.

Chief Uba did just that when he felt he had had enough from his 'unreliable' political *godson*. One of the resignation letters said to have been signed by Dr Ngige was tendered to the Speaker of Anambra State Assembly, Mrs. Eucharia Azodo (now impeached), who eagerly accepted it as an authentic resignation. She quickly got the House to approve it, to make way for the Deputy Governor, Dr. Ude - the Governor 'wannabe'- to proclaim himself the new Governor of Anambra state. Dr Ngige was duly abducted to ensure that he did not interfere with the process. But as mentioned earlier, their abduction plan was foiled. As Omonobi (August 10, 2003) noted, those implicated in the abduction saga were Chief Chris Uba (the *godfather*) Mrs. Eucharia Azodo, Ikechukwu Abana and Mr. Chuma Nzeribe.

It was alleged that Chief Chris Uba and his group forced Dr. Ngige "to sign post dated cheques" but when he refused to oblige they threatened him with death (The *Guardian*, July 13,

2003). Dr. Ngige himself alleged that Chief Chris Uba demanded N3 billion from him as refund of election expenses he (Uba) incurred in sponsoring him (Ngige). But as one would expect, Chief Chris Uba denied this when he said:

"When I heard that allegation by the governor...that I demanded N3 billion, I had a terrible shock of my life because I saw it as a cheap blackmail. The state as a whole doesn't have N3 billion and the man in question, if he had N3 billion he wouldn't have approached me for sponsorship."

There are many stories on the reasons why Dr Ngige fell out with chief Uba. One of these was that Chief Uba was angry that Dr Ngige did not want to 'settle' those who "worked hard for the victory of the party in the state"(Edike, July 13, 2003 and *Vanguard* of July 20, 2003). As mentioned earlier, Mr. Raphael Ige, Assistant Inspector general, Zone 9, (now retired), with about 200 of his errand police boys led the unsuccessful *'coup'* against Ngige. In fact, Ngige alleged that Mr. Raphael Ige told him on the fateful day that he was authorised by the powers-that-be in Abuja (apparently, the President and the Inspector General of Police (IG), Mr. Tafa Balogun) to arrest him. Many have wondered whether such a high ranking police officer and Chief Chris Uba himself could not have realised the legal implications of a *coup d'etat* (attempt at forcible seizure of power from a duly constituted authority). Chapter 1, Part 11 (2) of the 1999 Constitution of the Federal Republic of Nigeria says:

"The Federal Republic of Nigeria shall not be governed, nor shall any person or group of persons take control of the Government of Nigeria or any part thereof, except in accordance with the provisions of this Constitution."

By the laws of the land, the actions of Chief Uba and his associates are acts of treason. However, given the 'Nigerian factor', it is not yet clear what would be the fate of the coup plotters. Already, Mr. Raphael Ige, who led the coup attempt, was allowed to retire instead of dismissal from office. The public is not keeping mum; it is pressing that those involved in the 'Anambra Shame' must be tried for *treason*. However, this group (like the Mafia in Italy) is believed to be strongly connected with the authorities in Aso Rock at Abuja, the state capital.

Godfatherism: Methods of Manipulation and Impacts on the Polity

There are several *godfathers* and *godsons* in Nigeria. Their deals are littered throughout the political landscape of Nigeria, but the case of Chief Chris Uba and Dr. Chris Ngige exposed the negative impacts of crude political *godfatherism* in Nigerian politics. Like other forms of political corruption, the present-day form of political *godfatherism* is a threat to Nigeria's democracy project because it prevents the people from freely exercising their rights to participate in the political process.

Political *godfatherism,* it could be argued, thrives on the *ignorance* and *poverty* of the people because of its crude forms of extracting favours from the political *godsons,* and the primitive method of wealth accumulation that it glorifies. In addition, the crude form of political *godfatherism* is possible only in an environment lacking functional political structures and institutions. As a result, the rent-seeking individuals (the *godfathers* who perceive any expense in politics as an investment) employ terror, brute force, thuggery, blackmail, deal making and even corrupt political institutions and the media to force their *godsons* to submission. Some of them would create parallel party structures against the government and fabricate charges to chop off "pounds of flesh" from their godsons and their government.

For instance, during the time of Mbadinuju in Anambra State Chief Emeka Offor set up a parallel pressure group, *Anambra Peoples' Forum* (APF) with the sole purpose of frustrating his government (*Vanguard* 13, 2003). To achieve their selfish purpose the *godfathers* would segment the political environment into zones, form their own party caucuses and personal loyalties (and community groups) to achieve their purpose. As Nnamani (July 2003) noted, some of them would resort to 'ethnicism' or manipulate community groups 'to garner support' so as to escape the wrath of the law if their 'business' proved unsuccessful.

The impacts of the crude form of political *godfatherism* are enormous. It leads to political assassinations, unreasonable politics of decampments and rigging of elections such as declaring somebody that did not participate in an election the winner as was allegedly the case in Anambra State (*The Guardian*, July 27, 2003). Community development programmes are neglected and civil servants are often not paid because funds are either diverted or wasted to repay the *godfathers* or to fight them. Consequently, the delivery of services - roads and schools, healthcare services, electricity and water supply suffers. For example, during the tenure of Mbadinuju as the Governor of Anambra State public schools were shut down for about a year and teachers (and other public servants) were not paid for over 10 months because of the trouble created by Emeka Offor in the State (*Vanguard*, July 13, 2003). As a form of political corruption, political godfatherism undermines the credibility of the judiciary and police who are often employed by the godfathers in their single-minded pursuit of their goals (Mohammed, July 26, 2003, Dike, August 5, 2003 and Ezomon, July 27, 2003).

Thus crude political *godfatherism*, as Sagay, (July 20, 2003) notes, also perverts justice and liberty, and opposes the truth. For instance, the Election Petition Tribunal sitting in Anambra State nullified the Senate seat of Dr Ugochukwu Uba (the elder brother of Chris Uba) and Ikechukwu Godson Abana because it found that the Anambra State Resident Electoral Commission (REC) declared them winners of an election they did not even participate in. To redress the injustice, Prince Nicholas Ukachukwu and Chief Ben Ndi Obi whose elections were invalidated by the Anambra State REC were both re-declared winners by the Tribunal (Onyekamuo, August 8, 2003 and Okoli, July 23, 2003). It is proper to note at this juncture that this type of election fraud is not peculiar to Anambra State; it was common throughout Nigeria during the 2003 elections.

The bravado of the *godfathers* could also 'destabilise and subvert' the democratic political process, policies and governance and increase the misery of the people. Because of their connection to those in the corridors of power, these individuals become very powerful politically, personalise politics, make the entire business of governance their private business and expect the political activities in their enclave to revolve around them. This often leads to mediocrity because they (godfathers) would appoint whomever they want to any political position without minding whether the person is qualified for that position. It also leads to the building of a non-productive society and provides a negative role model to the youths because they would perceive thuggery and sheer bravado as traits. Nnamani (July 2003), citing Richard Joseph - *Democracy and Prebendal Politics in Nigeria* - noted, that the *godfather* phenomenon could lead to "the failure of orderly succession in government." This is because the godfathers could forcefully abduct a governor at will and replace him or her with their brothers or close friends and "expose the state to the fetish tradition of patrimony." Therefore, the personal abilities and character of a *godfather* in an area – and not the law of the land - would determine how a state could be administered. In this sense, the state becomes, according to Callaghy (1987), a "battleground for political, economic and social struggle" among competing 'groups' or 'classes' for control of state apparatus for personal gain.

Seeking Solutions to the Problem of Political Godfatherism

To avoid the crude form of political *godfatherism* from destabilising and subverting Nigeria's democracy project, the government (Federal, State and Local) must prosecute any person found guilty of plundering state resources - if it wants its avowed war on corruption to be taken seriously. It must also curtail the influence of money in politics by controlling individual contributions to political campaigns. Without this, the influence of money will curtail people's rights to participate in the political process. As Sagay (July 20, 2003) warned, "if we do not remove money from politics, money will remove our politics from us" because the *moneybags* would hijack the political process, purchase an electoral victory and pillage the treasury. Thus the issue of election campaign funding must be central in Nigeria's *Electoral Reform Bill*, with serious financial limitations on political contributions. This will limit the amount of money available to the corrupt politicians to buy votes, bribe the INEC officials and the police and pay their thugs. As *ThisDay* noted in its editorial (July 27, 2003):

> "...Moneybags and [political] contractors have hijacked the political process, unduly monetising our politics and distorting the political process. To run for elective posts, candidates need a lot of money. The bulk of such money is spent not in selling ideas to the electorate... but on what ordinarily should have been illegal: bribing the voters, the police and the electoral officials, and in paying for thugs."

Many Nigerians are poor and ignorant of their rights as citizens of Nigeria and, therefore, are susceptible to bribery and intimidation. There is therefore a need for massive public education by appropriate non-governmental organisations (NGOs) and state agencies. The Centre for Social Justice and Human Development (CSJHD), an NGO I founded, which has its headquarters in Sacramento, California, USA, will be willing to participate in such a public awareness programme in Nigeria. It is crucial that the public is made aware of the dangers of selling their conscience to the highest political bidders.

Many Nigerians for instance believe that Chief Chris Uba and his 'co-travellers' hijacked the political process in Anambra state, and carried out his unsuccessful coup attempt only because he successfully bribed the police, the judiciary and INEC officials. The suspicion of the public is buttressed by the roles played by Mr. Raphael Ige in the abduction saga and Mr. Justice Samuel

Wilson Egbo-Egbo in his ex-parte order asking Dr. Chris Ngige to "stop parading himself as Governor" and hand over to his Deputy Governor, Dr. Okey Ude. The controversial judgement, which was reported by the national dailies, including *ThisDay* (July 23, 2003) and the *Guardian* (July 27, 2003) read in part:

> "In the interim, the Deputy Governor of Anambra State, Dr. Okey Udeh should take over and perform the functions of the Governor of Anambra State pending the determination of the motion on notice."

This order attracted condemnation from the public, including from Chief Audu Ogbe, National Chairman of the ruling party, PDP, who noted that Justice Egbo-Egbo's order "sounds like the first endorsement of treason in the country." Justice Egbo-Egbo is not new to controversy; he issued similar *ex-parte* order in the case between Senator Wabara and Mr. Dan C. Imo. However, the public was furious about his order and that apparently made him to retract it (*Guardian*, July 27, 2003). Thus to control the political corruption that goes with political *godfatherism* in Nigeria, judges who grant frivolous *ex-parte* (one-sided or partisan point of view) orders should be fired without delay, prosecuted and jailed. This would help to sanitise the judiciary and help it regain public trust in the judicial process.

Nigerian politics is presently dominated by money and not issues. This is partly because having rich and powerful 'godfathers' seem all that is required to become successful in Nigerian politics or win elections. There is therefore an urgent need to restructure the political process to make it issues-based by taming the political godfathers. Making politics issues-based will also help to weed off the chaffs and allow those with good ideas about how to solve the country's numerous problems to enter the fray.

Deterioration in the quality of education, high unemployment and distorted value system have also forced the youths to 'worship' money and look up to the barely educated *moneybags* and political *godfathers* as role models. In the case of chief Chris

Uba, his obvious connections to Aso Rock appeared to have given him an extra audacity.

This book does not pretend to have all the solutions to the issues of corruption and political *godfatherism* in Nigeria. I however believe the suggestion above will be good starting points. There is also a need to restructure INEC to make it truly independent.

Notes and References

Ajani, Jide; "Why Anambra coup plotters should be tried;" *Vanguard,* July 21, 2003

Callaghy, Thomas M; "The State as Lame Leviathan: The Patrimonial Administrative State in Africa;" in Zaki Ergas (Ed), *The African State in Transition* [New York: St. Martin's Press], p. 91

Dike, Victor E; "Tackling the insecurity problem in Nigeria;" *Daily Trust,* August 5, 2003

Edike, Tony; "I'm out to rescue Anambra from bad leadership – Uba;" *Vanguard,* July 13, 2003

Ezomon, Ehichioya; "The Judiciary as a threat to Democracy; *The Guardian,* July 27, 2003

Igboanugo, Sunny; "Crushing another madness in South East politics;" *Daily Independent,* July 15, 2003

Joseph, Richard; Democracy and Prebendal Politics in Nigeria, as cited in Namani (July 2003)

Madunagu, Edwin; "Godfathers and political contractors;" *The Guardian,* July 31, 2003

Mohammed, Aminu; "Political Corruption and its Nemesis;" Weekly Trust, July 26, 2003

Nnamani, Chimaroke; "The Godfather Phenomenon;" *see* www.nigerdeltacongress.com, July 2003

Nwakanma, Obi; "Treason in Anambra State;" *Vanguard,* July 20, 2003

Odili, Paul; "Inside story of the coup in Anambra State;" *Vanguard,* July 13, 2003

Odivwri, Eddy; "The Governors, Their Godfathers;" *ThisDay,* July 19, 2003

Okoli, Anayo; "'INEC didn't register Abana'" *Vanguard,* July 23, 2003

Omonobi, Kingsley; "ANAMBRA: Why Police can't arrest Uba, others;" *Vanguard,* August 10, 2003

Onyekamuo, Charles; "Abana, Anambra Senator, Loses Seat;" *ThisDay*, August 8, 2003

Puzo, Mario; *The Godfather*; Mass Market Paperback, Dec 1995

Rasheed, Olawale; "How Ngige signed away Anambra;" *Nigerian-Tribune*, July 23, 2003

Sagay, Isaac; Political warlords: Threat to Nigerian democracy;" *Vanguard*, July 20, 2003

Sen, Amartya; *Development As Freedom*; [New York, Anchor Books, 1999]

The Guardian: "My Ordeal, By Ngige;" July 13, 2003

------------------: "We Won't Give Up On The Senatorial Election Case, Says Akpamgbo;" July 27, 2003

ThisDay: "A Law on Campaign Finance;" July 27, 2003

-----------: "Court Orders Ngige to Vacate Office;" July 7, 2003

Ushigiale, Joseph; Anambra: The Sudden Fall of a Godfather;" *ThisDay*, July 21, 2003

Vanguard: "Nine judges sacked over exparte motions – Babalakin;" August 01, 2003

-------------: "Treason in Anambra;" July 15, 2003

Williams, Alabi; "A History Of 'Treasonable' Offences;" *The Guardian*, July 27, 2003

Chapter 11

Conclusions: Understanding and managing the Challenges of 2003 elections

We have seen in the preceding chapter that crude political *godfatherism* is one of the problems that affected the 2003 elections because it contributed to the issues of insecurity, election frauds, decampment and political assassinations, which were rampant in the run-up to, and after the 2003 elections. I feel there is a need for a more detailed discussion of the 2003 elections because of the lessons to be learnt from that.

Since the inception of the new civilian administration, Nigeria has been rocked by a series of conflicts. All the agitations point to the people's feelings of injustices, domination, oppression, denials and marginalisation (either suffered or enjoyed) by the ethnic groups concerned. It could also mean that these groups who are complaining are feeling the pinch of the overbearing influence of the federal government. Many countries have addressed their unity or disunity problems using different methods.

2003 Elections: Fraud and Public Outcry

There seemed to be no appropriate words to describe the shock and sadness felt by majority of Nigerians over the magnitude of assassinations, unprincipled decampments and election riggings that took place during the 2003 elections. As it turned out, Chief Olusegun Obasanjo and the PDP apparently rigged their way into a second term, with the other political parties questioning the integrity of the elections. The people shouted 'fraud' and the PDP also cried 'fraud' in some constituencies. The parties that were rigged-out protested. Chief Chukwuemeka O. Ojukwu, the All Progressive Grand Alliance (APGA) Presidential candidate, decried the fraud and noted that if things were properly done, he should have been declared the winner of the presidential elections. He however said he would use "non-violent" means to get his message to the people. Major General Muhammadu Buhari, the All Nigeria Peoples Party (ANPP) was equally angry over the outcome of the elections. The party charged that "Gubernatorial and Presidential elections did not take place in the three southern zones, according to INEC guidelines and the electoral law, [but] rather figures were manufactured in government houses or collation centres to abide by pre-determined results for Obasanjo and PDP victory..." (*ThisDay*, May 11, 2003). General Buhari called for the cancellation of the election results and for fresh elections to be conducted in areas in which mass rigging were perpetrated, especially, in the Southeast and South-South zones. He also requested that fresh elections be conducted in Bauchi, Katsina, Benue, and Nasarawa (the areas he expected his party to win), "Otherwise, there would be no government from 30th of May [2003] in this country" (*ThisDay*, April 24, 2003). Gani Fawehnmi and Dr. Chuba Okadigbo (now, late) went a bit further by insisting that the Chief Obasanjo administration should hand over to an "interim government" (see Ekwowusi, May 14, 2003).

Local and foreign election observers also observed that there were widespread frauds during the elections. The European Union Election Observer Mission (EU EOM) noted that the elections were marred by monumental frauds. In particular, the *AP Africa* (April 22, 2003) noted that the chief European Union Election's observer pointed out that there were "widespread election frauds" in six Nigerian states. The Transitional Monitoring Group (TMG) observed that votes were recorded in some areas without elections (The *Guardian*, April 22, 2003 and *ThisDay*, April 24, 2003). Others noted that the results of the elections in many states lacked 'credibility' (*ThisDay*, April 27, 2003). Because Nigerians do not have personal identity cards, voter IDs were not checked, leaving room for under-aged voters (and non-citizens) to participate in the elections. It is not certain though how much influence this had in the outcome of the elections, but the effects could not be discounted.

In as much as there were mass rigging and fraud during the 2003 elections, many Nigerians do not seem to support the calls by aggrieved individuals and political parties to set back the ticking clock of democracy in Nigeria. The people seem to be looking toward the future, hoping that the kind of frauds that took place during the 2003 elections would not repeat again in the history of elections in Nigeria. Like the elections conducted in 1999, the people lost again in 2003. In the weeks and days preceding the elections 'Ghana-Must-Go' bags exchanged hands. It would appear that the sheer quantum of the money pumped into the election by the PDP defeated the energy of those who were working hard to make the elections free and fair. My personal opinion is that regardless of the obvious frauds that characterised the elections, people should accept the outcome in good faith. It is important that people do not give up hope despite what happened. The perverted outcome of the elections should rather increase people's resolve to stand up and continue fighting for justice and fair play in Nigeria. This in my opinion, is the only way to ensure the sustainability of the democracy project in the country.

2003 Elections: How they were manipulated

Was 2003 any way to organise a credible election? The answer is a resounding 'No!' Though there should be no form of intimidation in a free and fair election, the 2003 elections was on the contrary marred by intimidation, harassment and assassinations. Perhaps, it is time for political parties to assume responsibility and liability for crimes committed by their members during elections in the country. And it is time for the media in Nigeria to play truly a watchdog role in reporting the violations and not to look the other way, or being one-sided in their reports. Nigeria must go forward, not backward, and declare that any electoral outcome tainted by fraud and intimidation will be unacceptable. The country must move, not only resolutely but also quickly to address all the issues of fraud that were substantiated during the 2003 elections. Elections and their victors come and go, but the problems remain, if they are not resolutely solved. At this juncture it is apropos to review some of the methods by which the unscrupulous politicians and INEC officials manipulated the votes.

1) **Inflated census count:** (inflating of census figures of localities for political gain);

2) **Voter registration exercise:** (Some politicians use crooked means to register more voters than really existed in their constituencies);

3) **Printing of fake electoral materials:** (Crooks printed fake ballot papers after seeing the original ballot paper, to stuff ballot boxes);

4) **Party Primaries** (Manipulation of the process to select a party's flag-bearer);

5) **Colluding with electoral officers:** (Bribing electoral officers, security agents, police officers, and thugs to stuff ballot boxes with fake votes, snatch ballot boxes in transit, allow multiple voting and underage voters and the stealing of ballot boxes, and so forth; *Vanguard,* May 5, 2003);

6) **Voter intimidation and political thuggery:** (To scare away voters by threatening to kill or hurt them, and actual political assassinations. This was rampant during the 2003 elections as many people were killed in election-related violence (*Daily Trust*, May 5, 2003);

7) **Stuffing of ballot boxes:** (Indiscriminate thumb printing of ballot papers and putting them in ballot boxes to ensure the victory of their candidates; (*The Guardian*, April 22, 2003; Dike: Daily Trust, May 15, 2003,);

8) **Multiple Voting:** (Some voters casting more than one vote due to multiple registration and fake papers);

9) **Underage Voting:** (Voting by people who were below the stipulated voting age; this was common during the 2003 elections due to lack of national ID Card);

10) **Inducement of Voters:** (Some politicians buy votes by distributing food items -beans, rice, onions, garret, yam tubers, stock fish, salt and money to the population);

11) **ECOWAS Voting:** (mobilising immigrants from neighbouring countries to vote; *ThisDay,* May 11, 2003);

12) **Colluding with Gatekeepers:** (Gatekeepers in voting and collation centres, in alliance with electoral officers, could manipulate election figures);

13) **Deliberate counting mistakes:** (Unscrupulous election officers in polling centres could deliberately omit counting the votes of some candidates and inflate the votes of the candidates that bribed them to ensure that they get the required votes to win an election); and

14) **Deliberate technical errors:** (Results at polling centres could indicate that a particular candidate is winning or has won, but a wrong result could be posted; the officers could call it a technical error if the trick is discovered (*ThisDay,* May 11, 2003)

Seeking Solutions: Tackling Fraud in future Elections

Having identified the flaws in the electoral system, the political parties should, instead of wasting their time crying 'fraud' and instigating 'mass action' begin to search for real solutions to the problems. This is because the fiasco is likely to re-occur unless changes are made. As mentioned earlier, threatening 'hell-fire' because one lost an election is not necessary at this point in time. As we seek solutions to these election-related problems, we should also realise that Nigeria must go forward and not backward. This, however, does not mean that I support the massive frauds that allegedly characterised the elections. Democracy is both a serious and an expensive undertaking. Therefore any victory tainted by corruption must be condemned and the injustice redressed, but this must be done in a civilised fashion!

Some strategies to control electoral malpractice in future elections in the country include:

1) The use of Identity Card (to check under-aged voters and weed out illegal immigrants (non-citizens).

213

2)Chairman of INEC should not to be appointed by the Presidency or one person.

3)INEC should be fully independent, with its own annual budget, to avoid being manipulated by the presidency.

4)Checking and comparing fingerprints on the voters' card with that at the polling centre; people should be denied the right to vote if they don't tally.

5)INEC should conduct civic and voter education seminars to inform the people of their political rights and voting procedures; this will improve the development and growth of democratic institutions in the society (see New Nigerian, August 1, 2003).

6)Print only numbers on the voters card issued to voters and leave the voter's name and number at the polling centres; then match each voter's number with that at the polling centre to make sure that they match.

7)Appoint people of proven integrity to serve on electoral tribunal; and those appointed should be paid well to avoid them taking bribes from complainants or petitioners.

8)Check every voter's card for fake ballot papers and attach photographs on voters' cards, if possible; and make ballot papers fraud-proof.

9)Employ state-of-the-art technology to check for frauds. Multiple registrations and voting must be rejected.

10) Begin voters' registration drive on time, so as to have enough time to prepare for elections and review logistic plans and processes (*New Nigerian*, August 1, 2003) and ensure that voting materials are at the voting stations on time.

11) Discontinue with, or reduce the use of ad-hoc staff in elections.

12) Use high ranking and reliable police officers (if necessary military officers) and security personnel to guard polling stations during elections;

13) Set up permanent dates for elections; this will enable the country to become conscious of the time and prevent unnecessary election postponements, as the LGA elections have been.

14)   Make and implement tougher electoral laws; this can discourage political assassinations, intimidation, thuggery, violence, electoral frauds, cheating and *godfatherism*. A wild, corrupt, lawless and chaotic society cannot conduct free and fair elections.

15)   Disqualify political parties that encourage political assassination and violence and "provide a level-playing field for all contestants"(*ThisDay*, August 6, 2003);

16)   Automatic transmission (or release of results) at polling centres. The movement of ballots boxes to other locations after elections must be discontinued to reduce the incidence of result manipulation.

17)   Improve the standards of living of the people- poverty makes them vulnerable to corruption.

18)   Redress the injustices strewn all over the country; injustice breeds violence and anger.

19)   Install surveillance cameras at each polling station to track activities during elections; and this should be controlled by people of integrity;

20)   Fasten ballot boxes to poles or rods in secured rooms to avoid crooks and thugs from snatching them from polling officers.

21)   Restructure and nurture the nation's essential political institutions to fight corruption and reduce poverty among the officers of the judiciary, police, INEC, and so forth.

22)   The country should demand accountability from the politicians, by using their votes wisely.

23)   Reject parties and politicians that are not issues-based; society should demand that politics, which are presently fuelled by money, should be issues-based. This would make politics to be a game for politicians, and not for 'area boys and area girls.' As noted earlier, lack of principles caused the political 'doves and vultures' to shift from one party to another when they failed to realise their selfish political ambition during the 2003 elections.

24)   Courts and Judges should be stopped from declaring losers of elections the winners (or granting frivolous *ex-parte*

orders one - sided or partisan point of view- (*Vanguard*, August 1, 2003) thereby encroaching into the administrative duties and functions of the electoral tribunal, which is supposed to settle election disputes. The duties of the court and electoral tribunal should be clearly defined.

25)   Political parties involved in elections should be represented at every polling station, and must certify every election results to make them official; and prosecute (jail) those connected with any electoral malpractices.

26)   The electoral bodies and the police should continuously review their security plans to fix any loophole.

27)   Reduce the term for State and Federal House of Representatives to 2 years to enable the people to timely replace any member that is not performing up to expectation;

28)   Eliminate all conditions that would politicise the position of the chairman of INEC and other officials; and

29)   Set up a watchdog or agency to supervise the activities of the INEC.

Final Conclusions

WE have discussed some of the key issues in Nigerian politics during Obasanjo's first term in office (1999-2003), including the conduct of the 2003 elections, and the problems thrown up by inappropriate handling of some of those issues. In some cases I have gone beyond this period to properly contextualise the problem or show the history of that problem, and how it has mutated over time. One crucial observation is that many of the politicians now running around in billowing *babariga* jostling for political positions, are hardly the type of leaders to lead the nation to the 'Promised Land' of true democracy. Most of the politicians (and their cohorts) must change their attitude in their pursuit of political power, as politics should not be a *do or die* affair in the country. We also noted that the political leadership, at both the federal and state levels, have not made any serious efforts to enlarge or improve community services and facilities, such as schools, medical services, water, roads, urban planning, resources and energy development.

We argued that the barriers to economic growth must be removed, and people-oriented policies undertaken to arrest the devastating effects of poverty on many Nigerians. We noted that qualitative education plays a role in the gap between the developed and underdeveloped nations, as it reflects in technology and their standard of living. Without a good educational system, the development of any society would be very difficult, if not impossible. Based on this, we suggested that the government should focus on improving the welfare of the people by addressing the issues of poor education, healthcare, equal opportunity and the increasing insecurity of life and property. The people, we argued, must also work harder to reclaim Nigeria from the politicians by making proper use of their votes and avoid being manipulated by the unscrupulous politicians in future elections.

We also noted the lack of distributive justice. We agued that the injustices in the Niger-Delta area must be resolved quickly without further delay. The starting point, we said, should be the devolution of more power to individual states and allowing every locality to control their resources - be it oil, groundnut, cocoa, palm oil, tin, and so forth. Social injustice and inequity in the society (caused by the undue concentration of power in the centre) has robbed local governments the power and resources for community development programmes.

We argued that for Nigeria to move forward, it must be re-structured into a new society where freedom, security, justice, fairness, economic opportunity and socio-political stability shall be the cornerstone. The leaders of a restructured Nigeria should not be left in doubt that the purpose of political leadership is to provide services to the people and not an avenue for personal enrichment.

We called for serious efforts to be made in enlarging the national 'economic pie' because the poverty of the people often leads them into fraudulent and criminal activities.

We also discussed the 2003 elections and offered suggestions on how to avoid 'the politics of unreason' that characterised and marred the elections.

References

Daily Trust: "Commissioner, 4 others killed in Nassrawa poll violence;" May 5, 2003

Dike, Victor E; "Looking beyond the 2003 elections." *Daily Trust,* May 15, 2003

------------------; "To Sustain the Unity of Nigeria;" *Daily Independent* of January 30, 2003

Ekwowusi, Sonnie; "Redressing the Electoral Fraud;" *ThisDay,* May 14, 2003

Nnanna, Ochereome; "Lessons from elections 2003;" *Vanguard,* May 5, 2003

ThisDay: "Buhari: Don't Recognize Obasanjo After May 29;" April 24, 2003

-----------: "How the Polls Were Rigged;" May 11, 2003

-----------: May 11, 2003

-----------: "Resolving the Electoral Crisis;" April 27, 2003

-----------; See Joseph Ushigiale on "Can National Assembly Ensure Free, Fair Elections?" August 6, 2003

Vanguard; "Our agenda for Mr. President – Nas, Akande, Udoma, others;" April 26, 2003

-------------; "How to get a credible electoral body –Ebri;" May 10, 2003

-------------; See Sina Babasola and Innocent Anaba on "Nine judges sacked over ex parte motions- Bablakin;" August 1, 2003

The Guardian: "Obasanjo meets target to be named winner;" April 22, 2003

------------------: April 22, 2003

The Associated Press (AP): "Obasanjo Wins Re-Election in Nigeria;" April 22, 2003

E

economic development, 17,
18, 65, 109, 111, 116, 154, 165
Economic freedom, 18
economic growth, 65, 67, 73,
86, 90, 136, 137, 149, 159, 217
economic policy, 62
education, 9, 11, 49, 65, 82, 91,
101, 102, 115, 119, 141, 145,
146, 147, 148, 149, 150, 151,
152, 153, 154, 155, 156, 157,
158, 159, 160, 161, 162, 164,
165, 168, 170, 185, 190, 205,
206, 214, 217
electioneering campaigns, 8,
9, 11, 15, 28, 48
Electoral Commissions, v,
26, 31, 32
electoral fraud, 31
electoral process, 31, 39
Embezzlement, 57
ethnic identity, 16
ethnic militias, 15, 181, 182,
184
Ethnic politics, 15
Ethnicity and religion, 174
Extortion, 57, 194

F

First Republic, 26, 32, 197, 198
foreign financial
institutions, 40, 72
Fraud, 57, 64, 82, 209, 213, 218
Fulani, 15, 182, 186

G

General Abdulsalami
Abubakar, 28, 138
general elections, 14, 26, 27,
28, 32
General Sani Abacha, 27, 28,
40, 42, 72, 99, 112, 115, 138,
174, 176, 198
Ghana-Must-Go bags, 45, 211
globalisation, 119, 120
Go Back to Land Programme,
98
governance, 9, 20, 80, 100, 141,
147, 160, 170, 176, 185, 188,
199, 204
Grassroots Democratic
Movement, 28
Gross Domestic Product
(GDP), 86
Gross National Product
(GNP), 86

H

Huasa, 15
human rights abuses, 177,
191
human rights violation, 176,
177, 190
Human Rights Violations
and Investigation
Commission, 177

I

Ibos, 15, 173, 186
Ikechukwu Abana, 16, 200

221

National Primary Education
Commission (NPEC),, 148
Nepotism, 57
Niger-Delta, 46, 100, 217
Nigeria Labour Congress
(NLC), 129
Nigeria Ports Authority
(NPA)., 138
*Nigerian Agricultural and Co-
operative Bank*, 98
Nigerian Bar Association,
178
Nigerian Custom service, 74
Nigerian Deposit Insurance
Corporation (NDIC), 61
Nigerian External Tele-
communications (NET),,
138
Nigerian factor, 109, 201
Nigerian Maritine
Authority, 75
Nigerian National Alliance,
26
Nigerian National
Petroleum Corporation,
75
Nigerian National Shipping
Lines (NNSL), 138
Nigerian politicians, 20, 28
Nigerian politics, 9, 14, 20, 34,
46, 126, 172, 175, 197, 198,
202, 206, 216
Nigerian Ports Authority, 75
Nigerian Railways, Post and
Telegraphs (P&T),, 138
Nigerian's educational
institutions, 148

Nkrumah, 41, 52
Nnamdi Azikiwe, 9, 41, 197
Northern Elements
Progressive Union, 26

O

Obasanjo, 13, 15, 18, 24, 25, 30,
33, 35, 37, 44, 46, 47, 48, 49,
52, 53, 55, 60, 70, 71, 72, 73,
74, 83, 98, 99, 108, 110, 129,
136, 138, 152, 153, 161, 166,
173, 175, 177, 178, 180, 184,
195, 209, 216, 218
Oodua Peoples' Congress
(OPC)., 182
Operation Feed the Nation, 98
Organisation of Petroleum
Exporting Countries
(OPEC),, 109

P

Paris Club, 108
*Peoples Bank of Nigeria and
the Community Bank, of
Nigeria,,* 98
Peoples Democratic Party,
13, 28, 178
Petroleum Trust Fund, 44
political assassinations, 11,
28, 44, 178, 191, 203, 209, 212
political *godfatherism*, 182,
196, 198, 199, 202, 203, 204,
206, 207, 209
political *godfathers*, 9, 14, 56,
191, 196, 198, 206
political ideology, 14, 19, 20
political modernisation, 65

Ordering this Book

*Wholesale inquiries for this book should be directed to any of the following:

Wholesale inquiries in the UK and Europe should be directed to one of the following:

Bertram, The Book Wholesaler:
+44 1603216 666: email: orders@bertrams.com

Gardners Books Ltd
+44 1323 521777: email: custcare@gardners.com

In the USA, wholesale inquiries should be directed to one of the following:
Ingram Book Company (ordering)
+1 800 937 8000 website: www.ingrambookgroup.com

Baker & Taylor (General and sales information)
+1-800-775-3700 Email: btinfo@btol.com

*Online Retail Distribution: www.amazon.co.uk, www.amazon.com

*Shop Retail: Ask any good bookshop or contact our office:
http//: www.adonis-abbey.com
Phone: +(44) 020 7793 8893
The ebook version of this print is also available in PDF format. Please contact: sales@adonis-abbey.com

Other Books by Adonis & Abbey include:

Broken Dreams (fiction)
By Jideofor Adibe

Wooden Gongs and Drumbeats: African Folktales, Proverbs and Idioms (fiction)
By Dahi Chris Onuchukwu

The Making of the Africa-Nation Pan-Africanism and the African Renaissance (politics/political economy/history)
Edited by Mammo Muchie

The Challenge of Authenticity: African Culture and Faith Commitment (religion/philosophy/theology)
By Jacob Hevi

www.ingramcontent.com/pod-product-compliance
Lightning Source LLC
Chambersburg PA
CBHW020702270326
41928CB00005B/230